The JONI MITCHELL Companion

The JONI MITCHELL *Companion*

Four Decades of Commentary

Edited by

STACEY LUFTIG

Schirmer Books
New York

Schirmer Books
An Imprint of The Gale Group
1633 Broadway
New York, NY 10019

Library of Congress Catalog Card Number: 99-046732

Printed in the United States of America

Printing Number
10 9   8   7   6   5   4   3   2   1

Library of Congress Cataloging-in-Publication Data

The Joni Mitchell companion : four decades of commentary.
   p. cm.
  Discography: p.
  Includes bibliographical references (p.) and index.
  ISBN 0-02-865333-5 (alk. paper)
  1. Mitchell, Joni—Criticism and interpretation.
ML420.M542 J66 2000
782.42164'092—dc21
                                       99-046732
                                          CIP

This paper meets the requirements of ANSI/NISO Z.39.48-1992 (Permanence of Paper).

To Debi, who loved her first.

Contents

PART FIVE: Charismatic Siren. . . Doom-Laden Seer

PART SIX: The Music: Craft, Process, and Analysis

Acknowledgments

I have many people to thank for their help in the preparation of this book.

First, I would like to thank the writers of these articles, without whom there would be no book. Thanks to Richard Carlin, my editor at Schirmer Books, for his support and his time-saving ideas throughout the process. A special thanks to Joel Bernstein for giving me generous access to his archives of Joni Mitchell facts, memories, insights, and articles.

My gratitude also goes to two creators of wonderful Web sites: to Wally Breese, for the multifaceted Joni Mitchell Homepage at http://www.jonimitchell.com; and to Les Irvin, for cheerfully, speedily, and tirelessly helping me track down all sorts of Joni-related facts and for his library-of-a-site at http://www.jmdl.com. Thanks also to the jmdl discussion group for their open-hearted support; and particular thanks to John Melchert of the jmdl discussion group, for his feedback and editorial support, and for his listening.

Many thanks also to the following people, for their ideas on assembling and writing the text, for help in collecting the music, and for technical and emotional support: Ken Blum, Debi Elfenbein, Steven Goldleaf, Jackie Lund, Lisa Najavits, Martha Silano, Devan Sipher, Alison Sprout, Adam Vane, Penny Weingarten, and especially Daniel Jussim.

Finally, thanks to my parents (all four of them), to my sister and her family, and to the rest of my friends, for being there.

Introduction

How gratifying to see today's concert review of Joni Mitchell's music in the *New York Times*. There's a colorful picture of a beautiful and beaming Joni, her arms open wide. Above the headline—"It's All Joni Mitchell Onstage, but She's in the Audience"— are the words "Jazz Review." But this passage is the part I like best:

> More and more these days, her music, with its serpentine melodies and dramatic key changes, has been claimed by improvisers, and "Joni's Jazz," a Summerstage concert in Central Park on Thursday night, was a milestone in the furthering of Ms. Mitchell's status as an artist broader than the pop world that initially embraced her.

Joni Mitchell, appreciated. Compare that to her portrayal in that same paper less than nine months before. The piece, "The Hissing of a Living Legend," starts:

> At 54, Joni Mitchell has suddenly found herself in possession of a daughter, a grandson and a desire to write light songs. Yet she compares herself to Mozart, hates popular music and has nothing but contempt for the whole notion of the Lilith Fair.

It's a negative, gossipy story, with a large, unflattering head shot, that mentions her music only incidentally. It's a contrast to today's story—but not a surprise.

Joni Mitchell, like many celebrities, has had a difficult relationship with the press. They have praised her, created mythologies about her, slammed her, ignored her, and praised her again. She has been quoted extensively, quoted out of context, shown as joyous, as bitter, as innocent, as jaded, as pure, as promiscuous, as pretentious, as fresh, and as pioneer, trend follower, and oddball. (And that doesn't even address the confusion about her music.) The truth about Joni Mitchell, though subjective, of course, and ever-changing, is somewhere between the lines.

The facts, however, are these. It has been three and a half decades since Joni Mitchell, a.k.a. Roberta Joan Anderson, first strummed and sang at the folk clubs of Toronto. She began her career as a singer, songwriter, musician, and producer when such a combination, for a woman, was unheard of. At the same time, she was also a painter. After enormous success with her early albums, which were solo and acoustic, she branched out, adding a band and incorporating jazz-inflected rhythms. As her musical style continued to evolve, she alienated many fans, while gaining a smaller number of new ones. Yet she continued to make her musical choices based on what pleased her, and not, for the most part, on whether the results might be commercial.

From the mid-1970s to the mid-'90s, she paid for those choices with mixed reviews and lower album sales. Recently, however, she has also been honored, and with some of the most prestigious awards in the business: the National Academy of Songwriters' Lifetime Achievement Award, *Billboard*'s Century Award, the ASCAP Founders Award, and her induction into the Rock and Roll Hall of Fame, to name just a few.

This book is a chronicle of Joni Mitchell's career, as told by the many voices of the press. It is a collection of the most interesting, informative, and sometimes provocative pieces—articles, essays, interviews, and reviews—that I could find, fit, afford, and get permission to reprint. The articles are arranged in a way that is mostly chronological and completely subjective. While my bias is a positive one and my choices reflect that, I also made sure to include negative reviews and less-than-kind articles and interviews. My hope is that a broad range of attitudes will help shed light on so complex a subject.

Part One charts the rise of Joni Mitchell's popularity, starting with gigs that predated *Song to a Seagull*, her first album. "The way you enter the game in this business is usually the way you stay," says Mitchell in a long and informative article written by William Ruhlmann. And if you do change, the press may take time to catch up: though Mitchell stopped singing folk songs in 1965, the *Variety* notices from 1966 and 1967 call her a "folksinger," and that misnomer was to stick for years to come.

The section continues with a short, amusing piece about Joni and musician Chuck Mitchell, at that time her husband. Other highlights include a 1968 review of a folk festival in Pennsylvania and a 1969 profile from the *New York Times* called "Joni Mitchell: In Her House, Love."

Part One ends with a 1971 review of perhaps her most beloved album, *Blue*.

Part Two, From Folk Waif to Rock and Roll Lady, looks at a still-ascendant Joni. It is bracketed by two interviews and covers the time between *For the Roses* and *Court and Spark*. In the first interview, Mitchell talks about dreams, disillusionment, and the reasons for her retreat from the music business. She mentions her admiration for Miles Davis, a theme repeated throughout these articles. (For a wonderful story about Miles Davis and his feelings about Mitchell, see Daniel Levitin's interview with Joni in Part Five.) Though she speaks frankly and earnestly in these early pieces, it's clear she's also wary. British journalist Penny Valentine, quoting Mitchell, writes: "'I have in my time,' and she grins at the pseudodramatic air in her voice, 'been very misunderstood.'"

Misunderstood, perhaps. Praised, certainly—at least for a while. Part Two contains two glowing reviews: one of *For the Roses*, by Robert Hilburn, the other of a London concert that includes her first appearance with a band, Tom Scott and the L.A. Express. "Self-Portrait of a Superstar," the interview at the end of this section, shows a reflective and open Joni Mitchell at the height of her fame with the 1974 *Court and Spark*. Mitchell declares, "I still feel young as an artist. I don't feel like my best work is behind me. I feel as if it's still in front."

Parts Three and Four do in fact chronicle some of her best work. But these albums, produced between 1975 and 1979, are also among her least well received. In 1994, looking back in an interview with Barney Hoskyns (excerpted here in Part Five), Mitchell says, "I was completely out of whack with the public taste throughout the late '70s and the '80s. People aren't always going through changes at the same time as me, and sometimes I get so far ahead I look like I'm behind."

Part Three, Singer/Songwriter, Composer, Musician, includes reviews, mixed, of four of Joni Mitchell's most jazz-inspired albums: *The Hissing of Summer Lawns, Hejira, Don Juan's Reckless Daughter,* and *Mingus*. Michael Watts, in an article for *Melody Maker* magazine (not included here), calls Mitchell "a lyricist of exquisite subtlety" who, with *Hissing*, has "devised a delightful torture." The *Village Voice* writer reviewing *Hejira*, however, declares Mitchell has "failed" as a lyricist. In *Don Juan's Reckless Daughter*, according to Blair Jackson, "there is so much . . . it will take months, perhaps years, to absorb it." And Ed Ward, with his fascinating take on *Mingus*, offers some wisdom that transcends the review of this particular album: "People who don't let labels trap them can have a very good time exploring what's here to hear." Another highlight of this section is an interview, by Leonard Feather, titled "Joni Mitchell Makes Mingus Sing."

Charles Mingus called Joni Mitchell "a nervy broad" after seeing her dressed as a black man on the cover of *Don Juan's Reckless Daughter*. In the first piece in Part Four, we see an exuberant and philosophical Joni telling tales of working with Mingus, sharing stories about paradox and synchronicity, and generally whooping it up with Vic Garbarini soon after she and then-husband Larry Klein coproduced the ultraromantic *Wild Things Run Fast* in 1982. Iain Blair, in his piece "Lucky Girl," reports on Mitchell shortly after the release of the acerbic *Dog Eat Dog*. And Phil Sutcliffe, writing for *Q* magazine around the time of *Chalk Mark in a Rain Storm*, gets Mitchell to reminisce. Her memories include how "Woodstock" got written, the angry soldier who inspired "Beat of Black Wings," and the strange events that led to "Furry Sings the Blues." Part Four ends with a piece by Stephen Holden, written in 1991 about the gentle *Night Ride Home*, called "Joni Mitchell Finds the Peace of Middle Age."

The articles in Part Five continue the tale of Mitchell's career through the late 1990s. They include a light piece from the *New Yorker* about an impromptu club performance where a fistfight broke out between Chrissie Hynde and Carly Simon, an entry from *The Billboard Encyclopedia of Record Producers* that pays homage to one of Mitchell's most unsung professional roles, and an in-depth article from *Maclean's* magazine that describes how Mitchell finally reunited with the daughter she gave up for adoption.

Yet the pieces from the 1990s also bring us a starker, more defiant Joni Mitchell. It's no wonder. In addition to surviving a decade of failing health, falling record sales, and endless litigation woes, Mitchell found herself in yet another difficult position: that of the celebrity against the journalist. In the interview, "Our Lady of Sorrows," she is asked: "How did you feel when *Rolling Stone* dubbed you 'Old Lady of the Year' in 1972?"; "What do you consider the most neglected or underrated music of your career?"; and "Have you been disappointed by the sales of your albums since *Mingus*?" In another interview, this one first published in the *Austin Chronicle*, Mitchell addresses the question that keeps recurring, like a bad dream: How does she feel about the so-called "new Joni Mitchells"—that is, the female musicians who claim her as an influence, yet have none of her musical sophistication? In the same interview, she

Joni Mitchell at the Newport Falls Festival, 1967. © David Gahr

makes unsentimental observations about her recent honors and notes the difference in the way she's depicted in the "white press" as opposed to the "black press." With the final piece of this section, by Neil Strauss of the *New York Times*, we are left to imagine Mitchell's reaction to lines like these: " . . . Mitchell can be humorless. People describe her as 'bitter' and a 'loose cannon,' and those are her friends. Over the course of three days of conversations, Mitchell will compare herself to Mozart, Blake and Picasso . . . and describe her music as so new it needs its own genre name."

Fade out. In the final section of this book, the focus is on the music. It starts with two wonderful pieces from *Acoustic Guitar* magazine. The first is about "Joni's weird chords"—the nitty-gritty of the music she makes and how she makes it—and the second is a short history of her guitars. From theory and instruments we go to Mitchell's inner process of creating a song, with an excerpt from the book *Musicians in Tune*. Next is a scholarly analysis from the very first volume of the journal *Women in Music,* about the theme of flight in Mitchell's songs. From there it's a charming, light piece from Robert Hilburn in which Mitchell tells the inspiration behind many of her most popular songs, including "Chelsea Morning," "Amelia," "Both Sides, Now," and "Big Yellow Taxi." Finally, Part Six ends with another piece from *Acoustic Guitar* writer Jeffrey Pepper Rodgers on the vocal and lyrical craft of Joni Mitchell.

There's so much more I wanted to include in this book. More album reviews, more concert reviews. More about Mitchell's two live albums, *Miles of Aisles* in 1974 and *Shadows and Light* in 1980. (For additional articles, see the bibliography.) But I think that from what I did include in *The Joni Mitchell Companion*, you'll get a sense of the artist and her music that may surprise you. Thrill you. Anger you. Delight you. Frustrate you. And, I hope, enrich you.

Stacey Luftig
July 3, 1999

Part One

THE SEAGULL FROM SASKATOON
1966–1971

Joni Mitchell and Leonard Cohen at the Newport Falls Festival, 1967. © David Gahr

JONI MITCHELL: FOLKSONGS
47 Minutes
7 of Clubs, Toronto

Some early notice.—SFL

Variety, September 21, 1966

Canadian-born folksinger and songwriter Joni Mitchell is a fresh talent. In a 47-minute set of her own songs that all share a midwestern, prairie texture, she shows herself a creative spark in the current folk scene.

Her pattern is autobiographical and explanatory. It fits hand in glove with the songs, which range from "Lazy Summer" to a tribute to guitar accompanist David Rea, "Play, Little David, Play" [*sic*].

Miss Mitchell, with high cheekbones, flaxen-color hair and a crystal clear voice, is bound for bigger things.

JONI MITCHELL:
$1.50, $2.50 COVER
Riverboat, Toronto
Toronto, Feb. 14

Variety, February 22, 1967

Canadian folksinger Joni Mitchell, now married and living in Detroit, is a bright, engaging performer and a sensitive, original folk composer.

In her return date at Toronto's Riverboat coffeehouse following a successful November booking, she displays an ever ripening voice, and is an eyeful in a tight-fitting mini silver lamé dress, and sporting flaxen hair that falls below her shoulders.

Opening with her own song, "The Daisy Summer," she introduces her newest, "The Wizard of Is," and continues on with a Mitchell sampler, "Just Like Me," "Blue on Blue," and "Night in the City."

The numbers have much appeal and rate recording by folksingers on the lookout for new material. They are quiet songs, sometimes forlorn and always evocative.

Miss Mitchell, or rather Mrs. because she is married to Detroit folksinger Church [*sic*] Mitchell, is a talent to watch. She's booked here to Feb. 26.

BY A. L. MCCLAIN

TWO SINGLE ACTS SURVIVE A MARRIAGE

About a first marriage and a short-lived collaboration. Note the last paragraph.—SFL

Detroit News, February 6, 1966

In this era of computers serving as matchmakers, it seems unlikely that Chuck and Joni Mitchell would have been paired off as matrimonial partners. But seven months after their marriage, they seemed to have beaten the machines.

Their wedding required more sacrifice than the average couple's. Each was a folksinger. Chuck had played numerous engagements as a single in the Detroit area; Joni filled dates in her native Canada as a soloist.

They decided to combine single acts into one, and the honeymoon took a slight detour. Chuck explained it, "We are both strong-minded people, and we both had our own ways of doing a number. There were some hectic times until we blended our styles."

Joni's disposition also suffered when he took her home to his apartment in the Wayne State University area. They had to climb five flights of stairs, and he was too exhausted to carry her across the threshold. Joni walked in herself.

"But I carried her the last flight of stairs," laughed Chuck.

Chuck grew up in the Rochester area. Joni was used to Canadian customs. She had wanted to be an artist and had gone to school to study art.

The girl who bears a striking resemblance to Mia Farrow, of TV's "Peyton Place," explained it: "I got interested in a ukulele, and from there I turned to the guitar and folk singing. Thirty-six hours after I met Chuck, he asked me to marry him. But we waited two months."

Now their marriage and careers are on firmer ground. They recently finished an engagement together at the Chess Mate, and hope to get a try-out at the Playboy Club in Detroit.

Occasionally, they break up the act for separate engagements. This weekend, Joni backed up Blues singer Jesse Fuller at the Chess Mate and Chuck sang at the Alcove on Woodward.

On Feb. 15 they join forces again for a week's stand at the Chess Mate, and on Feb. 22 they appear together at the Living End, a nightclub.

Chuck said, "Joni and I have developed our act. We are not just folksingers now. We do comedy, sing some ragtime and do folk-rock. We're ready for the big clubs now."

Joni nodded her approval, as any dutiful wife would do.

BY WALTER F. NAEDELE

OUTSIDE SCHWENKSVILLE: JONI MITCHELL BREAKS UP OPENING OF FOLK FESTIVAL

*Joni, with only one album produced (*Song to a Seagull*), performs at a Pennsylvania folk festival and brings thousands to their feet. (By the way: A final act that night was 17-year-old Janis Ian, who sneered at the Pottstown police force and dedicated a song to Hubert Humphrey.)—SFL*

The [Philadelphia] Evening Bulletin, August 24, 1968

In an open field outside Schwenksville last night, a girl with blonde hair long as uncut wheat brought several thousand listeners to their feet, cheering for a voice echoing words that haunted.

Joni Mitchell had stopped the opening night of the seventh annual Philadelphia Folk Festival dead in its tracks.

Only her plea that she was not permitted any encores beyond her 20 minutes of five songs silenced the shouting that proclaimed this girl a sensation.

It was her first appearance here since her only album appeared earlier this year.

Joni Mitchell—a 24-year-old Canadian, with only one album, and a reputation that has blossomed her into the most exciting girl singer since Judy Collins, since Joan Baez.

For Joni is a writer and an influence.

Like Tim Hardin, her songs have been heard through other singers: Judy Collins singing "Michael from Mountains"; some group making popular "Both Sides, Now."

Joni Mitchell is also a phenomenon.

Like the crashing surf, you have to feel her voice hitting you hard to gain the exhilaration of something yet unexperienced.

The awful thing about Joni has been that she seemed to have two voices, a deep, open-throated tenor and a thin soaring soprano. She could not sustain a song without breaking across into what seemed a weakness.

But last night, she was stronger than in her album, each of her voices a richness, singing "Being Free," "Chelsea Morning," "Both Sides, Now" and a medley of "The Circle Game" and "Little Green."

The crowd sang "Circle Game" with her, a song she's never recorded.

Her awareness awakened by the bitterness of the cities in these, her voice carried the awe of a country girl affronted, the humility of a girl warning against what she had lived through.

Joni, herself, was in bad shape, suffering from the effects of hepatitis.

BY KARL DALLAS

JONI, THE SEAGULL FROM SASKATOON

A perspective from England on the musical phenomenon from Canada. Later interviewers will also mention the sort of instant intimacy with Joni that Karl Dallas refers to here.—SFL

Melody Maker, September 28, 1968

Talking to Joni Mitchell about her songs is rather like talking to someone you just met about the most intimate secrets of her life. Like peeping in a window on someone and then discussing with her what you have seen. Her songs are so personal.

They're honest, too. The girl in the songs on her Reprise album isn't all sweetness and light, and she doesn't seem to win the whole-hearted approval of the writer, herself.

"Her heart is full and hollow like a cactus tree while she's so busy being free," she sings, in a full round voice that has a lot of Judy Collins in it—which is interesting, since Judy has recorded two of her songs and is putting more on her next album.

"I've always admired Judy ever since I first started singing in Saskatoon, Canada, where I come from. Now we are close friends. But in those days I think I sounded more like Joan Baez.

"Since I started writing songs, the range of my voice has extended downwards something like two octaves, which gives me a lot more freedom in the sort of melodies I'm writing."

She certainly uses that freedom with long, free-ranging tunes that swoop down and soar up in ways that few except perhaps Mesdames Baez and Collins could handle.

In this they are unlike the deadpan, almost banal melodies used by her fellow Canadian, Leonard Cohen.

"My lyrics are influenced by Leonard," she admits. "We never knew each other in Canada, but after we met at Newport last year we saw a lot of each other. My song 'Marcie' has a lot of him in it, and some of Leonard's religious imagery, which comes from being a Jew in a predominantly Catholic part of Canada, seems to have rubbed off on me, too."

"Marcie" is about a girl waiting for a letter that never comes, who walks out of the last verse to go west again. Is Marcie Joni?

"I suppose so, really. Marcie is a real girl, she lives in London. I used her name, because I wanted a two-syllable name. But I'm the girl in all these songs.

"And the first song in the album, 'I Had a King' is about the breakup of my marriage."

The album is one of the few I can think of—the others that spring to mind are *Sgt. Pepper* and the Mothers of Invention LPs—which successfully hangs together as a complete whole.

The title, written so subtly by the wings of flying seagulls on the cover that few people notice it, is "Song to a Seagull." The first side is called "I Came to the City" and the second side is called "Out of the City and Down to the Seaside." Both are lines from songs on the second side.

"The album does tell a story, though not necessarily in chronological order. Certainly the songs aren't placed in the chronological order that I wrote them. As we were working on it, songs came up that would fit in. And since it was finished, I've written others that could go into the sequence, too."

Joni is not doing too much writing at the moment. "I'm too hung up about what's going on in America politically. I keep thinking, how can I sing 'night in the city looks pretty to me,' when I know it's not pretty at all, with people living in slums and being beaten up by police?

"It was what happened in Chicago during the Democratic Convention that really got me thinking. All those kids being clubbed. If I'd been wearing these Levis, they'd have clubbed me, not for doing anything, but because this is the uniform of the enemy. That's what they are beginning to call the kids today, the enemy.

"I keep trying to put what I feel into words, but it's all been said so much better by other people. Strangely enough, a song I wrote at the end of last year, 'The Fiddler and the Drum' [*sic*] expresses what I feel now, though I wasn't conscious of feeling that way then."

Because Joni Mitchell was originally a painter—she designed the sleeve for her own album—the things that stick in the mind from her songs are all visual. The king she lost, painting the pastel walls of her home brown, thinking of ladies in gingham while she is a girl dressed in leather.

Michael, stirring puddles with a stick to change the taffeta patterns of an oil slick.

Neon sign colors in the city "waltzing in time."

Traffic lights that are red for anger and green for envy.

And all through this album, the seagull that wheels above you cries, and then is suddenly gone.

I think Joni Mitchell is that seagull.

BY SUSAN GORDON LYDON

JONI MITCHELL: IN HER HOUSE, LOVE

A glimpse into Joni's life—colorful, rich, and intense—while she was living with Graham Nash.—SFL

New York Times, April 20, 1969

Joni Mitchell lives in Laurel Canyon, in a small pine-paneled house lovingly cluttered with two cats, a stuffed elk's head, stained glass windows, a grandfather clock given her by Leonard Cohen, a king's head with a jeweled crown sticking out from the brick fireplace, votive candles, blooming azaleas, a turkey made of pine cones, dried flowers, old dolls, Victorian shadow boxes, colored glass, an ornamental plate from Saskatoon, Saskatchewan, where she grew up, an art nouveau lamp in the shape of a frog holding a lily pad, a collection of cloisonné boxes, bowls and ashtrays, patchwork quilts, Maxfield Parrish pictures, various musical instruments, and Joni Mitchell and Graham Nash.

It's a lovely house, sunny and friendly and filled with the easygoing good spirits of the Laurel Canyon music scene. There's a lot going on there: Joni is in the midst of recording her second album, and Graham, who used to be with the British group the Hollies, has just finished a super-group album with David Crosby, formerly of the Byrds, and Steve Stills, formerly of Buffalo Springfield. There are new tapes being played and album details being worked out. During the day, a friend came by to show Graham the photograph for his album cover, and Joni's manager dropped in to talk about her progress on the album.

With her long blonde hair in braids, and wearing a peasant blouse and sailor pants, Joni looks younger and less mysterious than one might expect from hearing her songs. Her face, lacking the forcefulness and luminescent quality it takes on when she performs, looks like a forthright farm girl's, with freckled pale skin, watery blue eyes, and prominent teeth and cheek-bones. She speaks softly and gently, with great earnestness.

The night before, she had completed two cuts for the new album, an almost unheard of feat for her, and both she and Graham were elated by the result. "She's the only one who can sing this song," Graham said, putting on one of the tapes, "Both Sides, Now." Her version, mellowed by the experience of having written it and having sung it many times, and by the meanings added to it by Dave Van Ronk and Judy Collins, sounded infinitely rich, and definitive. "That was magnificent, Babe. I'm gonna kiss you for that," said Graham. "You would've kissed her, man, if she would've spit," said Joni's manager. "There sure is a lot of love in this house."

Though she's only become famous in the last year and a half—since Judy Collins included some of her songs on her album, *Wildflowers*, and [Mitchell's] own excellent album, *Song to a Seagull*, was released—Joni Mitchell, who is now 25, has been performing for a long time. During the folk boom, she was singing in small coffeehouses in Toronto. In 1965 she married Chuck Mitchell (the short marriage she describes in "I Had a King") and went with him to live in Detroit, where Tom Rush heard her sing and included one of her songs, "Urge for Going," in his repertory. Her reputation was high with other folksingers, but she had a hard time get-ting work. "The year Dylan went electric," she said, "the folk clubs started closing all over the country. It was like an epidemic. The only people being hired were people who had records out. I was always bringing up the rear. In those days, if you only played acoustical guitar, club owners treated you as though you were a dinosaur.

"Now everybody's branching out and there's room for all styles. People are playing where they feel their music. I feel my music with a solitary voice and a solitary guitar." Her music has a haunting, unearthly quality produced by the strangeness of the imagery in her lyrics, the unexpected shifts in her voice, and the unusual guitar tunings she uses. She is one of the most original and profoundly talented of all the contemporary composer-performers—Gordon Lightfoot, Leonard Cohen, Tim Hardin and Buffy Sainte-Marie, many others—who have evolved folk music into art-rock.

It's more than mere coincidence that she and Leonard Cohen are both native Canadians. "We Canadians are a bit more nosegay, more Old-Fashioned Bouquet, than Americans," she said. "We're poets because we're such reminiscent kind of people. I love Leonard's sentiments, so I've been strongly influenced by him. My poetry is urbanized and Americanized, but my music is influenced by the prairies. When I was a kid, my mother used to take me out to the fields to teach me bird calls. There was a lot of space behind individual sounds. People in the city are so accustomed to hearing a jumble of different sounds that when they come to making music, they fill it up with all sorts of different things."

Joni is quite a gifted painter, too. She did the paintings for both her album covers, and the imagery in her song lyrics is that of a person whose orientation is more visual than verbal: "Colors go waltzing in time," from "Night in the City," for example, or "The sun poured in like butterscotch and stuck to all my senses," from "Chelsea Morning." "I hardly read anything at all," she said. "I would rather paint or play the piano or write a song. I'm taking four months off at the end of the summer, because I haven't had much time to write new songs. A lot of the songs on the new album are old ones. I want to do more songs for the piano; that's where I'm moving now. The piano gives me a new melodic sense, as the guitar tunings used to.

"I'm more prolific with melodies than with words, but quite often I write poems and then set them to music. I guess I'm primarily an artist; what I like best is making new music. It's like going into a trance; I sit down with a melody and reminisce. I find it easier to think about my feelings in retrospect. The way I'd like to work from now on is to go into a studio as soon as a song is finished, when the feeling of the song is most intense. You should record songs when you believe them most.

"Most of my songs are about myself, songs of personal experience. It's very important to me how I sing them. I just played in Saskatoon, my home town, and it was a tremendously emotional experience. When I sang 'Both Sides, Now,' it was like singing the words for the first time. But it's funny—after a song's been written, it becomes a whole different thing; you don't own it anymore. I love to hear men sing my songs, because they're written from a feminine point of view, and men bring totally different things to them."

Joni has been working on the new album since December, but she decided only recently to take over the production of it herself. "I was working with a producer, and we were pulling each other in opposite directions," she said. "I was working within this framework of sound equipment, and the sound was fantastic, but I felt stifled. Now the sound isn't so good, but at least I know I'm doing what I want to do."

There isn't much any outsider could do to produce a Joni Mitchell record. It's as though she conceived each of her songs as a perfect entity, and only she knows whether or not the way she performs it measures up to her ideal of how it should be. She worked intensely at a recording session that night, trying a song over and over, not varying her singing or accompaniment, and breaking it off when the feeling didn't seem right to her. Graham, who is thin and funny and ebullient and looks a bit like George Harrison, offered loving encouragement, pep talks and jokes when things seemed to be going badly. "She bakes better pies than Myrtle," he joked, the Myrtle coming out in indescribably Manchester glottal stops. Her co-producer stood over the dials, turned down the lights in the studio and made small suggestions in the softest voice imaginable.

Joni was trying "That Song About the Midway" and "Chelsea Morning." They'll probably be the last two cuts for the album. "I can't make it cook," she said about "Chelsea Morning." "I can't get any life into it." Working, she looked very serious and womanly, an artist intent on creating perfection from visual images made into words, guitar chords providing a vessel to hold them and a voice to carry them as deep and as far as they'll go. She is essentially alone with her music.

"Do you want to pack it in, Luv?" Graham asked helpfully, after she'd broken off take eight. "Just sit there and look groovy," she said with a smile in the gentlest way possible, and went on to try it again.

BY STEWART BRAND

THE EDUCATION OF JONI MITCHELL

Jerry Brown, then Governor of California, was planning a public debate on education when he turned to Stewart Brand (later, founder of The Whole Earth Catalog*), for consultation. Brand suggested that the debate be three way and include a musician. "Joni Mitchell," said Governor Brown.*

In preparing materials for the debate, Brand asked Joni for an account of her education. Here is what he learned.—SFL

The CoEvolution Quarterly, Summer 1976

Stewart Brand: Where'd you go to grade school?

Joni Mitchell: I went to different schools in Saskatchewan, all along one highway. Then high school in Saskatoon, Saskatchewan.

SB: Was much education happening for you there, or was it just a holding tank?

JM: I was fortunate in the public school system to have one radical teacher. He was an Australian and a handsome, spirited man and a reverer of spirit. The year before he taught me, he approached me in the hall where I was hanging my drawings for a parents' day. He criticized my habit of copying pictures. No one else did. They praised me as a prodigy for my technique. "You like to paint?" he asked. I nodded. "If you can paint with a brush, you can paint with words." He drew out my poetry. He was a great disciplinarian in his own punk style. We loved him. He was more of a social worker or a renegade priest. I wrote an epic poem in class—I labored to impress him. I got it back circled in red with "cliché, cliché." "White as newly fallen snow"—"cliché"; "high upon a silver shadowed hill"—"cliché." At the bottom he said, "Write about what you know, it's more interesting."

I think at that time there was very good academic opportunity. However, I was only interested in art—painting and music and things which weren't supplied by the school system until a later time. I went back to my high school last summer and found it to be extremely progressive—theatre in the round, advanced study rooms with provision for

Joni Mitchell, Newport, 1969. © David Gahr

video tape, individual music practice rooms, a fairly advanced musical school, two classes devoted to fine arts.

When I was there it was an academic school of a very high order. It did attempt to make you do things for yourself, and function in a more adult way, but it was wasted on my particular interests. I must add at this point that this marvelous teacher who extracted the individuality of his pupils created monsters who were almost ungovernable within the rigidity of that system. We nearly drove our next year's teacher nuts!

SB: If they had had the art stuff then that they have now, do you think that would have made a difference?

JM: I'm not really sure if it would have or not. I mean, the pattern that it produced in me was independent thinking. I have no regrets definitely in retrospect. I do know that some of my art education has been something that I've had to undo. It's been a long time coming for me to find myself as a painter because I was educated badly in that area.

SB: Badly means what?

JM: Badly means being taught to copy things rather than to use my own imagination. And not to copy masterpieces, even, but the covers of magazines and postcards. Bad education in a small town, not progressive enough. They didn't know what to do with a creative child in that environment.

SB: *Was the art you were doing mostly painting and that sort of thing, or were you doing music by then?*

JM: No, I wasn't into music. It's interesting; I wanted to play the piano, but I didn't want to take lessons. I wanted to do what I do now, which is to lay my hand on it and to memorize what comes off of it and to create with it. But my music teacher told me I played by ear, which was a sin, you know, and that I would never be able to read these pieces because I memorized things. So again there was a misunderstanding. In my drive to play the piano I didn't fall into the norm for that system, so I dropped that. And I finally dropped my art lessons too through a similar disillusionment. I belonged to an extracurricular writers' club in my school, although I was a bad English student because I was good in composition, but I wasn't good in the dissection of English, you know. So even in a subject which I later enjoyed, I wasn't scholastically good in it because I didn't like to break it down and analyze it in that manner, and I liked to speak in slang.

I failed the twelfth grade, finally. It just caught up to me that I would cram at the end of the year, and then I would go into the new year with not enough knowledge to continue to build on that subject. So finally in the twelfth grade I ended up repeating a couple of subjects, and at the end of that year I went to art college, where I became an honor student for the first time in my life. And I found that I was an honor student at art school for the same reason that I was a bad student—an equal and opposite reason—because I had developed a lot of technical ability. I was already aware of tonality and light source, and a lot of things that were taught in the first year. As a result, I found that I seemed to be marked for my technical ability so that in free classes, where I was really uninspired, my marks remained the same standard. Whereas people who were great in free class, who were original and loose, who didn't have the chops in a technical class, would receive a mark that was pretty similar to their technical ability. So I became pretty disillusioned with art college, even though I enjoyed being near the head of my class for the first time in my life.

SB: *What was the name of the college?*

JM: Alberta College of Art, situated at a technical institution in Calgary, Alberta.

SB: *You were there how long?*

JM: One year. And the first year was like a time to decide whether you wanted to be a commercial artist or fine artist. They were going to decide what your fate would be. So I quit there and went to Toronto to become a musician. In that town there were about 18 clubs supporting singers, so I went up to see if I could get work. This was in '61.

Well, in Toronto there was a very strict [musician's] union. It cost $160 to get into the union. If you weren't in the union, you couldn't play. So I had to take a job in a clothing store which paid $36-something a week, you know, the minimum wages at that time, out of which a very high rental had to be paid, black dresses for the department I was working in had to be paid, and I could never get ahead to get in the union. And I couldn't write home, because my parents were pissed off at me because I didn't go finish out my art college.

SB: *You were what about now—18?*

JM: No, I was 20 at this point. Anyway, I finally found a non-union club in the city that took a chance on me that I worked at for a while. So I made a little money.

SB: *Did you ever get in a Canadian union?*

JM: I finally did, yes. I finally got enough money saved up. And then I came to the States and gradually began performing around the country.

SB: *Have you done any schooling since then?*

JM: No, but I've learned a tremendous amount from personal encounters. I continue to paint. I continue my work as a fine artist and a commercial artist.

SB: *I wonder where that distinction comes anymore.*

JM: Well, I still feel there is a distinction. You've got to remember that at that time, for modern abstractionism there was no real commercial vent. That was what the fine arts were. You didn't see too many Christmas cards, album covers, car ads, or anything like that which incorporated that aspect of painting.

SB: *Maybe the distinction is: a commercial artist is any artist whose audience is anybody besides personal friends.*

JM: I think that's about it. The fine artist decides that there are only about 13 people in the world who understand him and resigns himself to it. I don't get much from most contemporary art. I find it too noncommunicative.

SB: *You're still doing some of that sort?*

JM: I'm still experimenting with very personal painting as well as more commercial illustration of my own album jackets and things. I haven't taken any formal training, but I have discovered my own educational system. I know how I learn best and I know how I learn most rapidly and how to feed myself information for my particular kind of growth, so I'm out of this a self-educator, but people do feed into me. I'm aware of sources of growth, people who have laid short cuts on me. I can mark the days of those encounters as points of departure. So I'm continuously in school. I do read some, though I seldom finish a book. I read it till I come to a point of inspiration and then work from that point into my own work.

SB: *Do you ever look for more in the same book?*

JM: Some books I do. Rather than overload myself with fact—like in the school system, where they gave you so much information that at best all you could do was regurgitate—I've found that at certain points in a book I would say, "Oh, that's interesting," and I would want to spend some time to develop it or pursue it. I'm interested in the relativity of one thing to another. That's a thing that I do continually, collect information and seek what may seem to be strange correlations. For instance, I know a great studio guitarist, Larry Carlton, whose linear aesthetic tends to arc and splash—Dolphins, I used to call his lines, until I found out he was a weekend flycast fisherman. I find that I interview people all the time. I feel like I'm more in a state of growth and education at this point of my life than when I was in the school system.

SB: *Do you think that's true for most of your contemporaries?*

JM: I can't speak for them.

SB: *Do you find yourself hanging out with people who are more in the learning mode or ones who tend to know something that you feel like you can learn from them? They're not mutually exclusive, I realize.*

JM: In my early twenties I met two men who were best friends from childhood—one a sculptor, one a poet. My association with them was catalytic in opening my gifts in two areas. The sculptor, Mort Rosengarten, gave me a very simple exercise which freed my drawing—gave it boldness and energy. He gave me my originality. The poet Leonard Cohen was a mirror to my work and with no verbal instructions he showed me how to plumb the depths of my own experience. It's funny the way information falls in for me, you know. There are people at large . . . I wanted so badly to go and visit Picasso, even on the fan level that people come to me, even with the possibility that I would be turned away, I wanted desperately to go and see him. Picasso is one of my teachers, although I never met the man, I have applied some of his philosophy of painting to my song writing. I don't seek out those things. I'm very fatalistic about the reception of information.

SB: *Are there others like that?*

JM: Yes. But they live in books. The [Carlos] Castaneda books are a magnificent synthesis of Eastern and Western philosophies. Through them I have been able to understand and apply (in some areas) the concept of believing and not believing simultaneously. My Christian heritage tends to polarize concepts; faith and God—doubt and the Devil—it creates dualities which in turn create guilt which impedes freedom. Jean Grenier and Camus also are teachers of freedom. I feel closer to Camus since he is more savage—Grenier being somehow to me wise but passive.

SB: *Is there anyone you've looked up personally? I should explain partly why I'm curious about this. I've just spent some time with Marlon Brando, and he is very much an adult educating himself by going around hanging out with people whom he admires. He just shows up at their door.*

JM: That's a wonderful way to do it. Warren Beatty also approaches things that way. He calls people that interest him and flies to meet them. Warren and Marlon have that ability—who's going to turn them away from the door? That's why I was hoping Picasso would like my music and wouldn't turn me away. I wanted to go and play him a song while he painted or something, because I had so much respect for his prolonged creativity. I've chosen books, I guess, because I lack the chutzpah to just go up and knock at somebody's door.

SB: When kids come around now to see you, wondering what they should be doing about their own education, do you give them any counsel?

JM: Well, the last time I had contact with a group of kids they had come over here because they had a class in career choice. They live in the valley, and they were all interested in music, but music again in the school was not considered a career and they were being channeled into what they would describe as straight jobs. So they asked me to tell them how I had come to have an outlet for my music, how I had achieved success. Well, in talking to them, most of them felt they had to make it like the Beatles—by the time they were 21. They seemed to have a feeling of urgency, they didn't seem to have the patience to develop and hone their craft over a long period of time. They were rushing, which I felt would interfere with their growth in a way—setting their goals too high and too close at hand.

SB: You can tell them if they're famous by the time they're 21, it will turn their brains to hamburger and they'll be sorry.

JM: I told them, "You should see the Beatles now, at 30, with all of their glory behind them." I said, "Wouldn't you rather come to fruition later on in life, sort of slow and gradual, so you're still working toward something when you're 30?" I said, "I am 30," and I looked them right in the eye, because 30, you know, to a kid is that magic number where you begin to fall apart or something.

SB: Middle-aged.

JM: Right, they can't conceive of it. So anyway, anybody that comes to me, I don't have any stock thing to say, because they all ask different questions. I find one thing: they'll ask a question and they'll get an answer that I feel could be useful to them. I can tell by how they relate to it that it's interesting enough for them to use for themselves. Then instead of taking that one bit of information, they get excited and they get greedy in a way, so that they wind up with more information than they can do anything with.

SB: *One handball instructor I know of tells you one thing during the course of an afternoon's workout, and that's all you get.*

JM: That's why I never finish books, I think. I get to a point where something hits me so strong that it takes me out of the reading, the non-active activity of intake, and puts me into an output situation; it inspires something, it triggers my work habits, it triggers my . . . at that point I put that book down.

SB: *What books have done that for you lately?*

JM: The Boho Dance in Tom Wolfe's book *The Painted Word*. He described the Boho Dance as that period in an artist's existence when he's a bohemian, when he's established all of his moral justifications for poverty while still striving for success. The second stage is the consummation which he has aimed himself toward, when the public says, "Yes, we like your work, we would like to buy it," and he is celebrated, he finds himself sucked into a social strata which he deplored as a bohemian. There are different reactions. Picasso went right into it, you know, and bought himself a Rolls Royce and some little black and white maids, and everybody said, "Look at Picasso, man, he's going to blow it," like he sold out. Jackson Pollock said, "I won't sell out," went to all of these fancy cocktail parties and pissed in the fireplace and did everything just to show he wasn't going to enjoy it. That's the point in that book when I said, "Oh, my God, that is a liberating statement and an understanding to me," and I created a song called "The Boho Dance," taking his title and taking my own experience. I experienced my own understanding of what he was saying so strongly that it almost paralyzed me from reading further. Do you know that feeling? Carlos Castaneda, Rimbaud, Leonard Cohen—they do that for me too.

SB: The only way I can continue is if I can get hold of a pencil and make some mark on the page, turn down the corner, and then I can go on. I've done at least something to acknowledge the hit, and I can come back to it if I need to.

JM: I am fatalistic about my reading lessons. I was working on a song when I was up in Canada. I had gone up to this lake with John Guerin and we got into a discussion about Genesis and Adam and Eve, and I said let's look up the story. I'd taken two books with me, and there happened to be this Gideon Bible in the cottage, in the dresser drawer. One book I took was a book on the history of modern art from a lot of critics' points of view. They were critical essays on the modern art movement through history, and I was still trying to understand. As I said before, I don't understand this period of modern painting, which is why I was reading Wolfe's book. We were looking for how they had arrived at this, since a lot of it seemed humorous and they wouldn't cop to it being funny. And there was such an elitist attitude.

Well, this other book I had was called *The Disorderly Poet*, which was an explanation of the creative trance, you might call it, taken to different extremes—drug-induced, natural chemical body disorders such as epilepsy and speaking in tongues. And these three pieces of information were so related. In the art book I came upon a passage about witches and how they had actually been used to further the scientific method, and out of the whole book that's all I recall—that's it in a nutshell, believe me. It was as if the rest of the book wasn't intended for me to discover at that moment. And the information from those three books, in conjunction with one another, was my lesson for the day. And it was completely random, it was, you know, opening the book on page 92 or something. It was almost like the *I Ching*. It was almost like an oracle. But it was the perfect information for that moment. It connected for me in its randomness. So I do feel kind of mystical too about education. I feel that somehow the answers come to you through your inquiry.

BY WILLIAM RUHLMANN

JONI MITCHELL: FROM BLUE TO INDIGO

Written in 1995, this article is packed with details from Joni Mitchell's career, particularly from the '60s and '70s. This is only an excerpt—the piece in its original form is nearly a biography in itself. Note: Some slight revisions to the originally published piece have been made by the author to correct factual errors pointed out to him by the eagle-eyed Mitchell.—SFL

Goldmine, February 17, 1995

In 1964, Mitchell got on a train and went east to Toronto to attend the Mariposa Folk Festival and see folksinger Buffy Sainte-Marie. On the way, she wrote her first song, "Day After Day." She did not return to college. As she put it, "I allowed my disappointment in the education offered me to lead me to the East Coast, where there were 17 thriving coffeehouses in Toronto."

In his book, *Neil Young: Don't Be Denied* (Quarry Press, 1992), John Einarson provides a description of the thriving music scene in Toronto in 1964. "The 'scene' of Toronto music at that time was the Yorkville district," Einarson wrote. "Within the downtown Yorkville village district, a two-block stretch between Avenue Road and Yonge Street one way, and Davenport and Bloor Streets on the other side, some ten to fifteen different coffeehouses could be found amid the closely knit artistic community that thrived there. On any given night one could easily hear the strains of Eric Andersen, Tom Rush, or Odetta wafting from these tiny enclaves. These coffeehouses were literally houses, old, brick two- and three-story homes with folksingers or small groups performing in the front room or basement."

And there wasn't only folk music, as Levon Helm recalled in his book *This Wheel's On Fire: Levon Helm And The Story of The Band* (written with Stephen Davis, William Morrow and Company, 1993). "It was a great time to launch a band in Toronto," noted Helm, who was a member of Ronnie Hawkins' rockabilly-playing Hawks then, "because the place was jumping. On a weekend night on that Yonge Street strip you could catch Oscar Peterson, Carl Perkins, Ray Charles and his band, Cannonball Adderley, Charles Mingus. You could see a local band like us or one of our competitors, the Paupers. There was a folk music scene. . . . And it wasn't just music. Toronto was also the publishing, fashion, and style capital of Canada. The city was swinging at least a year before so-called Swinging London."

Sounds great, but for 20-year-old Joni Mitchell there was just one problem. "When I got there," she recalled, "it cost $160 to get into the [musicians'] union, which was a fortune for me, just an impossible goal. And there wasn't much scab work around, and coffeehouse doors slammed in my face, and it was pretty insulting. There were some dues in that town."

She stuck it out, however. As Einarson put it, "Living in one of the dozens of communal pads on Huron Street in the village, Joni perfected her . . . craft in the coffeehouses at night, working during the day at a Simpsons-Sears department store to pay the rent."

Apparently, there was more department store than coffeehouse work, but, "then I finally found a scab club in Toronto that allowed me to play," Mitchell told Joe Smith in his book *Off the Record: An Oral History of Popular Music* (Warner Books, 1988). "I played for a couple of months.

"In 1965, I was playing in the cellar where they kept the Canadian talent and where the imported American talent played upstairs," she said, elaborating, "and I met a folksinger named Chuck Mitchell. I was at an indecisive time in my life, and he was a strong force. He decided he was gonna marry me. So, he dragged me across the border, and he got me some work, and we were kind of quickly married. It was not a marriage made in heaven. He was relatively well-educated. He was in contempt of my lack of education and also my illiteracy. I did all my book reviews [in school] from *Classic Comic Books,* and I had a kind of a contempt for what I called pseudo-intellectuals, and in a way I was right. I mean, I was developing as an original, unschooled thinker, and I had the gift of the blarney. I had a gift of metaphor. But he kind of ridiculed me in the same way that [Canadian prime minister] Pierre Trudeau ridiculed his wife, Margaret, when she wrote her book. He said, 'My wife is the only writer I know who's written more books than she's read.' So, there was this aristocratic—the educated pride versus the uneducated, and that marriage didn't last very long."

It did last for almost two years, however, and they were important years in Joni Mitchell's development. For one thing, she began to write songs in earnest. "I began as a folksinger," she said, meaning a singer of traditional folk songs. "I would say I was a folksinger from 1963 until '65.

'65, when I crossed the border, I began to write. Once I began to write, my vocal style changed. My [Joan] Baez/Judy Collins influence disappeared. Almost immediately when I had my own words to sing, my own voice appeared."

Writing also led Mitchell to her own guitar sound, based on unusual tunings and conditioned by a physical infirmity. "The moment I began to write I took the black blues tunings which were floating around," she said. "Tom [Rush] played in open C. Eric Andersen showed me an open G, which I think is Keith Richards's tuning, he mainly writes in that. Then there was D modal. Buffy [Sainte-Marie] had a couple of original tunings. But I began to experiment because my left hand is somewhat clumsy because of polio. I had to simplify the shapes of the left hand, but I craved chordal movement that I couldn't get out of standard tuning without an extremely articulate left hand. So, to compensate for it, I found the tunings were a godsend. Not only that, but they made the guitar an unstable thing, but also an instrument of exploration, so that you could put the thing in a new tuning, you had to rediscover the neck, you'd need to search out the chordal movement, and you'd find five or six chords, and then there was the art of chaining them together in a creative manner. It was very exciting to discover my music. It still is, to this day."

"Her unusual tunings and lilting voice drew the attention of those in the know who tipped her to be a future major talent," wrote Einarson. "Unfortunately, not enough people took notice of her genius to keep her in Canada." Chuck and Joni Mitchell moved to Detroit, where Chuck was from, in late 1965.

Unlike nearly all aspiring songwriters, the Mitchells put their business together properly at the start. "The one thing I had was my own publishing company," Joni said. "Chuck and I set up two publishing companies. That was at his instigation. That was very insightful." Joni's company was called Siquomb Publishing, and the name came from one of her many writing projects. As she would explain on Philadelphia radio station WMMR in March 1967, she was writing a mythology, the names of its various members derived from acronyms based on descriptive phrases. There were, for instance, a race of miniature women, the Posall ("Perhaps Our Souls Are Little Ladies"), and men, the Mosalm ("Maybe Our Souls Are Little Men"). Siquomb was the queen of the mythology, her name meaning "She Is Queen Undisputedly Of Mind Beauty."

Indisputably, Siquomb saved Joni Mitchell from the kinds of schemes that typically rob songwriters of their work. One of her first songs was

"Urge for Going," which eventually concerned romantic parting, though in its original form it was about the difficulty acoustic folk performers were starting to have finding places to play in the wake of the folk-rock movement ushered in by Bob Dylan's decision to use an amplified backup band. "The clubs were going electric," she recalled, and the first draft [of "Urge for Going"] was about that: 'I've got the urge for going, but there's no place left to go.'"

Another early composition was "The Circle Game," Mitchell's song about a young boy's rites of passage. It was inspired by another song, Neil Young's "Sugar Mountain." Mitchell had met Young in 1964 at the Fourth Dimension folk club at the University of Manitoba, and encountered him again in the Yorkville district of Toronto in 1965. Young, a member of the Squires rock 'n' roll group, had written "Sugar Mountain" on his 19th birthday, November 12, 1964, as a lament for the approaching end of his teenage years ("You can't be 20 on Sugar Mountain"). Mitchell took the story to its logical conclusion, but offered hope. "So the years spin by and now the boy is twenty / Though his dreams have lost some grandeur coming true / There'll be new dreams, maybe better dreams and plenty / Before the last revolving year is through."

And then there was "Both Sides, Now."

"I think at 21 I was quite old," she said. "'Both Sides, Now' is like an old person reflecting back on their life. My life had been very hard. I had gone through a lot of life. When I wrote 'Both Sides, Now,' Chuck Mitchell said to me, 'Oh, what do you know about life, you're only 21.' But I knew a lot about life. I'd gone through a lot of disease and personal pain. Even as a child. I'd had three bouts with death. I was not unaware of my mortality. But somehow, still, I was very young for my age, in spite of my experience."

Based in Detroit, Chuck and Joni Mitchell traveled to folk clubs in the northern Midwest and along the East Coast, and when they were at home, they played host to fellow folk musicians in town to play the Chess Mate, the local folk club.

"In Detroit, everybody was kind of scuffling, and we had a big apartment, Chuck and I, so we billeted a lot of artists," Mitchell said. "Eric Andersen stayed there, and Tom Rush stayed there. It was a fifth-floor walkup in the black district, basically, it was two white blocks, Wayne campus housing. The rent was really cheap, and we had three or four bed-

Joni Mitchell and David Crosby, 1968. © Corbis/Henry Diltz

rooms in this old place. So, artists stayed with us frequently. I was just beginning to write, and Tom, I think, first carried off 'Urge for Going.' So, he played that around, and the next time he came to play the Chess Mate, he said, 'You got anything else?' and I played him some songs. It was usually the one that I thought was too feminine, a little too light for a man to sing, that I withheld—'Any more?' 'Well, yes, this one, but it's not right for you'—'The Circle Game' or something—'That's the one I want.' So, he'd cart that off, and in that way the songs became known in places that I hadn't gone. There were no records."

Soon enough, however, there *were* records. The first, curiously enough, was by country singer George Hamilton IV, who cut "Urge for Going." In a March 1967 live appearance, introducing the song, Mitchell told her audience, "It's currently on the country hit parade. However, I don't think it really is a country song, if you can classify songs. As a matter of fact, it's #13 with a bullet. That means it's moving up rapidly. It's by a fellow named George Hamilton IV. The song is by me, but he does it, with Chet Atkins and a whole Nashville chorus and a Carter Family type and all sorts of people and a recitation and electric rock 'n' roll mandolin. But originally the song went like this. . . ."

Hamilton's cover of "Urge for Going," released as a single by RCA, entered *Billboard*'s Hot Country Singles chart for the week ending January 21, 1967, and peaked at #7 during a 21-week chart run. (Unless otherwise stated, all chart figures cited here will be from *Billboard*, as reported in Joel Whitburn's various chart books, published by Record Research, Inc. On occasions when a record performs better on charts published by the rival trade paper *Cash Box*, this will be noted.)

Mitchell isn't sure how Hamilton got hold of the song, but she credits Tom Rush, who may also have pitched it—unsuccessfully—to Judy Collins. "At one point, George came to Detroit, and I remember meeting him," Mitchell said, "but I think he must have heard the song first from Tom." By the time "Urge for Going" had ended its chart run, other Joni Mitchell compositions were coming onto the market. In February, Vanguard Records released Canadian duo Ian and Sylvia's *So Much for Dreaming* album, containing their rendition of "The Circle Game." In June, Vanguard released Buffy Sainte-Marie's *Fire and Fleet and Candlelight* LP, which included "The Circle Game" and "Song to a Seagull."

"I picked up music more for fun," Mitchell said. "I had no ambition to make a career of it at all." But when her songs started to become popular, this changed. "Of course, once I began to write my own songs, I was slightly ambitious for them," she admitted. "I was a stage door mother to them. I wanted to display them. I thought that this was a superior work to selling women's ware, which was all I was really trained for. I had a grade 12 education. So, waitressing, hairdressing, that was about all. This was slightly more lucrative and a lot more fun at the club level."

And at the club level, her increasing renown as a songwriter was boosting her as a performer, helping her break the one city she'd been having trouble playing, New York. "I had difficulty initially in finding work in the clubs [in New York]," Mitchell said, "but I had a kind of a circuit on the Eastern seaboard from Miami to Boston, and a little bit in the Midwest around the Detroit area. New York was difficult without a record. The major clubs were hard to crack until some people started singing my songs. When Buffy and Tom Rush initially began to play [them], then the circuit that they played on opened up to me because they were kind of a herald of the writer of these songs. So, 'Circle Game' and 'Urge for Going,' [Dave] Van Ronk with 'Both Sides, Now' [which he retitled "Clouds"] and 'Chelsea Morning,' all helped to make club work possible for me."

This, in turn, seems to have given Mitchell the impetus she needed to split up with her husband and go out on her own. The dramatic circumstances of that move suggest it was anything but an amicable parting.

"I was in the middle of a poker game some place in Michigan late in the evening," Mitchell recalled, "and I turned to a stranger, basically, next to me, and I said, 'I'm leaving my husband tonight. Will you help me?' We rented a U-Haul truck. We drove back to Detroit.

"I had polio, and a lot of the muscles in my back are deteriorated. So, you can imagine the will. I separated what I considered was a fair split, 50 percent of the furniture, and the stranger and I hauled it on our own backs down a fifth-floor walkup in the middle of the night, and I moved out. The song 'I Had a King' kind of tells a bit of the aftermath of that. I moved to New York. I moved to West 16th Street, and I set out looking for work in that area."

Despite the success she had found with her songs and the increased club work, Mitchell was not naive about her chances for making it big in the music business. She considered those chances small, and, in fact, in 1967, the year of the Summer of Love, the year of *Sgt. Pepper*, the chances for a songwriter with only an acoustic guitar could not have been considered very great. The people who were recording her songs were folkies, none of them big sellers, all of them essentially sideswiped two years earlier by the rise of folk-rock, which was itself already giving way to other pop trends.

Mitchell could see all this by the time she got to New York. "I came in late," she said. "Basically, clubs were folding, and bands were the new thing, and I wasn't ready for a band. It would take me five albums to find a band that could play with me without squashing the intricacy of the music."

At this point, though, she wasn't thinking about five albums, or even one. "Record companies offered me terrible slave labor deals in the beginning, and I turned them down," she said. "I turned down Vanguard. They wanted three albums a year or something. In the folk tradition, they come and stick a mike on the table in front of you, and they collect it in an hour, and that's the album. And that output—I already saw Buffy struggling under the weight of it. So, I thought, no way. This'll take the fun out of it. There's no remuneration. It was a terrible contract, the highlight of which was, they would provide little folding table-top cards that said I was a

Vanguard artist, and it would have driven my price up slightly, I guess. To be a recording artist, I could have made a little more in the clubs, but not that much, and it would have required that I have a manager."

A manager was another thing she didn't want. "Of course, the managers wanted a big hunk of [my song publishing], and I turned down a lot of managers," Mitchell said. "I said, no way, this is my little business. You're not writing these songs. It's kind of like the story of the little red hen. You know, 'Who will help me sow the wheat?' I didn't understand the way that management was structured at that time."

Nor did Mitchell understand how she was going to make it when she was perceived as a folksinger, even if she had ceased thinking of herself that way. "I looked like a folksinger, even though the moment I began to write, my music was not folk music," she said. "It was something else, maybe closer to German lieder, or it had elements of romantic classicism to it." Nevertheless, it sounded to a lot of people like folk music, and folk music was on its way out.

"I wasn't keen waiting for my big break or anything," Mitchell said. "As a matter of fact, I entered into the game thinking that this was the tail end of an era. The minimum wage at that time was $36 a week, you could barely eat and pay your rent on it, and I was able to make about $300 a week in the clubs. Traveling, of course, ate up some of it. But I had no manager, I had no agent, I had no liens on me. So, I viewed it initially as a way to get a little nest egg ahead, and then I would fall back on salesmanship. I would go back into women's ware. My idea of a little bit ahead was, the rent paid and enough for the next month, like, $400 in the bank."

In fact, she achieved her goal in 1967. "That's probably the richest I ever felt," she recalled, "because after I had my recording deal, I had a lot of people on my payroll, and unless you're an arena artist, it's a lot of work, and everything you do is self-promotion."

Despite that $400 nest egg, Mitchell kept accepting engagements, including in the early fall of 1967, an offer by British-based American record executive and producer Joe Boyd to undertake a brief tour of Great Britain. "Joe set up a tour with the Incredible String Band, and some isolated little gigs without them in small coffeehouses," she recalled.

Boyd was especially interested in Mitchell as a songwriter, and he arranged a U.K. publishing deal for her with Essex Music. She left a 10-song demo tape with Boyd, who played it for his clients the folk-rock group Fairport Convention. Fairport recorded a demo of "Both Sides, Now" at sessions for their debut single, "If I Had a Ribbon Bow," released in November. "I Don't Know Where I Stand" and "Chelsea Morning" would turn up on their debut album, *Fairport Convention*, released in June 1968, and they added "Marcie" and "Night in the City" to their concert repertoire.

(In January 1969, they would include "Eastern Rain," a song Mitchell herself has never released officially, on their second album, titled *What We Did on Our Holidays* in the U.K. and *Fairport Convention* in the U.S.)

"The first time I heard 'Both Sides Now,'" Judy Collins wrote in her autobiography, *Trust Your Heart* (Houghton Mifflin Company, 1987), "was on the phone in 1967 during the middle of the night. I got a call from Tom Rush, who was very excited. Tom, a great fan of Joni's, had earlier introduced me to her and to her fine song, 'The Circle Game.'

"'Joni has a new song, and I want you to hear it. I think you'll love it.' He put Joni on the phone, and she sang 'Both Sides Now.'

"I immediately fell in love with the song and knew it was a classic. I had to sing it."

Judy Collins recorded "Both Sides Now" (while Van Ronk had changed the title completely, Collins merely removed the comma after "Sides") on September 28, 1967, at Columbia Studios in New York with a string arrangement by Joshua Rifkin, who played harpsichord on the track. Collins also recorded Mitchell's "Michael from Mountains," and the two songs were used as the opening tracks on either side of Collins's album *Wildflowers*, released in November

Like Joan Baez, Judy Collins had begun as a singer of traditional folk songs and, in the wake of the folk songwriter boom led by Bob Dylan, begun to champion the work of new writers. Unlike many of her folk peers, she had neither ignored the rise of folk-rock in 1965 nor entirely given in to it, instead branching out into tasteful arrangements and adding theater music to her repertoire. She had been rewarded in 1967 by the audience that greeted the LP *In My Life*, making it her most successful album so far. *Wildflowers*, on which she introduced both Mitchell's songs and her own, was intended to consolidate that success and extend it. It would.

Mitchell, meanwhile, was still having some trouble with the New York club circuit and beginning to think that maybe having a manager wouldn't be such a bad idea. "I had a hard time playing in New York," she said, "I cried and pleaded, said, I'm good, I'm good. I had no manager to, like, front for me. Finally, this place [the Cafe Au Go Go] hired me as an opening act to an opening act. Ian and Sylvia were the headliners, and there was a comic in the middle and I was in really foot soldier position. I had all of the songs at that point that would constitute my first two albums.

"Elliot [Roberts] came in. He was a manager of comics. He came in to hear the comedian, Howard Hesseman. And people were talking, you know, the opening act to the opening act, nobody was really listening to me. Elliot thought that, God, this girl is really good. Why is nobody listening to her?"

Elliot Roberts (born Elliot Rabinowitz in the Bronx), then working at the William Morris Agency, represented a new type of manager, appropriate to the new type of entertainers who were emerging in the second half of the 1960s. For one thing, he didn't want a piece of Mitchell's publishing. As he told Steve Chapple and Reebee Garofalo for their book *Rock 'N' Roll Is Here to Pay: The History and Politics of the Music Industry* (Nelson-Hall, 1977): "People see now that they can become millionaires by doing it right. People used to think you had to beat someone for all their publishing to hit the jackpot. We showed them that it was the other way around. If you left the publishing there and did the right thing by the artist, and the artist was good, then you'd make it."

Beyond that crucial matter, Roberts was ready to adapt himself to the special needs of his clients. "Let's say you wanted me to manage you," he said. "Well, we'd have to get together. I'd have to find out what you wanted, what you're like, whether you're abrasive and hard, or soft and sensitive. I'd have to find out what you're capable of. Whether you can go on all these interviews or whether you would get shell-shocked. All this varies from person to person. It's all in the person. What do you want to be? Do you want to retire in three or four years? You know, that's all part of it. It depends on what the person wants."

What Roberts found out initially was what Joni Mitchell didn't want. "He pitched being my manager, and I said, 'I don't need a manager. I'm doing quite nicely. Why should I cut you in?' Mitchell recalled. "But he was a funny man. I enjoyed his humor. So, I said, 'Okay, let's do a trial run. I've got a gig coming up in the Midwest near Detroit. Why don't you accompany me, and we'll see how we get along?'" The resulting trip, which, according to Roberts, began the next day, sounds like a folkie version of *This Is Spinal Tap*, but it solidified their relationship.

"We went to this town, Ann Arbor, Michigan," Mitchell recalled. "Pot was legal there, and Elliot was a pot smoker, but people were very secretive about that. He was also dressed in a suit with silk shirts with his initials on the pocket. So was [his friend and later partner David] Geffen at that time. They were very Madison Avenue.

"So, we get to this hotel, and it's before the gig, and we don't let each other know that we smoke pot. But I get to his room, and I can smell that he's been smoking pot, and he's got a towel under the door and everything, and I realize he's as bad as me. He has no mechanical aptitude. He can't find the light switch, he can't turn his TV set on. Anyway, we end up on our way to this gig. We get lost in the hotel. The hotel was, like, kind of a square donut shape, and we literally could not find our way out [laughs], and we wandered through soup kitchens and all kinds of places, and he was so funny.

"When we finally got to this club, it was packed not only to capacity, but there were people standing in the back. It was the biggest crowd I ever drew at that point. I got up on the stage and I sang my first song, and there was, to me, a thunderous reception. I broke out into a wide grin, and my upper lip stuck to my gums and I couldn't get it down! I had to peel it with my tongue. Elliot was doing loud shtick from the audience. He was making a lot of jokes, and everybody was giggling 'cause everybody knew why. And so, I said to him, 'Okay, you're my manager.' I enjoyed his company on the road so much. He was good, and I was a great straight man for him. So, in this way we began."

Roberts quit his job at William Morris and began working full-time for Joni Mitchell. His first goal, of course, was to obtain a record contract for her. But if independent folk labels like Vanguard were interested, the majors were not. Roberts tried Columbia Records, the home of Bob Dylan, with its self-professed talent scout of a company president, Clive Davis. They weren't interested, maybe because Roberts's friend David Geffen was pitching them another female singer-songwriter, Laura Nyro, whom they signed instead.

Roberts next tried RCA. "We brought them Joni's songs and demos," he told Chapple and Garofalo, "and they said, 'That's nice, a girl and some songs, but it's not making it. We're looking for the Rascals or Wilson Pickett.'"

Many people are credited with "discovering" Joni Mitchell, from Tom Rush to Joe Boyd to Elliot Roberts, and Mitchell graciously admits them all. "These all, in their own way, were kind of discoveries," she said when the list was read off to her. But it would take one more discoverer to get her career going: David Crosby.

"I was playing the Gaslight South," she recalled [referring to a club in southern Florida]. "He came into the club one night and was very interested in my tunings."

There was a little more to it than that. "Right away I thought I'd been hit by a hand grenade," Crosby told biographer Dave Zimmer (*Crosby, Stills & Nash: The Authorized Biography*, with photography by Henry Diltz, St. Martin's Press, 1984). "Her voice, those words . . . she nailed me to the back of the wall with two-inch spikes. I went up to her afterwards and said, 'You're incredible.' She said, 'You really think so?'"

—

Mitchell, with Crosby in tow, arrived back in New York and met with Roberts in his office on West 57th Street. "He was," Roberts said in *Long Time Gone*, "the first hippie that I met in that era." Roberts had succeeded in getting Mitchell signed to Warner Brothers Records, and the three took off for California to record her first album.

Probably, her first album would have been tricked out with folk-rock arrangements if it hadn't been for David Crosby, who came in to produce it. "To many corporate executives, I looked like a second-generation Judy Collins or Joan Baez because I was a girl with a guitar," Mitchell explained. "The same thing they do to young women now, they liken them to me. [Did someone say "Tori Amos"?] So, basically they wanted a folk-rocker. David believed in my music as it was. He knew that it was taking that some place, and the people in power couldn't really hear that it was taking it some place but it didn't look like it was taking it that some place. As a matter of fact, I was an oddity on the scene."

Under Crosby's laissez-faire production style, the album was cut quickly at Sunset Sound in Los Angeles. Far from a folk-rock record, it featured Mitchell alone on guitar and piano. The only added instrumentation was some bass guitar played by Stephen Stills of Buffalo Springfield, who were recording at the studio next door. Also in the Springfield, of course, was Neil Young, Mitchell's old friend from Canada, and they were able to renew their acquaintance. Roberts, meeting these various artists for the first time, would wind up managing all of them.

The album was finished by February, when Mitchell took off for her club circuit back on the East Coast, starting in Ottawa. While there, she was introduced to Graham Nash, who was on tour with the Hollies and had heard of her from his friend Crosby.

When Mitchell got back to Los Angeles, Crosby set out to showcase her to various people in the business, playing an advance copy of her album or having her sing in person. In *Long Time Gone*, Roberts describes one such impromptu concert. "Sure, they played [disc jockey] B. Mitchell Reed's house too. David invited some people over one day. I remember

Cass [Elliot] was there, John Sebastian, Michelle Phillips, about seven or eight people, all heavy players. David says, 'Joan,' and called Joni out. She was upstairs and came down with her guitar and she played eight or nine of the best songs ever written. The next day B. Mitchell Reed talked about it on the radio, how there was this girl in town named Joni Mitchell that's recording an album and there's nothing he can play now, but whenever this album comes out, it's going to be one of the great albums of all time. David set it up so that when the album finally came out, everyone in L.A. was aware of Joni Mitchell. The first club date we played, at the Troubadour, was standing room only for four nights, two shows a night."

The Hollies, meanwhile, arrived in L.A. on tour, and Nash came to see Crosby, setting off a turn of events that would inspire several songs. "I was living with David," Mitchell said in *Long Time Gone*. "Graham and I had had kind of an ill-fated beginning of a romance because we had met in Ontario. . . .

"He ended up at David's place, and I was staying with David until my house was ready. Graham came down sick in David's house, and I took him home to my new house to play Florence Nightingale. At first it wasn't really for romance's sake . . . I took him home and was looking after him and I got attached—here was a mess. What was I going to say? I'm kind of going with David and we sort of staked claims, but I'd written all these independent songs, trying to explain my position to him; that I'm still in an independent mode. But I got really attached to Graham and I guess that's the first time I harbored the illusion of forever. I really felt for the first time in my life that I could pair bond."

"I went with her," said Nash, "and I didn't leave for a couple of years."

The author of "Triad," meanwhile, said, "The thing with Joni and Graham was that I felt great about it." Crosby went back to his old girl-friend, Christine Hinton. And the world was treated to such songs as Mitchell's "Willy," Nash's "Our House" and Crosby's "Guinnevere" (which is partially about Hinton, partially about Mitchell).

Joni Mitchell was released in March 1968, and the first thing to say about it is to confirm that the title was *Joni Mitchell*. The album's cover, a painting by Mitchell surrounding a tiny photograph of her, features a grouping of birds that spell out the words "Song to a Seagull," the title of one of the songs and the title Mitchell actually intended for the album. Not only has this led many people to call the album *Song to a Seagull*, but several reputable rock 'n' roll history books (one example being *The* Rolling Stone *Rock & Roll Encyclopedia*, edited by Jon Pareles and Patricia

Romanowski [Rolling Stone Press/Summit Books, 1983]) list two different albums, one called *Joni Mitchell*, the other *Song to a Seagull*.

Mitchell, when informed of this, expressed surprise. "People can't see them," she said of the birds, "and the 'L' [of Seagull] is cut off, 'cause even the graphic department, they didn't see it either. It's called *Joni Mitchell*."

To anyone who had been attending Joni Mitchell's club performances, the album must have been a surprise, at least in terms of the song selection. First, her best-known material—"Urge for Going," "The Circle Game," "Both Sides, Now"—was nowhere to be found. Nor were some of her lighter, funnier songs. Instead, more recent material, the "independent songs" she had been writing while living with Crosby, were here, arranged in a loose story line that followed her recent history. "Part One," the first side, was titled, "I Came to the City," and began with "I Had a King," her account of her split with Chuck Mitchell, followed by songs reflecting on city life. "Part Two," subtitled, "Out of the City and Down to the Seaside," included songs like "The Dawntreader," about life on Crosby's boat, "The Pirate of Penance" and "Cactus Tree," about "a man who's been out sailing" and "a lady in the city."

Whatever else such an arrangement of material may have meant, it presented a different Joni Mitchell from the one audiences were used to in clubs, where her sense of humor and wit balanced the ornamentation and preciousness of some of her lyrics. "See, there you're looking at a slightly different form," she explained. "An album was basically 22 minutes per side. In a club, you're writing for sets, which are a little longer. I forget now, it's so long since I played a club set, but I think it was about 10 songs, maybe 14 songs. You're doing three and four sets a night, and some people are staying for two sets, so there has to be some variation between sets.

"Also, as an entertainer, you're looking to keep your audience awake, and so there's kind of little comedic things like 'Dr. Junk The Dentist Man' and funny little songs from back where I felt, I need a laugh here, this is too much drama, and none of those things found their way onto albums. I must have 20 or 30 songs prior to the first album that never were recorded."

Later, when Mitchell began to introduce some of her humor on records, it sometimes contributed to the critical backlash she suffered in the late 1970s. Though she is referring to Crosby's preservation of her acoustic presentation, one of the comments she makes in *Long Time Gone* about the album is telling:

". . . The way you enter the game in this business is usually the way you stay. It takes a lot to break typecasting and the way you come into the game is crucial, which was something I didn't realize at the time. In retrospect, I realize the importance of it."

Actually, at the time, *Joni Mitchell* didn't get that much attention. It entered the charts on May 18 at #197 and peaked three weeks later at #189, lasting a total of nine weeks near the bottom of the Top 200.

But other events were conspiring to put Joni Mitchell before the public. For one thing, the musical climate, which, only the previous fall, had seemed to favor psychedelia and the elaborate eclecticism of *Sgt. Pepper*, had changed in favor of her approach. Bob Dylan's comeback album, *John Wesley Harding*, released the last week of 1967 on the same day as Leonard Cohen's debut LP *Songs of Leonard Cohen*, countered the new complexity with a new simplicity. Soon after, Simon and Garfunkel topped the charts with *Bookends* and the soundtrack to *The Graduate*, and soft, quiet folkie music seemed to be back.

Also, Judy Collins's recording of "Both Sides Now" became a Top 10 hit and an instant standard, appearing on albums by at least 15 different artists in 1969 alone, and it is no doubt the most widely recorded song Joni Mitchell ever wrote. It has been recorded by Frank Sinatra, Bing Crosby, Neil Diamond, Andy Williams and Willie Nelson, among many others.

The situation did not go unnoticed at Warner Brothers, of course, but the way the company chose to exploit its association with the hit offended its artist.

Its ads, designed by Stan Cornyn, were intended to appeal to the sly, irreverent side of the counter-culture. For example, when Randy Newman's debut album failed to sell despite glowing reviews in 1968, Warners took out an ad in the trades under a headline reading, "Want a free album? Okay." The ad noted that the company was unable to sell the album, had hundreds on hand, and would give a thousand of them away free to those who sent in an enclosed coupon. The tone of the ad copy was satiric: at one point, it speculated about what would happen after the offer was over. "Which brings us to the age-old dilemma: can the girl who gave it away ever hope to sell it?"

Today, such a remark might get somebody sued for sexual harassment, and that brings us to Joni Mitchell, who also had a poor-selling album in 1968, while her song "Both Sides, Now" (not contained on her record) became a big hit for Judy Collins. This inspired Cornyn to write an ad with a headline reading, "Joni Mitchell is 90% virgin."

The point, if you read the copy, was that Collins had sold 10 times as many records as Mitchell had, but the headline statement flagged a part of

Joni Mitchell's image that has both helped and hurt her, and that she has never entirely escaped.

In fact, Mitchell brought it up in her *Goldmine* interview, noting that, in an earlier interview as part of the press junket she's been on promoting *Turbulent Indigo*, she was "confronted" with a copy of the ad in Toronto, as well as Cornyn's followup ads, "Joni Mitchell takes forever," bemoaning the time it took her to finish records, and, announcing the release of her second album, "Joni Mitchell finally comes across."

"I must have seemed very peculiar to them," Mitchell said of Warners. "I had an innocence. By that time, I'd be about 25, but I felt and looked about 16. So, I think that innocence is—they want—the temptation with innocence is to corrupt it, and since I was not corrupting myself, I wasn't showing my tits, I had very low necklines, but they were demure. In a way, they didn't really know what to do with me. I was neither an anarchist nor—I wasn't rough-mouthed. I was a Canadian girl. Not that it wasn't within me, under the right circumstances. But under the wrong circumstances, if I was rough-mouthed, I would embarrass people because of their view."

Mitchell acknowledged that this innocent image had its advantages, just as it had back in Saskatoon when she was a teenager. "People tended to be protective of me," she said, "and even in the scene when cocaine was around, people would shelter me from it. Everyone would be doing it, but they wouldn't do it in front of me. So, somehow or other, I brought out protectiveness in people well into my 30s, which was all right. It helps you survive some pretty tough situations."

But Mitchell did not feel protected by the Warners ads, and they would be one reason she left the company in 1971.

Meanwhile, Roberts put her on the road to take advantage of her increasing success on records. In September 1968, she was in London at the Royal Festival Hall, appearing with Al Stewart and Fairport Convention in "An Evening of Contemporary Song." In December she played the Miami Pop Festival, appearing before 100,000 people. On February 1, 1969, she made her debut at Carnegie Hall in New York.

In the midst of touring, she found time to cut her second album, which, despite her objection to Dave Van Ronk's title change, was called *Clouds* and finally contained her version of "Both Sides, Now." Indeed, the album was a combination of older songs like "Chelsea Morning" and "I Don't Know Where I Stand" and newer ones that frequently took direct, personal glimpses at romance.

Clouds entered the charts on June 14 at #93, 96 slots higher than her previous peak, and reached #31 on July 19, lasting a total of 36 weeks. This time, when Judy Collins released a one-off single of "Chelsea Morning" in July, Mitchell's own version also was available. (It hit #78 in August and turned up on Collins's *Living* album in the fall of 1971, where it was heard by Bill and Hillary Clinton, who later named their daughter after it.)

Mitchell's friends and lovers Crosby, Stills, Nash and Young had formed a group by the summer of 1969, and Mitchell, currently living with Nash and handled by the same management (Roberts had by now formed a company with David Geffen called Geffen-Roberts), frequently traveled with them. During the first weekend of August, she performed at the Atlantic City Pop Festival in New Jersey where she quickly discovered that playing to an audience of a quarter million was quite a different experience than playing to a rapt club crowd.

Attempting unsuccessfully to grab the attention of the noisy festival-goers with her soft, acoustic songs, a frustrated Mitchell stormed off the stage after offering only a few songs, commenting something to the effect that if they weren't interested, neither was she.

Two weeks later, she was with CSN&Y in New York, but as reports of the first chaotic day of the Woodstock festival came out, it was decided that she would not accompany them to the site. She was scheduled to appear on Dick Cavett's talk show on the Monday night after the week-end festival, and it was feared they might not be back in time. Also, as she told Dave Zimmer, "I was the girl of the family and, with great disappointment, I was the one that had to stay behind." (As it turned out, Crosby, Stills and Young appeared on the Cavett show with her.)

Stuck in a hotel room while history was being made in the mud at Yasgur's Farm, Mitchell found inspiration. "The deprivation of not being able to go provided me with an intense angle on Woodstock," she told Zimmer. "I was one of the fans. I was put in the position of being a kid who couldn't make it. So I was glued to the media. And at the time I was going through a kind of born again Christian trip—not that I went to any church, I'd given up Christianity at an early age in Sunday school. But suddenly, as performers, we were in the position of having so many people look to us for leadership, and for some unknown reason, I took it seriously and decided I needed a guide and leaned on God.

"So I was a little 'God mad' at the time, for lack of a better term, and I had been saying to myself, 'Where are the modern miracles? Where are the modern miracles?' Woodstock, for some reason, impressed me as being a modern miracle, like a modern-day fishes-and-loaves story. For a herd of people that large to cooperate so well, it was pretty remarkable and there was tremendous optimism. So I wrote the song 'Woodstock' out of these feelings, and the first three times I performed it in public, I burst into tears, because it brought back the intensity of the experience and was so moving."

"Woodstock" is actually something of a throwback to Mitchell songs like "Both Sides, Now" and "The Circle Game," both in its sense of disillusionment and longing for an idealized world and in its circular imagery.

Mitchell continued to tour with CSN&Y, opening for them at the Greek Theatre on the campus of UCLA on August 20 and at the Big Sur Folk Festival in September. Like Woodstock, that festival was taped, and it would result, more than a year later, in Mitchell's feature film debut, *Celebration At Big Sur* (1971), one of many festival documentaries released in the wake of the success of Monterey Pop and Woodstock. Mitchell's "Songs to Aging Children," meanwhile, turned up on the soundtrack of a movie version of Arlo Guthrie's story song "Alice's Restaurant," in theaters in the fall and in the charts, up to #63. The version was sung by one Tigger Outlaw.

In two years, Joni Mitchell had gone from being the opening act to an opening act in a Greenwich Village club to being a worldwide headliner. But by the beginning of 1970 she had been on the road for a year, and it had become too much. On February 17, after appearing at the Royal Albert Hall in London, she announced that she was quitting live appearances.

Asked to compare the club work, which she seemed to enjoy, with the concert work, which she clearly did not, Mitchell said, "It's not the number of the people, because it all abstracts, but you can't see faces from the big stage, and you're subject to severe adjudication, and it's not as much fun. I never liked the big stage. The looseness and the heart went out of it for me.

"I got to the point where I kept asking my manager at that time, 'Let me quit, let me quit,' and he couldn't understand it till he came out one night for 'Circle Game' and it was towards the end of the show, and he saw my knuckles were white on the strings. It was very, very unpleasant for me to be up on that stage. There was no rapport. It didn't feel friendly."

In fact, there was even more to it than that, as she explained to

Joni Mitchell, 1968. © Corbis/Hulton-Deutsch Collection

Musician magazine's Bill Flanagan in an interview conducted in the fall of 1985 and later published in his book *Written in My Soul: Rock's Great Songwriters Talk About Creating Their Music* (Contemporary Books, 1986). "I really enjoyed playing clubs for about forty people," she said. "I liked being [the] center of attention. It was like being the life of the party. That I could handle. When it got to the big stage I found that I didn't enjoy it. It frightened me initially. I had a lot of bad experiences, including running off many a stage. I just thought it was too big for me, it was out of proportion. This kind of attention was absurd."

Part of the reason Mitchell didn't trust the adulation was that it came for the same performances that had attracted only scant attention before. "I don't like receiving things that don't mean anything," she said. "I couldn't get work in these little piddling clubs, and then I couldn't believe that suddenly overnight all these people loved me for the same songs. These same people sat in clubs when I was the opening act and talked through my show. Now suddenly they were rapt? I wanted to see where they were at. I wanted to show them where I was at."

In showing them, Mitchell moved toward the nakedly personal songs on her next several albums, songs that, rather than alienating her audience, cemented their commitment to her, so much so that it is this material that most of her longtime fans love the most.

BY PETER REILLY

JONI MITCHELL SINGS HER BLUES

In a 1979 interview with Cameron Crowe of Rolling Stone, *Joni says:*

"By the time of my fourth album [Blue, 1971], I came to another turning point—the terrible opportunity that people are given in their lives. The day they discover to the tips of their toes that they're assholes [solemn moment, then a gale of laughter]. And you have to work from there. And decide what your values are. Which parts of you are no longer really necessary. They belong to childhood's end. Blue was really a turning point in a lot of ways."

And later, in the same interview:

"The Blue album, there's hardly a dishonest note in the vocals. At that period of my life, I had no personal defenses. I felt like a

cellophane wrapper on a pack of cigarettes. I felt like I had absolutely no secrets from the world, and I couldn't pretend in my life to be strong. Or to be happy. But the advantage of it in the music was that there were no defenses there either."

The following is one of the many glowing reviews for Blue.—SFL

Stereo Review, October 1971

Joni Mitchell continues to demonstrate that she is not only an actress-singer but a composer of considerable power: her newest (and aptly titled) album *Blue* for Reprise is an unqualified success on both counts: It is a collection of what once were called "torch" songs, but Miss Mitchell adds an extra dimension to her "my man's gone now" theme by introducing a spare, satirical element that is sometimes directed at herself, sometimes at her partners. It is this balanced dispassion which makes her work truly womanly rather than merely girlish.

And, if her songs are based on personal experience, she certainly does seem to have had a rough time of it in the Game of Love. In the song "California" she meets a red-neck on a Grecian isle who "gave me back my smile / But he kept my camera to sell." The subject of "My Old Man" is apparently given to irregular disappearances, thus causing Joni to collide with the blues and to discover that "the bed's too big / The frying pan's too wide." That last phrase (think about it) is a *genuine* image, provocative and palpable. There are others like it running all through her compositions, and they regularly bring the listener to sharp attention with the unmistakable clang of sardonic truth.

Though the subject of all these songs is the blues, Miss Mitchell's extraordinary performances of them quickly remove any possibility that they might all add up to a bad case of the sulks. For instance, her nervous, slightly weird soprano makes "My Old Man" a touching and poignant story rather than a tiresome, weepy complaint. Also, the near-perfection of her arrangements and accompaniment (both Stephen Stills and James Taylor sat in on guitar during the sessions), the beautifully finished (in the sense of complete) sound of each track, all contribute to what may be her best album yet.

I think the finest thing about *Blue* however, is its message of survival. "Well, there're so many sinking now / You've got to keep thinking / You can make it through these waves. . . . Well everybody's saying that hell's the hippest way to go / Well, I don't think so." These words sound to me very like a pointed and pertinent warning to that part of a generation that talks a lot about getting it all together but begins to seem less and less capable of really doing so.

Blue. Joni Mitchell (vocals); orchestra. All I Want; My Old Man; Little Green; Carey; Blue; California; This Flight Tonight; River; A Case of You; The Last Time I Saw Richard. Reprise MS 2038 $5.98, M 82038 $6.95, © M 52038 $6.95.

Part Two

FROM FOLK WAIF TO ROCK & ROLL LADY
1972–1974

EXCLUSIVE JONI MITCHELL INTERVIEW

Joni disappeared from the public eye whenever she could, the better to write, compose, and paint. This interview, published in England, took place after an early retreat.—SFL

Part One—Sounds, June 3, 1972

The lady who walks on eggs is sitting in her hotel suite overlooking St. James Park with her legs tucked up, her chin resting on her knees.

She is wearing a pair of jeans, a tiny printed shirt and a plain sweater over the top. Her feet are bare where she's kicked her clogs off, and her fine, fair hair trails across her shoulders almost hiding the silver hoops she wears in her ears. There is a tidy casualness about her appearance, a cleanliness and unrumpled freshness. And after the perfunctory look at you there's an acceptance that's surprisingly warm when you consider the image that has been built up around her over the years.

It was Richie Havens that called Joni Mitchell "the lady that walks on eggs" some years back when we were discussing star signs and environmental characteristics. And not knowing her, it seemed from her music she was careful, delicate, going through life frightened of breaking it. It was quite a capsuled insight then—rightly capturing the fragility of a girl whose relentless pursuit of happiness appeared destined to fail. And yet here and now Joni Mitchell is a contradiction in terms that shows almost before you speak to her.

The star syndrome, though, produces contradictions in itself. The biggest with Joni is that metamorphosis on stage and off. At the Festival Hall she was like a Hans Christian Andersen snow queen, a throwback to her Scandinavian/Canadian origins, the vocal pitched to hang like icicles on the night air.

This Saturday in a rainswept London she is a comfortable encounter, and for all the outward initial purity the bright red painted toenails she wiggles while she talks make you smile—simply because they are in themselves a contradiction to the image.

After the Festival Hall she went to Europe for some concerts and then came back to London on Thursday. That night she took herself off to see Kurt Weill's *Threepenny Opera*, found it had moved, tried to see *Day in the Death of Joe Egg*, found it had started. Undismayed, and she laughs now telling it, she had gone back to the hotel, stuck her hair up in a beret and prowled midnight Piccadilly alone with her notebook of half-finished poems so that she could sketch people in bars. On Friday she had taped an "In Concert" for Stanley Dorfman and afterwards, at dinner, we'd talked about her newly completed house in Canada, and the plan in her own mind that had never materialized: "I thought I'd lead a kind of *Heidi*-like existence, you know—with goats and an orchard."

The interview she has promised on Saturday is her first for two years. She made a lot of decisions, back in '70, one of which was to give up working and travel around, the other to not give any more interviews. She'd had a rough time of it mentally and physically, a whole wrong outlook on her life and work. And to her, interviews were beginning to hurt: "All people seemed interested in was the music and the gossip—I felt then that the music spoke for itself and the gossip was unimportant.

"I have in my time," and she grins at the pseudodramatic air in her voice, "been very misunderstood." But you can feel that the constant intrusion into her private life got too much to bear.

A lot of new songs have emerged from the two-year hiatus and in themselves are interesting insights into the change in Joni's outlook. The loving humor of "You Turn Me On (I'm a Radio)," the pain in "Cold Blue Steel and Sweet Fire," retrospective bitterness in "Lesson in Survival," but then there is that feeling—haven't all her songs been directly autobiographical, total personal emotions?

"Well, some of them are, yes, directly personal and others may seem to be because they're conglomerate feelings. Like, remember we were talking about before about that song for Beethoven and I was telling you that's written from the point of view of his Muse talking to him. But that comes from an understanding that I thought I perceived. By reading books about Beethoven I got a feeling which I felt was familiar, as I had felt about people that are friends of mine. So that's from my own experience, because it's my feeling for other people."

And yet one had stuck particularly in my mind—"Cactus Tree"—the song about a girl who everyone loved and yet who was "too busy being free" to concentrate on returning that feeling properly. . . .

"I feel that's the song of *modern* woman. Yes, it has to do with my experiences, but I know a lot of girls like that . . . who find that the world is full of lovely men but they're driven by something else other than settling down to frau-duties."

But then, I say, there is this impression she gives out—someone on the move all the time, someone intent on having freedom even if it's a deceptive kind of freedom.

"Freedom is deceptive, though. It's like that line of [Kris] Kristofferson's: 'Freedom's just another way of nothing left to lose' [sic]. Freedom implies a lot of loneliness you know, a lot of unfulfillment. It implies always the search for fulfillment, which sometimes is more exciting than the fulfillment itself. I mean, so many times I've talked to friends of mine who are just searching for something and one day they come to you and they've FOUND IT! Then two weeks later you talk to them and they aren't satisfied. They won't allow themselves to think they've found it—because they've come to enjoy the quest so much. They've found it—then what?

"I think that there's a new thing to discover in the development of fulfillment. I don't think it necessarily means trading the search, which is more exciting than the actual fulfillment. I still have this dream that you can come to a place where there's a different kind of medium—a more subtle kind of exploration to do of one thing or one place or one person. Like, drifting through lives quickly and cities quickly, you know, you never really get to understand a person or a place very deeply. Like, you can be in a place until you feel completely familiar with it, or stay with a person until you may feel very bored. You feel you've explored it all. Then all of a sudden, if you're there long enough, it'll just open up and flash you all over again. But so many people who are searching and traveling come to that point where it's stealing out on them and they just can't handle that and have to move on."

We talk about the time she spent traveling and how—although songs came out of it and so it was a productive experience—there was an innate disappointment. A sense—and this came out in her spoken intros at the Festival Hall—of disillusionment that what she had believed would be magical somehow never turned out that way. She was affected by that too, she admits, and yet after a thought she smiles at her own naivete in expecting places to be untouched, in expecting to be totally absorbed into them and accepted.

"You tailor make your dreams to 'it'll be this way' and when it isn't . . . like, if you have a preconceived idea of anything, then inevitably it can't live up to your hopes. Hawaii had so many really beautiful parts to it, and the island of Kuwaii is still agricultural. I guess I had thought of [Hawaii] from all those *Occa Occa* movies I had seen—sacrificing the maidens to the volcano, rivers running with blood and lava, guava trees and," she laughs, "Esther Williams, you know, swimming through the lagoon. And you get there and have to sort through the stucco and the pink hotels. Crete was for the most part pretty virgin, and if you walked to the market you'd find farmers with burros and oranges on the side; it was wonderful. Matela was full of kids from all over the world who were seeking the same kind of thing I was, but they couldn't get away from ummm—I mean they may as well have been in an apartment in Berkeley as in a cave there because the lifestyle continued the same wherever they were. And the odd thing to me was that after my initial plans to be accepted into the home of a Greek family fell apart, we came to this very scene—the very scene we were trying to escape from—and it seemed very attractive to us. There were so many contradictions, so much I noticed about life generally on those trips. Like, the kids couldn't get used to seeing all the slaughtered meat hanging in the shops—they'd only ever seen bits of meat wrapped in cellophane, and to see it there on it's frame turned their stomachs. Most people have that reaction—look at last night over dinner when we started to complain because people were talking about eating birds. We got so upset, and yet at the same time we were eating chicken by the mouthful without even thinking. I go on vegetarian things every so often—well, fruitarian really. In California it's easy because it's warm most of the time. I think you need meat in winter. I have this friend who's a vegetarian and helped me build my house in Canada. We lived on fruit all summer, and he was a fanatical vegetarian—sneering at me when I looked at sirloin—but as winter approached he got colder and colder and I said 'Look you've got to eat some meat if we're going to finish this house.' I had visions of him collapsing. He actually did break down finally and have a steak, and I felt really terrible corrupting, breaking down a man's principles like that."

I wonder if the house in Canada is a permanent move, whether she's had enough of the California scene and is moving back to her roots.

"Not really—moving back is like burning your bridges behind you. For one thing, I don't want to lose my alien registration card, because that enables me to work in the States. So I have a house in California—not the one in Laurel Canyon I used to have—for an address. The house in Canada is just a solitary station. I mean, it's by the sea and it has enough physical beauty and change of mood so that I can spend two or three weeks there alone.

"The land has a rich melancholy about it. Not in the summer, because it's usually very clear, but in the spring and winter it's very brooding and it's conducive to a certain kind of thinking. But I can't spend a lot of time up there. Socially I have old schoolfriends around Vancouver, Victoria and some of the islands, but I need the stimulation of the scene in Los Angeles. So I really find myself down there almost as much now as when I lived there—because then I was on the road most of the time anyway.

"I'm so transient now that even though I have the house in Canada I really don't feel like I have a home—well, it's home when I'm there, you know, but then so is the Holiday Inn in its own weird way."

We get on to the two-year break and I wonder how she'll take the intrusion into her reasons and her personal kick-back. But she's relaxed and forthright and somehow you feel it's a question she feels right in answering now that it's in the past and she hasn't spoken of it before publicly.

"The first year I traveled, the second year I built my house and—in the process of building it and being alone up there when it was completed—I had written a lot of new songs. And it seemed to me that [they weren't] like a completed art until they were tried in front of a live audience. Well, not 'tried,' but there's a need to share them. I kept calling people in the bar of this lodge and saying, 'Listen, want to hear a song?' and they say, 'That's really nice—know any Gordon Lightfoot?' No, that's not really true—but I really did want to play in front of people, which was a strange feeling for me to get because two years ago when I retired I felt I never really wanted to do it again—ever.

"Like, I gained a strange perspective of performing. I had a bad attitude about it, you know. I felt like what I was writing was too personal to be applauded for. I even thought that maybe the thing to do was to present the songs some different way—like a play or a classical performance where you play everything and then run off stage and let them do whatever they want, applaud or walk out.

"I was too close to my own work. Now I've gained a perspective, a distance on most of my songs. So that now I can feel them when I perform them, but I do have a certain detachment from the reality of the story."

Did it help her in that troubled time to get her feelings out on paper?

"Yes, it does, you know, it translates your mood. You can be in a really melancholic depressive mood, you're feeling downright bad and you want to know why. So you sit down and think 'why?' You ask yourself a lot of questions. I find if I just sit around and meditate and mope about it all, then there's no release at all, I just get deeper and deeper into it. Whereas in the act of creating—when the song is born and you've made something beautiful—it's a release valve. And I always try and look for some optimism, you know, no matter how cynical my mood may be. I always try to find that little crevice of light peeking through. Whatever I've made—whether it's a painting, a song, or even a sweater—it changes my mood. I'm pleased with myself that I've made something."

Part Two, Sounds, June 10, 1972

Last week Joni Mitchell spoke for the first time in over two years about why she virtually "retired" from the music scene during a period of searching and self-exploration. How her writing had become a therapy for her to overcome something of a real crisis in her career and in her outlook.

In her London hotel, happily chain smoking her way through the afternoon, she continues our discussion of her life and attitudes. . . .

For Joni then, the emotional release to her problems came through her artistic involvement, her sense of achievement. But the subject brings up theories on psychiatrists and whether the ordinary person, who perhaps does not have the artistic satisfaction of creating, is ever helped through times of stress by them.

Surprisingly, it turns out, that despite her own forms of release, Joni did once visit a psychiatrist herself just before she made the decision to come off the road.

"A couple of years ago I got very depressed—to the point where I thought it was no longer a problem for burdening my friends with. But I needed to talk to someone who was very indifferent, so I thought I'd pay this guy to listen to me. I had done a lot of thinking beforehand as to what was eating me, so there wasn't a great deal of uncovering to do. I went to see him and said 'okay blah blah blah' and just started to rap from the time I came in through the door—which turned out to be 40 minutes of everything I thought was bothering me. Which included a description of myself as being a person who never spoke, which naturally he found hard to understand! But it was true that in day-to-day life I was practically catatonic. There were moments when I thought I had nothing pertinent to say, but there I was, blabbing my mouth off to him.

"So in the end he looked at me and said 'Well do you ever feel suicidal?' and I said 'Sometimes I feel very bad but I have to make another record . . .' telling him I had all these things to live for. So he just handed me his card and said, 'Listen—call me again sometime when you feel suicidal.' And I went out into the street—I'd come in completely dead pan, my face immobile even when I talked—and I just felt this grin breaking over my face at the irony of it all. At the thought that this man was going to help me at all. I don't see that [psychiatrists] really do much good. The idea that you disclose all these things to a person who remains totally anonymous seems not very helpful."

But isn't that why people go [to therapy]—that they are anonymous beings?

"Oh sure—that is why people talk to strangers on trains and buses, for a release. But I wanted more than a release. I wanted some wisdom, some kind of council and direction. He didn't know. He only knew the way to his office in the morning and the way to the bar afterwards."

Well, some people use them like a priest—almost as a confessional . . .

"True, but . . . did you read Hermann Hesse's book *Narcissus and Goldmund*? In reading that book—and I have never had any Catholic experience—but at the end when Narcissus the priest gives Goldmund a mantra to repeat over and over again, not reproaching him for his life, but just giving him a focus because he's so spaced out, kind of 'you're out of focus—get yourself in focus.' I thought that was so brilliant; so many priests and psychiatrists miss the whole point of getting right to the heart of the person. Giving him rehabilitation and setting up a solution. Hesse is certainly my favorite author—although I must admit I hardly ever read. As a result, I find difficulty in expressing myself—suddenly I find how limited my vocabulary is. I never was a reader, I always was a doer. To me, reading was a vicarious experience. But I have a hunger now; there are times when I am among my friends and I feel like an illiterate.

"It's like I came through the school systems completely unscathed in a way, and completely unlearned in another way. Which makes me feel terribly ignorant. I find now that the most common phrase in my vocabulary is," she lowers her voice sternly, "I DON'T KNOW, I just don't know."

Sadly, it's a common link between us—something we have to laugh at but knowing it's only a cover-up in exactly the same way as an excuse for scholarly learning is that "living is more important."

"Oh well, I think that both those sides are true. I think that a lot of people that [are] glued into books can only learn from books. Like, one thing I love is the exploration of learning. I love teaching myself things. In a way that handicaps me, because when someone tries to instruct me, I can't be instructed. This is particularly painful to me in my music, because someone will say, 'Oh, I like the way you play piano, will you play these key changes C to E?' And I can't do it. The only way I could is if they play the tapes and let me wander around and choose my own chords.

"I was constantly rapped on the knuckles at piano classes because I'd listen to what the teacher played and I'd remember it. So I never learned to sight read properly and she'd bust me on it. I'd fake it—like, I'd read the music and it wouldn't be quite right, there was a certain amount of improvisation in it. And she'd say, 'Those notes aren't in there.' That kind of killed my interest in piano for a good 15 years or so. From the beginning I really wanted to mess around and create, find the colors the piano had buried in it. You know, I always feel like such an irresponsible creature."

We move back to the songs. At the Festival Hall she debuted "Lesson in Survival," which now, having discussed the two years away from the business, seems even more pertinent than it did that evening. She apologized for it on stage, saying she didn't necessarily feel that way now, but obviously it was a very bitter time.

"Yes, that was when I came off the road. I had a friend at that time I was very close to and who was on the verge of tremendous success. I was watching his career and I was thinking that as his woman at that time I should be able to support him. And yet it seemed to me that I could see the change in his future would remove things from his life. I felt like having come through, having had a small taste of success, and having seen the consequences of what it gives you and what it takes away in terms of what you THINK it's going to give you—well, I just felt I was in no position to help. I knew what he needed was someone to support him and say it was all wonderful. But everything I saw him going through I thought was ludicrous, because I'd thought it was ludicrous when I'd done it.

"It was a very difficult time, and the song was actually written for that person: 'In the office sits a poet and he trembles as he sings, and he asks some guy to circulate his soul . . . okay on your mark red ribbon runner.' Like, go after it, but remember the days when you sat and made up tunes for yourself and played in small clubs where there was still some contact and when people came up and said they loved a song [and] you were really glad that they loved it. After a while, when people come up it begins to sound hollow and you meet so many people that misunderstood what you said—maybe they did before, but you didn't care, you know? Ummm, well, I've got to clarify that—it is appreciated when someone says it and genuinely means it and you can see it's moved them, maybe changed them a little. Like, I've been really moved by some performances and I've been unable to tell them from my side of it because I know what it's like to receive praise. It's a very difficult thing to give sincerely and communicate that sincerity."

Joni Mitchell and Graham Nash, 1969. © Corbis/ Henry Diltz

Having gone through all those feelings, didn't she find it hard to come back to concerts and get involved in it all again—knowing what she knew and how she'd reacted to knowing it?

"Well, that part of the song I apologized for the most was the bitterness, I had felt so pressurized. I don't feel pressurized by it now, mainly because I intend to express myself in more than one medium, so if I go dry in one, I'll move into something else.

"You come to dry periods as an artist, and you get real panicky. I've known people that haven't written for maybe a year, and they're chewing their fingernails right down to the wrist. And I've known people who maybe haven't put out such a good fourth record and they feel they're on some sort of decline. Either they feel it personally or they're led to believe it. Their record company [is] beginning to withdraw from them, the spark is going out. Or maybe it's the fact that at 17 they were so pretty and all of a sudden in the morning they have bags under their eyes.

"But now I feel personally unaffected by all that, in that I feel my creativity in one form or another is very strong and will continue. I may, of course, just dry up all around—hey, I may become the whole Gobi desert next year! You know, I always say to Elliot (Roberts, her manager), 'Oh, I haven't written anything for three weeks,' and he's always laughing at me because I'm very prolific. But I'm also very lonely—which is one of the dues you pay. I don't have a large circle of friends. I have a few very close friends, and then there's a whole lot of people I'm sort of indifferent to. And I sometimes think that maybe that's not so good, that maybe I should go out of my way and be nice to everyone, you know?"

But it must be difficult for her—the star system is a trap where it's hard to work out who is a friend for simply what you represent and who for the person you really are.

"I used to see that as a problem, but there was also this thing where I'd be nice to anyone who was nice to me—that I had this obligation to be nice back. But that's a discrimination I've learned. I'm older and wiser now."

The rain has stopped outside and the last rays of a 7:00 P.M. sun are filtering across the trees in the park. Joni plays a little piano, eats a little butterscotch, and we move on to the new album—her first for Asylum, the label that her co-managers Elliot and David Geffen started and which she joined as a friend to lend her support to.

"Well, I've started on it. I've been into the studio to cut a publisher's dub, when the songs were very new. I just cut most of them by myself. For 'Cold Blue Steel' I got in James Burton, who's really a great guitarist. Like, that song is a real paranoid city song—stalking the streets looking for a dealer. I originally thought it needed a sliding steel, but we tried that and it didn't work. Finally I ended up with James playing really great wah wah—furtive kind of sound. It's a nice track, but in the meantime the bass line and the drums didn't work solidly, so I have to recut that. I have a take of 'Lesson in Survival' which is really magical, the feeling is there, and I don't think I'll do it again—so I have that cut and finished.

"Then I tried to do 'You Turn Me On (I'm a Radio).' I've never had a hit record in America, so I got together with some friends and we decided we were going to make this hit—conjure up this bit of magic for AM radio, destined to appeal to DJs. Graham [Nash] and David [Crosby] came and Neil [Young] lent me his band, and he came and played some guitar and somehow it didn't work. There were too many chefs, you know. We had a terrific evening, a lot of fun, and the track is nice, but it's just . . . it's like when you do a movie with a cast of thousands. Somehow I prefer movies with unknowns. So I'm going to start looking for people who are untried, who have a different kind of enthusiasm that comes from wanting to support the artist.

"Like, Miles Davis always has a band that [is] really great, but [the musicians] are cushions for him, you know. That sounds very egotistical, that I should want that, but this time I really want to do something different. Like, the music is already a growth, a progression from *Blue*, the approach is stronger and melodically it's stronger, I think that will be noticeable whether I make a sparse record as I did with *Blue* or not. But I feel I want to go in all directions right now, like a mad thing right! I'd think, 'this is really rock and roll, this song, isn't it?' and I see it with French horns and everything and I really have to hold myself back, or I'll just have a monstrosity on my hands. No, I don't feel trapped in this held back careful image. I could sing much stronger than I do, you know, especially on the low register. I've got a voice I haven't used yet and haven't developed, which is very deep and strong and could carry over a loud band. And I'm very tempted to go in that direction experimentally.

"But rushing ahead of ideas is bad. An idea must grow at its own pace. If you push it and it's not ready, it'll just fall apart."

BY ROBERT HILBURN

JONI MITCHELL'S NEW *FOR THE ROSES*

Most of For the Roses *was written at Joni's retreat in British Columbia. It was, according to journalist Timothy White, "conceived as a possible farewell to the music business."—SFL*

Los Angeles Times, November 21, 1972

At a time when so many of our most successful and respected songwriters—from Carole King to Gordon Lightfoot to James Taylor—are having difficulty coming up with something fresh in their music, Joni Mitchell, as literate a writer as we have, continues to produce works of richness and value. Her new *For the Roses* album (Asylum SD 5057—distributed by Atlantic Records) is the latest case in point.

From the insights in her lyrics to the wholly distinctive vocal style, there is such quality in Miss Mitchell's albums that each one has a way of growing more impressive and personal as time passes—a fact that sometimes makes her new albums seem a disappointment until you have grown as familiar with them as you have with her earlier ones.

But a look back at her albums shows a remarkable consistency, each

From Folk Waif To Rock & Roll Lady
5 5

offering observations about love and human relationships that form a vital link in her total body of work. Looking at the four previous Reprise albums, for instance, we find such songs as "Michael from Mountains" and "Cactus Tree" in the *Joni Mitchell* album, such tunes as "Chelsea Morning" and "Both Sides, Now" on the *Clouds* album, such songs as "For Free" and "The Circle Game" on *Ladies of the Canyon* and such works as "All I Want" and "A Case of You" on last year's "*Blue*."

One of the reasons Miss Mitchell is able to produce works of merit so consistently is her willingness to explore and then honestly reveal—rather than soften, filter or glamorize—her emotions and experiences, both the joys and, more importantly, the sorrows. She is able to face her disappointments in love and deal with them in an instructive way in song.

Several of the 12 songs on the *For the Roses* album (among them "Lesson in Survival," "Woman of Heart and Mind" and "See You Sometime") deal with moments of defeat or insecurity in an open, honest way that few other major writers could duplicate. In "Lesson in Survival," for instance, she tells about the inadequacies a lover brought out in her: "Your friends protect you / Scrutinize me / I get so damn timid / Not at all the spirit / That's inside of me."

The album's other highlights include "Blonde in the Bleachers," a song about the difficulty one faces in holding on to a free-spirited, rock 'n' roll man; "Electricity," a well-designed song that plays the elusive nature of electricity against the elusive nature of love; "Judgement of the Moon and Stars," an ode to Beethoven or any passionate artist, and "You Turn Me On (I'm a Radio)," a light, bouncy tune about offering to comfort someone the way a radio station's music lends support.

But the album's best two songs are "Cold Blue Steel and Sweet Fire," a haunting, convincing account of the helplessness that heroin offers its victims, and the title song, a marvelously sensitive and moving account of the hopes, rise and fall of a pop music star.

In the song, Miss Mitchell traces the artist through the early loneliness and fright of getting started ("In some office sits a poet / And he trembles as he sings / And he asks some guy / To circulate his soul around") to the time, long after stardom has arrived, that the public tires of him.

Between the rise and the fall, however, there is the time his music becomes a product and Miss Mitchell tells about the parties in which the business people who have a slice of you celebrate your latest million seller: "They toss around your latest golden egg / Speculation —well, who's to know / If the next one in the nest / Will glitter for them so."

Handsomely designed, the album package contains original art work by Miss Mitchell and a tasteful somewhat distant photo of her standing nude on a rock looking out at the ocean. But the real value, as usual, is in the music and the value of Miss Mitchell's music, also as usual, is at the highest level in contemporary pop music.

BY MARCI MCDONALD

JONI MITCHELL EMERGES FROM HER RETREAT

This is Joni at the height of her popularity, both musically and as cultural icon. Writer Marci McDonald paints a portrait of the artist as Joni steps outs from another retreat, this time to promote Court and Spark.*—SFL*

The Toronto Star, February 9, 1974

The myth is spun in sacred vinyl and remembered spotlights. In swirling soprano self-portraits and worshipful press clippings, all cornsilk flashes and free-spirit poetry. There is no myth in the top of pop quite like it.

Carole King and Helen Reddy sell more records, but what is magical about women's lib or baking banana bread and driving your kids to school in a pick-up truck? Roberta Flack sings with more soul, but what is there to catch a body's imagination about living with your mother in Washington, D.C.?

No, Joni Mitchell clearly has the edge on enchantment, an edge totally untarnished by six albums of stark self-revelation, caustic self-accusation and the contrary indications of a sometimes sordid reality.

She sings that she is fickle, that her heart is full and hollow like a cactus tree 'cause she's so busy being free, but they only seem to remember the romantic elusiveness. She sings guiltily about her greed for fame and fortune, but they only seem to hear the artful imagery.

Through it all, though, through the 10-year career knocking around the Toronto coffeehouse circuit, booking herself right into recognition and sustained sometimes only by her own steely drive, through all the loves and the losses that read like a gossip roster of Who's Who in rock 'n' roll, she has emerged unscathed in portraits of enchanted dewdrop vulnerability.

And if absence only makes enchantment grow fonder, she will walk out onstage at the University of Waterloo tonight or Massey Hall tomorrow after a two-year retreat from the public glare as queen of the cults still intact, immaculate, preserved forever as the elusive pastel prairie wildflower, the misty wispy moonbeam princess lushly chording in her castle of bittersweet sorrows and stained-glass dreams.

They will not see a tall, thin blonde with features just a shade too sharp and teeth too numerous to be really pretty, a deft self-propelled superstar who has survived the millions and the minions and a decade of musical history, to live now in half a Beverly Hills' mansion that Julie Andrews used to own, see her psychoanalyst twice a week and date Warren Beatty and assorted rock stars as countless as "railroad cars," which is about as Hollywood as you can get; who likes to eat out at classy restaurants and go bowling, which is about as unpoetic as you can get; and who just passed her 30th birthday.

They will not see the girl who friends say has changed, no longer acts so strange, is more sophisticated, worldly, womanly, has let her decolletage dip down for her newest publicity photos and her folkie bangs grow out.

They probably wouldn't want to see her, either, just a week or so ago on this sleazy fringe of Sunset Strip just down the street from Deep Throat, the Venus Massage Parlor and the Institute of Oral Sex, up a darkened alley and behind a fortress-like grated iron gate here in this all-night rehearsal hall where she comes storming down the corridor past the pay phone and the pinball machines and the pool table in the lobby, muttering the unmistakable pear-shaped sounds of a four-letter word.

Joni Mitchell has just been told there's a journalist in the hallway and she is not exactly enthusiastic about journalists ever since *Rolling Stone*, the rock Bible, chronicled her romances with Graham Nash, David Crosby, Leonard Cohen and James Taylor, among others, complete with convoluted hearts-and-arrow graph charts, and somewhat unkindly christened her "old lady of the year." Now Joni Mitchell extends a limp and wary wrist and makes quite clear she doesn't do interviews anymore.

"I've had some bad experiences," she'll admit much later that night. "And besides, I just don't find these things very interesting reading."

So she writes her own press releases, like the one for her newest album in her child-like loopy longhand, a little short on details and a little long on preserving the mythology.

"I was born in Fort Macleod, Alberta, in the foothills of the Canadian Rockies—an area of extreme temperatures and mirages," she lyricizes.

"When I was two feet off the ground I collected broken glass and bats. When I was three feet off the ground I made drawings of animals and forest fires. When I was four feet off the ground I began to dance to rock 'n' roll and sing the top 10 and bawdy service songs around campfires and someone turned me on to Lambert, Hendricks and Ross and Miles Davis. And later Bob Dylan. Through these vertical spurts there was briefly the church choir, Grade 1 piano, bowling, art college, the twist, a marriage, runs in the nylons and always romance —extremes in temperature and mirages."

Others who have been a little less liberal with the mirages have recorded that she was born Roberta Joan Anderson, grew up in Saskatoon the daughter of a grocery man who used to blow trumpet and a onetime country schoolteacher who used to know the names of all the wildflowers, that she doodled her way all through school, learned her love of words from her Grade 7 teacher, Mr. Kratznan, but always wanted to be a painter till she was waylaid at Calgary art college with a romance with a coffeehouse called The Depression and a Pete Seeger do-it-yourself record that taught her to play guitar.

She dropped out to tote her dreams and schemes into the Toronto folk scene in 1964, where Riverboat owner Bernie Fiedler, now her friend and promoter, offered her a job as a dishwasher, which he says was just a joke, although she doesn't remember it quite that way. But, by that time Joni Mitchell knew just where she was going and she went there straight up, till suddenly it all got too much for her two years ago and she dropped right out of the glare.

Now, on this, the last night of rehearsal before she hits the road for her personal comeback, she is warmed up, wound up and admittedly nervous because it's the first time that she's shared the stage with a band, Tom Scott and the L.A. Express, and things are, she says, "a little shaky."

But she invites you in anyway, "not as the press but as a friend," although ironically, a week before she had talked to old folksinging friend Malka (of Malka and Joso), not as a friend, but as the press. She was glad to have the band, she told Malka on CBC radio's Entertainers, "to absorb some of the loneliness of the stage, even in the mass applause there comes a loneliness . . . I don't want to be vulnerable."

She perches on an equipment trunk to watch them warm up now, wedged between a bottle of vodka and Liebfraumilch, wearing the pastel colors she paints in, pink pants and high-stepping '30s pink slings, prim white blouse and yellow chamois jacket, her fingers all brand-new gold rings, her waist all flowers in an antique cloisonné belt. She sips white wine and a cigarette dangles through long languid fingers. "I'm excited," she says, "'cause I really like these guys."

But at the break it becomes clear that she's excited too because she really likes one of them, drummer John Guerin, a lean, elfin good-looker, a little better than the rest. They kneel together, arms entwined . . . and she brings him comic newspaper clippings, snaps polaroid photos of him and follows him out into the hall.

As one of her friends says, "There's no need for interviews. She says it all in her songs. Whatever's going on in her life, she says in her music. In her writing, Joni's the frankest person I know."

Indeed, she sits down now at the piano and chords out the reasons for her retirement in the song about the street busker who played real good for free . . . .

It [the song "For Free"] was written when "the money and success seemed distasteful. The fame and fortune seemed out of all proportion to what I was doing, although there were times I felt I deserved every bit of it. . . . I felt a little whorish about selling my soul, putting a price on it. I would get up and pour out fragments of it for money and applause, not only my life but sometimes the life of someone I was with in a close personal relationship."

She had poured out the end of her three-year marriage to Detroit folksinger Chuck Mitchell years ago in "I had a king in a salt-rusted carriage / Who carried me off to his country for marriage too soon."

Thirty-six hours after they'd met they formed a duo; he gave her his name and in many ways her start. It was his friends like Tom Rush staying at their house who first heard and recorded Joni Mitchell tunes. As she told Malka, "Then I began to long for my own growth. As soon as the duo dissolved, the marriage dissolved."

But years ago she confessed, "I guess the thing that bust it was when I started making more money. That hurt a lot."

But that wasn't what made Joni Mitchell want to quit the business. The relationship that left [the] most marks on the singer and her songs was the one with James Taylor, who she met on Toronto Island after a Mariposa Folk Festival, all chronicled in bittersweetness and goodbyes on her last two albums, *For the Roses* and *Blue*.

She belts out his battle with heroin in "Cold Blue Steel and Sweet Fire," keens at her own lonely sense of feeling left out as she gave up working and traipsed after him as he made his one abortive movie, *Two*

Lane Blacktop: "Your friends protect you / Scrutinize me /. . . . Oh baby, I can't seem to make it / with you socially."

She sings now, "You can't hold the hand / Of a rock 'n' roll man."

"The rock 'n' roll industry is very incestuous," she confesses. "We have all interacted. James, he's written songs for me, I've written songs for him. A lot of beautiful music came from it, a lot of beautiful times. And a lot of pain came from it too, because inevitably relationships broke up."

When Joni Mitchell and Taylor started slowly coming apart two years ago, she retreated to the house she'd built out of rock on a promontory of Half Moon Bay on Vancouver Island, a house that she hasn't been near in a long time now, though it stands there still. "Almost like a monastery. All stone and hardwood floors and hardwood benches, everything that would be corrective. No mirrors. Fighting for all that good virtue in myself," she says. "When I left my house in Laurel Canyon I looked around and it seemed too soft, too comfortable, too dimly lit, too much red upholstery. . . . It was really ridiculous. I just made this place really uncomfortable, like a corrective shoe."

She retired into traveling and painting, and that Christmas all her friends got a special, exquisite limited edition silver book of her songs, handwritten out beside bright fine-line felt-pen drawings, one of them unmistakably a picture of James Taylor on a bright green bedspread, pale and unstrung.

She started psychoanalysis "to talk to someone about confusion," she says, "and I was willing to pay for his discretion. . . .

"An artist needs a certain amount of turmoil and confusion and I've created out of that, even severe depression. But I had a lot of questions about myself, the way I was conducting my lives—life, what were my values in this time. Most of it was moral confusion . . . I'm your average quiet-ridden person," she says.

Still, it might not have been quite as easy as she makes it sound, for later there's a truer ring as she sings "Trouble Child." "So why does it come as such a shock / To know you really have no one / Only a river of changing faces / Looking for an ocean. . . ."

But out of all the soggy dreams and isolation and time on her hands, one answer came back loud and clear.

"I heard it in the wind last night," she sings. "It sounded like applause. . . ."

The lure of what she calls onstage "an almost euphoric feeling . . . sometimes I've felt out of control with it, I no longer was myself. I was transported . . ." in the end transported Joni Mitchell right back into the spotlight.

As she says, "I was too young to be retired at 27. I didn't know what to do with myself."

She played a James Bay Indian benefit in Montreal and another in Topanga Canyon last summer to get over the old loss of nerve that had once gotten so out of hand she'd stalk off a stage in mid-song "if anything fluttered in the room."

Now, up on this tiny rehearsal stage, going through the set a second faultless time, there's little doubt about how glad she is to get back. The first set's gone well, but something still finer is happening this time. The horns and heavier percussion take off with her high, piercing soprano. The room goes electric. A long, liquid brown beauty, all flying hair and turquoises, takes to the floor and starts to boogey to the rhythms, all alone, oblivious. "Magic," she moans, "has arrived."

You watch the face up on the stage that changes almost as fast as the incredible guitar fingerwork, from the toothy, giggling schoolgirl gossiping at the break about short haircuts and new silver earrings, to the shy, moony-eyed maid eyeing her new man, now to the wanton rocker, all grit and tumbleweed.

And you realize that it wasn't just a slip of the tongue when in mid-sentence she caught herself talking about not her life but "lives." There are paradoxes here beneath the myth, myths buried deep still beneath the bowl-o-rama cool-rocker reality. "It's all part of that [I] guess," she says, "will the real me please stand up."

Joni Mitchell's still singing about waiting for her prince to ride up, only this time she sounds a little more upbeat about it, a little less wild-flower vulnerable, a little less victimized. The songs are mellower, matured and maybe some of the best work she's ever done.

She tosses her long blonde mane back, but now there isn't quite so much to toss.

"The thing is," says Joni Mitchell eyeing her myth separately across the studio's back-wall mirror, "you can express all these high and beautiful thoughts, but your life may not back it up."

FROM FOLK WAIF TO ROCK & ROLL LADY

Joni wows 'em in London. She's touring with her first band, Tom Scott and the L.A. Express.—SFL

Sounds, April 27, 1974

Joni Mitchell's first appearance in Britain with a band was a triumph.

Joni's last appearance here was for a Festival Hall show where the sound came through as if it was being transmitted on shortwave radio from Mars by a Martian eating a giant bowl of Rice Krispies.

Understandably she'd come across as a nervous, rather fragile lady, embarrassed by the spaces between songs—as breakable as a guitar string that's been strung a little too tautly.

The difference couldn't have been more complete. At The New Victoria Theatre on Saturday night, the sound was excellent, and, as on Joni's last two albums, the gaps that used to be left to your imagination are now filled with a superlatively appropriate band who do the job a lot better than my imagination. I have to admit it.

Miss Mitchell seems to have changed in much the same way as her music, to judge from her stage persona. Striding onstage in a loose-fitting top, jeans, center-parting and rather more makeup than she used to wear, Joni looks a little harder and tougher, and a whole lot freer. Confident for sure. Folk waif into rock and roll lady, happy to let things roll along.

This time, she was enjoying herself instead of trying to pass some kind of test.

Since Bob Dylan took to stages to meet the folkie purists' hostility with The Band about eight years ago, solo acoustic performers have been turning themselves into bands as soon as they could afford to. Joni's one of the last to get around to it, but now that she's made the step, it's hard to see how she could have waited so long: Joni's voice is so much stronger for the backdrop. It's like a puppy can have a lot of fun playing with you and chasing the ball or the stick, but when you see him frisking with another puppy, it's a whole different ball-game. Joni's voice stands up now like a proud confident instrument in the knowledge that there's a whole pack of other instruments to bounce off.

Right off, she was trading off Robben Ford's guitar quite beautifully in the second number, "You Turn Me On (I'm A Radio)," lilting and whooping without a sign of strain.

Robben Ford was the guitarist who amazed a lot of people when he was playing in Jimmy Witherspoon's band supporting Eric Burdon in the armpit of the Marquee. If that band proved his technique and ability to dominate a band, Saturday's concert proved he's equally capable of hanging back and throwing in just the right phrase at the right time.

Ford apart, this was the band that provided the main part of the accompaniment on *Court and Spark*: leader Tom Scott on various woodwinds and reeds, and once even a triangle; with Melanie's arranger/keyboard man Roger Kellaway (also a new addition), Max Bennett on Fender bass and John Guerin on drums. The band played their own set first, which provided much flexing of instrumental muscles, but not a great amount of corporate inspiration, at least until a Coltrane composition, which gave Scott, Kellaway and Ford their heads.

But the entrance of Joni with her amplified acoustic guitar seemed to provide everyone with a place and a purpose, and they played superbly throughout the night, leading off aptly with "This Flight Tonight." Then to "Radio," with the band providing a good blare at the right moments, and the lighting hitting bright red to point up the fact.

Then with little ado, it was right into *Court and Spark* with "Free Man in Paris" and "The Same Situation," archetypal Joni lines here—"Tethered to a ringing telephone in a room full of mirrors / A pretty girl in your bathroom, checking out her sex appeal." Like Dory Previn, Joni always has those lemon-haired ladies just next door, birds of prey, and her situations always ring true.

Listening to her albums over all those years since I picked up the first one by ferreting through a rack years ago, when she was just an oddity on Frank Sinatra's label, has its ups and downs. It's a little like living next door in the canyon—one day she's round smiling with a bottle of champagne, and the next she looks just awful and you have to put the black coffee on the stove and sometimes she's a little too close for comfort and wants a little too much advice. But it's always worth it, and the amazing thing is that every one of those golden eggs in the nest is actually better, deeper, more lasting than the last one. I don't think anyone else has managed that over the same period of time.

She gets a little lost in the middle of "The Same Situation"—the only time during the whole concert—but it worries her not at all. She doodles a little on the piano, shouts to the band, "OK, on your spots," and we're

Joni Mitchell and girl, 1970. © Corbis/ Henry Diltz

off again—like a lot of the numbers, it starts off solo and gets gradually embellished.

"I used to count lovers like railroad cars, I counted them on my side / Lately I don't count on nothing, I just let things slide," she sings, and maybe it's giving her time to get the music even that much better.

The older songs are approached with a slightly cool reappraisal in the new light of the band and of other experiences, slightly muted jazz-accented funk. At times, L.A. Express sound a lot like the sound the Section put together for Carole King. When she sings "Both Sides, Now," she sings "I look at life that way, sometimes still!" as if she's surprised that the song still has any relevance.

She does "Woodstock" and "Big Yellow Taxi," as well as the newer material, and it's a long concert, never too long. Nobody can complain that their favorite's been left out, and still there's time for two long meandering introductory rambles to a couple of the songs. "Speedfreak!" someone in the audience shouts (there's always one of those). "No, I'm just a naturally compulsive talker," she says, carrying on in slight bafflement.

Joni comes back after the interval in a long blue dress and plays a few songs solo before being rejoined by the band. And the standard stays at an incredibly high level right through. Especially notable was a chilling version of her incredible "Cold Blue Steel." Singing with the deep siren voices of addiction, and wiggling gracefully behind her guitar at the same time, she made the song even more unsettling than it was on *For the Roses*. There are times when the lady's lyrics seem like they'd been dragged protesting right out of your subconscious.

A frantic "Raised on Robbery" was a natural closer. "The Last Time I Saw Richard" and "Twisted" ("I finally understood what jazz was all about playing with these guys") provided a pleasing encore.

A great night. I could tell you I saw Rod Stewart in the foyer and all that gossip column stuff, but it really was irrelevant. What mattered was seeing Joni Mitchell, caught and sparkling like a well-fed cigarette lighter. No sweat, no fuss: just an effortlessly great concert.

BY MALKA

JONI MITCHELL:SELF-PORTRAIT OF A SUPERSTAR

One of the first places Joni performed in the mid 1960s was the Riverboat, a tiny coffeehouse–folk club in Toronto's Yorkville district. Among the performers she met there was Malka, an Israeli-born folksinger who later branched out to a career in broadcast journalism. In this interview, Malka and Joni speak for the first time since the folk music heyday back in Yorkville.—SFL

Maclean's, June 1974

MALKA: You're on the road performing again. Why the silence of two full years?

JONI MITCHELL: I like to retire a lot, take a bit of a sabbatical to keep my life alive and to keep my writing alive. If I tour regularly and constantly, I'm afraid that my experience would be too limited, so I like to lay back for periods of time and come back to it when I have new material to play. I don't like to go over the old periods that much; I feel miscast in some of the songs that I wrote as a younger woman.

MALKA: How do you feel, then, about listening to your records?

JONI: I don't enjoy some of the old records; I see too much of my growing stage; I've changed my point of view too much. There are some of them that I can still bring life to, but some that I can't. Let's take the *Ladies of the Canyon* album; there are good songs on there which I feel still stand up and which I could still sing. There's a song called "The Arrangement" which seemed to me as a forerunner and I think has more musical sophistication than anything else on the album. And the *Blue* album, for the most part, holds up. But there are some early songs where there is too much naivete in some of the lyrics for me to be able now to project convincingly.

MALKA: Your name has been linked to some powerful people in the business, James Taylor and Graham Nash, for instance. Do you feel that your friends have helped your career in any way?

JONI: I don't think so, not in the time that James and I were spending together anyway. He was a total unknown, for one thing—maybe I helped his career? . . . But I do think that when creative people come together, the stimulus of the relationship is bound to show. The rock and roll industry is very incestuous, you know; we have all interacted and we have all been the source of many songs for one another. We have all been close at one time or another, and I think that a lot of beautiful music came from it. A lot of beautiful times came from it, too, through that mutual understanding. A lot of pain too, because, inevitably, different relationships broke up.

MALKA: But isn't there a certain amount of danger, when you surround yourself with musicians and troubadours doing the same kind of work you are doing, that you really create your own special world and are not so open to what's happening in the rest of the world?

JONI: A friend of mine criticized me for that. He said that my work was becoming very "inside." It was making reference to roadies and rock 'n' rollers, and that's the very thing I didn't want to happen, why I like to take a lot of time off to travel some place where I have my anonymity and I can have that day-to-day encounter with other walks of life. But it gets more and more difficult. That's the wonderful thing about being a successful playwright or an author: you still maintain your anonymity, which is very important in order to be somewhat of a voyeur, to collect your observations for your material. And to suddenly often be the center of attention was . . . it threatened the writer in me. The performer threatened the writer.

MALKA: When you were a little girl, did you think that you would be a singer one day, or a songwriter? How did it all start?

JONI: I always had star eyes, I think, always interested in glamour. I had one very creative friend whom I played with a lot and we used to put on circuses together, and he also played brilliant piano for his age when he was a young boy. I used to dance around the room and say that I was going to be a great ballerina and he was going to be a great composer, or that he was going to be a great writer and I was going to illustrate his books. My first experience with music was at this boy's house, because he played the piano and they had old instruments like auto harps lying around. It was playing his piano that made me want to have one of my own to mess with, but then, as soon as I expressed interest, they gave me lessons and that killed it completely. My childhood longing mostly was to be a painter, yet before I went to art college my mother said to me that my stick-to-itiveness in certain things was never that great, and she said you're going to get to art college and you're going to get distracted, you know. Yet all I wanted to do was paint. When I got there, however, it seemed that a lot of the courses were meaningless to me and not particularly creative. And so, at the end of the year I said to my mother I'm going to Toronto to become a folksinger. And I fulfilled her prophesy. I went out and I struggled for a while.

MALKA: Did you ever think you'd make it so big?

JONI: No, I didn't, I always kept my goals very short, like I would like to play in a coffeehouse, so I did. I would like to play in the United States, you know, the States, the magic of crossing the border. So I did. I would like to make a certain amount of money a year, which I thought would give me the freedom to buy the clothes that I wanted and the antiques and just some women trips, a nice apartment in New York that I wouldn't have to be working continually to support. But I had no idea that I would be this successful, especially since I came to folk music when it was already dying.

MALKA: *Many of your songs are biographical—do you think that the change in your lifestyle now has affected your songs?*

JONI: I don't know. I had difficulty at one point accepting my affluence, and my success and even the expression of it seemed to me distasteful at one time, like to suddenly be driving a fancy car. I had a lot of soul-searching to do as I felt somehow or other that living in elegance and luxury canceled creativity. I still had that stereotyped idea that success would deter creativity, would stop the gift, luxury would make you too comfortable and complacent and that the gift would suffer from it. But I found the only way that I could reconcile with myself and my art was to say this is what I'm going through now, my life is changing and I am too. I'm an extremist as far as lifestyle goes. I need to live simply and primitively sometimes, at least for short periods of the year, in order to keep in touch with something more basic. But I have come to be able to finally enjoy my success and to use it as a form of self-expression, and not to deny. Leonard Cohen has a line that says, "Do not dress in those rags for me, I know you are not poor," and when I heard that line I thought to myself that I had been denying, which was sort of a hypocritical thing. I began to feel too separate from my audience and from my times, separated by affluence and convenience from the pulse of my times. I wanted to hitchhike and scuffle. I felt maybe that I hadn't done enough scuffling.

MALKA: *But success does have some rewards. The Beatles, for instance, before they disbanded, translated it into a movement for peace. How do you think it affected you, the success?*

JONI: In a personal way it gives me the time to be able to pick and choose my project, to follow the path of the heart, which is really a luxury. So that I can be true to myself. I know a lot of artists who don't have that freedom, friends of mine who are still struggling to buy themselves that independence. Then there comes the question of do you take it all for yourself or what do you put back into the world? I haven't really found what I am to do. People are always coming up with great causes for me to get involved in, and they have wonderful arguments and reasons why I should be. The ones I select are the ones that I am genuinely interested in because I feel that they will show some sort of immediate return. Maybe this is impatience, like in Greenpeace, we raised some money to buy the ship which went to Amchitka with the hopes that they were going to sit in the territorial waters in this area where they're exploding bombs ridiculously close to the San Andreas fault. That inflamed me. That was a project I wanted to be a part of. In Montreal I played at a benefit for Cree Indians who were being displaced by a very stupidly run dam project. I know that money can be put to positive use, even if it's just to support people struggling in the arts. I believe in art, I believe that it's very important that people be encouraged in their self-expression and that their self-expression ping-pongs someone else's self-expression. That's what I believe in the most. If I'm going to distribute some of my windfall, it would be among other artists.

MALKA: Do you consider yourself a Canadian, Joni?

JONI: I definitely am Canadian. I'm proud of that and when it came to settling [on] the place where . . . I wanted to spend my old years, I bought some property north of Vancouver.

MALKA: You were once quoted as saying that your poetry is urbanized and Americanized and your music is of the Prairies.

JONI: I think that there is a lot of Prairie in my music and in Neil Young's music as well. I think both of us have a striding quality to our music which is like long steps across flat land. I think so, although I'm getting a little New Yorkish now with this jazz influence that's coming in. It's got to be urbanized. I talk about American cities, about Paris, about Greece; I talk about the places where I am.

MALKA: On your new album, Court and Spark, *for the first time you've recorded a song that isn't yours, "Twisted." Why did you decide to record something that is not your own?*

JONI: Because I love that song, I always have loved it. I went through analysis for a while this year, and the song is about analysis. I figured that I earned the right to sing it. I tried to put it on the last record, but it was totally inappropriate. It had nothing to do with that time period, and some of my friends feel it has nothing to do with this album either. It's added like an encore.

MALKA: *I hope I'm not encroaching on your privacy, but why the analysis now?*

JONI: I felt I wanted to talk to someone about the confusion which we all have. I wanted to talk to someone and I was willing to pay for his discretion. I didn't expect him to have any answers or that he was a guru or anything, only a sounding board for a lot of things. And it proved effective because simply by confronting paradoxes or difficulties within your life several times a week, they seem to be not so important as they do when they're weighing on your mind in the middle of the night, by yourself, with no one to talk to, or someone to talk to who probably will tell another friend, who will tell another friend, as friends do. I felt that I didn't want to burden people close to me, so I paid for professional help. And I went through a lot of changes about it, too. It's like driving out your devils—do you drive out your angels as well? You know that whole thing about the creative process. An artist needs a certain amount of turmoil and confusion, and I've created out of that. It's been like part of the creative force—even out of severe depression sometimes there comes insight. It's sort of masochistic to dwell on it, but you know it helps you to gain understanding. I think it did me a lot of good.

MALKA: *When I listen to your songs I notice that there are certain themes that kep appearing; one theme that comes up often is loneliness.*

JONI: I suppose people have always been lonely but this, I think, is an especially lonely time to live in. So many people are valueless or confused. I know a lot of guilty people who are living a very open kind of free life who don't really believe that what they're doing is right, and their defense to that is to totally advocate what they're doing, as if it were right, but somewhere deep in them they're confused. Things change so rapidly. Relationships don't seem to have any longevity. Occasionally you see people who have been together for six or seven, maybe 12 years, but for the most part people drift in and out of relationships continually. There isn't a lot of commitment to anything; it's a disposable society. But there are other kinds of loneliness which are very beautiful, like sometimes I go up to my land in British Columbia and spend time alone in the country surrounded by the beauty of natural things. There's a romance which accompanies it, so you generally don't feel self-pity. In the city when you're surrounded by people who are continually interacting, the loneliness makes you feel like you've sinned. All around you you see lovers or families and you're alone and you think, why? What did I do to deserve this? That's why I think the cities are much lonelier than the country.

MALKA: Another theme I think is predominant in your songs is love.

JONI: Love . . . such a powerful force. My main interest in life is human relationships and human interaction and the exchange of feelings, person to person, on a one-to-one basis, or on a larger basis projecting to an audience. Love is a peculiar feeling because it's subject to so much . . . change. The way that love feels at the beginning of a relationship and the changes that it goes through and I keep asking myself, "What is it?" It always seems like a commitment to me when you said it to someone, "I love you," or if they said that to you. It meant that you were there for them, and that you could trust them. But knowing from myself that I have said that and then reneged on it in the supportive—in the physical—sense, that I was no longer there side by side with that person, so I say, well, does that cancel that feeling out? Did I really love? Or what is it? I really believe that the maintenance of individuality is so necessary to what we would call a true or lasting love that people who say "I love you" and then do a Pygmalion number on you are wrong, you know. Love has to encompass all of the things that a person is. Love is a very hard feeling to keep alive. It's a very fragile plant.

MALKA: I sometimes find myself envying people that seem to be able to handle love, people who have found a formula for marriage. You were married at one point yourself; how do you feel about marriage now?

JONI: I've only had one experience with it, in the legal sense of the word. But there's a kind of marriage that occurs which is almost more natural through a bonding together; sometimes the piece of paper kills something. I've talked to so many people who said, "Our relationship was beautiful until we got married." If I ever married again, I would like to create a ceremony and a ritual that had more meaning than I feel our present-day ceremonies have, just a declaration to a group of friends. If two people are in love and they declare to a room of people that they are in love, somehow or other that's almost like a marriage vow. It tells everybody in the room, "I am no longer flirting with you. I'm no longer available because I've declared my heart to this person."

MALKA: Do you think you'll get married again?

JONI: I really don't know. I wouldn't see a reason for marriage except to have children, and I'm not sure that I will have children, you know. I'd like to and I have really strong maternal feelings, but at the same time I have developed at this point into a very transient person and not your average responsible human being. I keep examining my reasons for wanting to have a child, and some of them are really not very sound. And then I keep thinking of bringing a child into this day and age, and what values to instill in them that aren't too high so they couldn't follow them and have to suffer guilt or feelings of inadequacy. I don't know. It's like I'm still trying to teach myself survival lessons. I don't know what I would teach a child. I think about it . . . in terms of all my talk of freedom and everything.

MALKA: *Freedom, and in particular the word "free," is another theme in your music. What does freedom mean to you?*

JONI: Freedom to me is the luxury of being able to follow the path of the heart. I think that's the only way that you maintain the magic in your life, that you keep your child alive. Freedom is necessary for me in order to create, and if I cannot create, I don't feel alive.

MALKA: *Do you ever envision or fear that the well of creativity might dry up?*

JONI: Well, every year for the last four years I have said, "That's it." I feel often that it has run dry, you know, and all of a sudden things just come pouring out. But I know, I know that this is a feeling that increases as you get older. I have a fear that I might become a tunesmith, that I would be able to write songs but not poetry. I don't know. It's a mystery, the creative process, inspiration is a mystery, but I think that as long as you still have questions the muse has got to be there. You throw a question out to the muses and maybe they drop something back on you.

MALKA: *Sitting from the outside, it seems that as a creative person you have attained quite a lot: you have an avenue in which to express your talent, affluence, recognition. What are your aims now?*

JONI: Well, I really don't feel I've scratched the surface of my music. I'm not all that confident about my words. Thematically I think that I'm running out of things which I feel are important enough to describe verbally. I really think that as you get older life's experience becomes more; I begin to see the paradoxes resolved. It's almost like most things that I would once dwell on and explore for an hour, I would shrug my shoulders to now. In your twenties things are still profound and being uncovered. However, I think there's a way to keep that alive if you don't start putting up too many blocks. I feel that my music will continue to grow—I'm almost a pianist now, and the same thing with the guitar. And I also continue to draw, and that also is in a stage of growth, it hasn't stagnated yet. And I hope to bring all these things together. Another thing I'd like to do is to make a film. There's a lot of things I'd like to do, so I still feel young as an artist. I don't feel like my best work is behind me. I feel as if it's still in front.

Part Three

SINGER/SONGWRITER, COMPOSER, MUSICIAN 1975–1979

Billboard for Joni Mitchell Live Album, 1975. © Corbis/ Henry Diltz

BY NOEL COPPAGE

MORE THAN A SPRINKLING OF SYMBOLISM IN JONI MITCHELL'S "THE HISSING OF SUMMER LAWNS"

In The Hissing of Summer Lawns, *Joni experiments with world music years before Paul Simon and others. She continues to develop a jazz-inflected pop style that will influence a generation of rock musicians, including Sting, Peter Gabriel, and the artist formerly known as Prince.*

Yet this album received a mixed and often negative critical response. In a 1994 piece in LA Weekly, *Joni offers a reason: "Because I suddenly had commercial success, it was time to get my ass." In the same article, the author writes: "Mitchell believed the backlash had a lot to do with her decision to write 'social description as opposed to personal confession. People thought suddenly that I was secure in my success, that I was being a snot and was attacking them.'"*

In his review of Hissing, *Noel Coppage notes this switch away from "first-person-singular." Though his writing style, a mid-'70s, stoned-at-three-a.m. way of saying things, can be off-putting, keep with it; Coppage's ideas on what make this album difficult and rewarding are, in themselves, difficult and rewarding.—SFL*

Stereo Review, February 1976

Joni Mitchell's viewpoint has usually been first-person-singular, with the world seen as an incidental part of the examination of the quandary inside a relationship. In her new album, *The Hissing of Summer Lawns*, the viewpoint seems more nearly general, less specific, and the stories she tells collectively yield some truths (or maybe they're only suspicions) that are social as well as personal.

There is still the question of how much romanticism balanced against how much "reality" is good for us, but it is complicated this time out by the irony of what has happened to the settings, the environments—the city has paradoxically become the place primeval, while the country (nowadays the suburbs) has become the place where too much civilization is beginning to take its toll. Joni Mitchell shows us people trying to recapture a certain irresponsibility or a spontaneity—the ability to dance, to play—and they come off looking either a bit tawdry or frantic. Or she has them (us) looking for something through "lifestyle" affectations in New York, city of cities, or trying to beat back boredom and rage in suburbia—especially this, I think. She has built a song around the Johnny Mandel–Jon Hendricks relic of jazzbo slickness called "Centerpiece" that deals not only with the problem of "living happily ever after" but with the problem of centerpieces—their having more to do with making an impression than with supplying nourishment.

It is a difficult album, you see, partly because Mitchell is not moralizing, not boiling a situation down so any right-thinking listener can interpret it in only one way. It is difficult too because it doesn't sound like anything we're accustomed to, familiar as we are with the machinery behind the popular song, nor does it go out of its way to be pretty or tuneful. "The Jungle Line," for example, is about an asphalt jungle—but seen as something a beautiful madman such as the "primitive" painter Theodore Rousseau might have created ("Beauty and madness to be praised," she says in another song, about a movie-style greed for the root flavor of life). It is an experiment, a successful one, exquisitely lyrical images enhanced by almost frightening synthesizer whoops and warrior drums, and it doesn't mind being pulled out of the album to be considered as a separate whole. Most of the other pieces don't disengage from the overall context quite so easily.

Throughout, I am alternately struck by the notion that she has done little work on her melodies, that she has just ambled along the path of least resistance, and by the opposite notion (fostered by the delicacy of the tune to "Shades of Scarlet Conquering," or that of "Shadows and Light") that she is up to something too subtle for me to detect at this early stage in my relationship with the music. The lyrics, too, sometimes remind me of what Wilfrid Sheed said about symbolism: if the reader (or listener) gets it, you've taken an unnecessarily roundabout way of communicating with him, and if he doesn't get it, you haven't communicated with him at all. That's just the trouble with symbolism, though, and certainly no reason not to use it. There's more to poetry than simple communication—otherwise telegrams would be literature. And so the appeal of Mitchell's metaphors lies in their richness, in how long you can continue to pull new ideas and fresh slants out of them, no matter how many of them came from her head, how many from yours.

I hope I've made it clear that this isn't much of a party record; you'll have to deal with it privately, as you would read a book. But it should keep you occupied for about as long as you want it to—and how often does "popular" music do that?

BY PERRY MEISEL

AN END TO INNOCENCE: HOW JONI MITCHELL FAILS

A *literary slice-and-dice of* Hejira *from the pages of the* Village Voice. *(Note: For those intrigued by the analysis of cultural contrasts and contradictions included in this review, see Meisel's book,* The Cowboy and the Dandy: Crossing Over From Romanticism to Rock and Roll, *Oxford Press, 1999.) —SFL*

The Village Voice, January 24, 1977

Despite Joni Mitchell's reputation as a lyricist, the poetic element in her work has been a growing source of embarrassment to many listeners over the years. Less a measure of ignorance than of optimism, Mitchell's verbal pretensions are a product of her innocence—an innocence that seems unwarranted by the crushed hopes her songs discern in everything from urban blight and stardom to motherhood and love. Usually, Mitchell's melodies have been so compelling that her songs stand up on purely musical grounds, at least until her last LP, *The Hissing of Summer Lawns*, which sounded so aimless that it put off many of Joni's oldest fans. It is the poetic/lyrical factor, though, that sustains the new album, *Hejira*, Mitchell's ninth disc in almost nine years and her best since *Court and Spark*.

The predominance of the verbal and vocal on *Hejira* is largely the result of its simple dearth of melody. The singing, lean and true as never before, is almost entirely in the service of Mitchell's verse, which flexes through a wide variety of thematic exercises in language sharper, but also more abstract, than one has come to expect from her. Recitative rather than swinging or rocking, the songs tend to hover low and somber over the flat and sometimes faceless surface of the backup rhythms (most of them without drums), making Mitchell's declamatory voice the disc's sole object of attention.

In fact, *Hejira* presents the Queen of El Lay more explicitly in the guise of a poet than ever before, festooned with cape, beret, slanted pinky, and the backdrop of a resolutely abstract landscape. Well, that's the way poets are supposed to look, I guess, and Mitchell's (self-)portrait here seems to be a little too aware of that. Mitchell, of course, has always tried to pass herself off as a poet by printing out her lyrics on the covers of her recordings. No mere listening aids, the printouts constitute a tacit commitment to the perils of scrutiny and rereading. Mixing your metaphors in ignorance is one thing, but flaunting your pretensions in black and white is quite another. Unless . . . unless . . . the vaguely ironic Mitchell that emerged after *For the Roses* is now becoming more overt.

Mitchell's paradoxical history, both personal and artistic, should have prepared us for such a contingency. Here was a lover of words who, by all accounts at least, had spoken for a generation in revolt against language, a prairie girl from Alberta who wailed about the garden she had willfully forsaken for the grit and darkness of adopted cities like Toronto, Detroit, New York, and Los Angeles. Above all, here was a capricious lover resisting fantasies of domesticity even while the hausfrau within her was rattling around the kitchen in a constant huff about how fickle her own lovers seemed to be. Despite the paradoxes, though, Mitchell managed to forge an ego-ideal for lots of women, and certainly an ideal for the female vocalizer who was also a versifier, not to mention the lousy poet who could sing.

But self-absorption in art, the city, and the emerging self was only half of it. On the other side was another cluster of dreams, all of them allied with the rhythms of nature, childbearing included. Beyond them, however, was the question whether matrimony and domesticity were parts of nature, too, or whether they were simply another expression of the same evil that had erected New York and L.A. in place of the garden. The categories got jumbled—what was nature and what was repression?

The new album seems to offer a new set of answers to the old questions, beginning with the familiar contrast between the world of "nylons" and the world of "jeans": "You know it was white lace I was chasing / Chasing dreams / Mama's nylons underneath my cowgirl jeans" ("Song for Sharon"). Surprising as it may seem to hear Mitchell opting for the "white lace," self-reliance capitulates to domesticity, the cowgirl to the family. Yes, what is real or natural—what is "underneath"—turns out to be an ego-ideal named "Mama."

Yet the rest of the stanza complicates this moment of self-discovery by scrambling the terms on which it is made: ". . . first you get the kisses

/ And then you get the tears / But the ceremony of the bells and lace / Still veils this reckless fool here." The "bells and lace," of course, turn out to be just as foolish as the "jeans." Neither is more real or natural than the other. The "veil" of the bride is also the veil of illusion. So the meaning of "underneath," in its Freudlan sense of discovery, gets called into question; depth itself becomes a fiction and the self a surface of images, ciphers, or signs. Epiphany is "just a false alarm" ("Amelia"), while "deep and superficial" ("Hejira") come to be one and the same thing.

If Mitchell's language denies the possibility of real discovery, though, what happens to the "nature" that Joni the romantic has always been hell-bent on recovering? If there is no ground, how can there be a garden? And if domesticity may be part of humanity's natural rhythms, where is a nature that is separate from society and its attendant constraints?

At this point Mitchell's mythology begins to crumble. Premised on a return to nature, her mini-allegories fairly reek with a nostalgia for the garden and, by implication, for a pre-fallen language as well. Such a paradisiacal language would identify the word with the thing, allowing Mitchell to speak about feelings with all the sincerity for which she yearns. Trouble is, we're all outside the gates of Eden. Language is not an innocent tool of expression; it leads a life of its own, and, more often than not, it helps to manufacture the world in which we live.

Mitchell, though, resists the power inherent in language as such, even the power her own language displays. Despite the fact that her words generate ambiguity and call their own meanings into question, she wants them to stay fixed and believes that they do. A relentless practitioner of figurative speech, Mitchell behaves as though her words are straightforward conduits of expression, "direct from the heart" as it were. I'm more than willing—in fact, I'm eager—to grant Mitchell the title of Ironist. Unfortunately, she's not willing to grant it herself.

Indeed, she clutches on to reactionary notions about history and anthropology as eagerly as she clutches her own sincerity. Without a belief, however metaphoric, in the garden beyond or before civilization, there could be no belief in the garden of pure feeling that Mitchell assumes to be growing "underneath" ego and superego in the terrain of the self. For the Mitchell of *Hejira*, "history falls / To parking lots and shopping malls" ("Furry Sings the Blues"). Though the trope's manifest meaning is simply that old buildings get torn down by property developers, Mitchell's figurative use of the word "history" also makes a clear (even if unintentional) rhetorical distinction between "history" and "shopping malls" that implies that shopping malls aren't part of human history at all. What's more, this trope is typical of her indulgence in nostalgic fantasies about a simple past she presumes to have existed before technology and industrialization. In this context, the phrase "history falls" turns out to be meaningless: history is a consequence of the fall, not the other way around. In this way the phrase even threatens to invalidate the Christian romance of Mitchell's quest for redemption—of personal, and, public histories alike.

The question of literary prototypes also raises the question of Mitchell's relation to real Romanticism. The High Romantics themselves were by no means the pantheists our high schools like to teach, nor were they the source of Mitchell's naive assumptions about the status of nature. Shelley, for example, begins his famous poem in awe of Mont Blanc, and ends by asserting that he has imagined it. Not only is there no way back to the garden that Mitchell's "Woodstock" once demanded—nature itself may not even exist. There is no state of innocence down "underneath," where she expects it to be.

So there is finally no paradox involved in Mitchell's having spoken for the nonverbalists of the '60s. Hers is a language on the verge of dissolution, though the dissolution is largely unwitting and unrecognized. Unlike Barthelme or Borges, whose language is intentionally designed to empty out its signifying power in a dissolution that is part of its significance, the dissolution of Mitchell's language falls outside her will and control. Her language is therefore clouded, vague, imprecise, immodest; above all, rampant with figures of speech that break down under scrutiny and that collide in implications they do not intend.

God knows, I've had my heartthrobs for Joni, and I've been moved almost to tears by her stuff. But that's when I've been listening to her sing. Joined with melody and the infinite nuance of her voice, Mitchell's words are something else again. At a batch of syllables no longer bound to the responsibilities of the page and its ironic preconditions, they acquire a new and different kind of life. Puns on "ego" and "eagle" ("Coyote"), for example, are entirely legitimate when they're sung, despite their nonexistence on the page. Even the dangers of imitative form are superseded when Mitchell's voice ascends to meet the heights of "ice cream castles in the air" on "Both Sides, Now."

Mitchell's language also creates the kind of phonemic density and variation that only singers like Ella Fitzgerald or Sarah Vaughan can impart to the relatively simple verbal mannerisms of most pop tunes as they are written. Because the phonetic density of Mitchell's lyrics is so high

(I'd wager she uses more syllables per song than any songwriter living, Dylan included), her songs are, formally speaking, almost like copied-down scat extensions of a simpler melody line embedded somewhere inside the tune as a whole. From this point of view, Mitchell's style of song-writing seems designed to catch up as best it can with its perception of the essence of jazz singing proper. What it more often resembles, however, is the effort of a patchworker or bricoleur in assembling fragments of inspiration from a bewildering panoply of half-understood sources—blues, folk, opera, music-half, cabaret, and so on.

Mitchell readily admits to knowing next to nothing about "real" bluesmen, like the pop composer W. C. Handy or the vaudevillian Furry Lewis, whom she pairs up in what is doubtless *Hejira*'s most distressing song, "Furry Sings the Blues." Despite its expressive flexibility Mitchell's voice is about as far removed from anything like real jazz singing (especially Ella's or Vaughan's) as her romanticism is from the Romantics themselves. Joni's voice doesn't get you in the crotch or gut the way real blues heartthrobbers do. Mitchell lacks the element of swing as plainly as she lacks a direct kind of sexiness—witness her version of Wardell Gray's "Twisted" on *Court and Spark* or even *Hejira*'s "Blue Motel Room."

If Mitchell's sexuality is hard to flush out into the open, her prairie-bred will is always plainly in evidence. Her instinctive professionalism yokes together all her half-digested musical influences, saving and polishing every scrap and displaying in the process a frugality and neatness that may signify a latent anality in this liberator of the repressed. Granted, when the compulsive Mitchell handles the crossfire from her various musical sources with perfect control, the results are melodies like those on *Blue*, which inhabit the mind as an unforgettable sweep of notes largely devoid of the lyrics with which they are sung. Without melody, though, Mitchell's singing gets boring and redundant despite its requisite subtleties and nuance as on the droning, recitative "Coyote," *Hejira*'s opener. Is it an accident that, even for Joni's greatest fans, her greatest songs have always been her most tuneful ones?

Bound to the page as they are, however, Mitchell's songs insist on being divided against themselves. There is no more striking example of this than the breathtaking moments on "Refuge of the Roads," in which the song's recurring melodic channel emerges with sudden splendor in a late chorus. The splendor is due to the ambitious words with which this melody is sung: "These are the clouds of Michelangelo / Muscular with gods and sungold / Shine on your witness in the refuge of the roads." Yet the lines are impossibly pretentious for a number of reasons, chief among them the vague relation between Michelangelo and the clouds, and the unfortunately successful identity it implies between Michelangelo's work and Mitchell's own. Both accomplishments, by the way, are signified by the figure of clouds, which have always been a cipher for all that is significant to Mitchell since "Both Sides, Now."

Hejira's title, however, is its most enticing trope. The word "hejira" refers to Mohammed's flight from Mecca in 622, a flight for personal survival that preserved the fledgling Islamic religion. Ever since, "hejira" has come to mean such a purposive flight from danger or oppression. Clearly, Mitchell means to take this meaning for her own, to signify her many flights from oppressive relationships the burdens of stardom, the dirt of the city. In this way, the album's recurrent images of flight—Icarus, jets, crows and so on—conspire to suggest a Mitchell whose only "refuge" is "the roads." Yet "flight" also signifies the transitory, the ephemeral, the flighty quality of Mitchell's own attempts at meaning. This kind of flight—escape or loss rather than departure for freedom—is far different from the Mohammedan sense of the word, which Mitchell wants to use to grant her own flightiness a weightier sense of purpose than it really possesses. The meanings are at odds, and they fight it out within the word itself.

Ultimately, though, we are left with a question of intentionality: Are all these meanings of "hejira" really "there," or does Mitchell's language comment on itself—indeed, deconstruct itself—outside her control and design? Just how naive is this airy lady of the canyons, whose new album seems a witness to the inauthenticity of all sincerity? Mitchell mocks herself on *Hejira*, though just how wittingly it is hard to tell. There seems to be something like bitterness on the album, even if it comes out as a diminished investment in the self and a decline in the earnestness with which the persona is presented. I suspect that this level of irony is firmly within Mitchell's conscious grasp, and that her absurd pose on the album's cover is a caricature she has willfully drawn to subvert her own pretensions as a personality.

As an artist, however, Mitchell clearly lacks any real understanding of what her work is and how it behaves. Aware as she may be of the ironies of her pose as a lover and a soothsayer, the finer ironies of what it means to work in language obviously elude her. These are two distinctly different kinds of irony, mind you, and they signify two distinct levels of knowing. The first is dramatic or situational, the way we have of knowing what we don't know, much as Mitchell the self-mocking artiste knows she no longer has the answers. The second, however, is far crueler, since it knows we can never mean what we say. It is this second style of knowing that characterizes a literary language, and that can transform any language into an aesthetic one so long as its syntax displays some delight in the hazards of signification and some deliberation as to how it means to handle them.

These hazards are not only beyond Mitchell's control but also beyond her ken. Her art lacks deliberation because it lacks a knowledge of the instruments it employs. The product of these shortcomings for the artist is the self-consuming artifact that finally consumes its own maker. *Hejira* signifies Mitchell's flight from precisely this fate. The mythology of the garden still has her in its thrall, and until she confronts it within her conscious imagination, her work will be haunted by the prospect of its own annihilation.

BY BLAIR JACKSON

DON JUAN'S RECKLESS DAUGHTER

In case you ever wondered, yes, that's Joni herself dressed as a black man on the cover of Don Juan's Reckless Daughter. *The writing of this album in 1977 clearly marked an important time for her; in a recent interview in the* Austin Chronicle, *reprinted in Part Five, Joni says she is writing her autobiography and plans to begin her story in the late '70s. Her opening line: "I was the only black man at the party."*

For the story behind the costume, see Phil Sutcliffe's interview in Part Four. For a well-observed review of Joni Mitchell's tenth album, read on.—SFL

BAM, January 1978

The significance of this album is easily explained: it's ambitious as hell; a double-record set of staggering depth, complexity and musical scope from one of the most talented artists working in pop music. It is also the album which will reveal Joni Mitchell's "singer/songwriter" tag to be shamefully inadequate. To those appellations, we most add "composer" and "musician": if you've ever thought that "Both Sides, Now" and "Help Me" are what Joni Mitchell is all about, listen to her guitar work on "Cotton Avenue" or "The Silky Veils of Ardor," her piano playing on the epic six-

Joni Mitchell, Joan Baez, & Bob Dylan at Madison Square Garden, 1975. © Corbis/Bettmann

teen-minute "Paprika Plains" and the intelligence behind the arrangements of the above tunes and "Dreamland." There is so much on this record it's going to take months, perhaps even years, to absorb it all. (If that sounds ridiculous, think back on how long it took you to digest Dylan's *Blonde on Blonde* or even the Beatles' *White Album*.) If *Don Juan's Reckless Daughter* is "about" anything, it is duality: the split-tongued spirit which reveals itself on side four's title track. It is about the serpent—"fighting for blind desire"—and the eagle—"for clarity." It is about dichotomous reality: "self indulgence to self denial / man to woman / scales to feathers / you and I." It is also about dreaming and being painfully awake.

The spirit/flesh duality crops up for the first time on the album's opening cut, "Overture/Cotton Avenue." It opens as an ethereal, free-form duet between Joni's arresting, metallic acoustic guitar work and her airy voice, double and triple tracked, soaring high in a vocal reminiscent of Flora Purim or Milton Nascimento. Then, in stark contrast to this shimmering voice, comes Weather Report's Jaco Pastorius, entering with a thundering, sensual bass, adding a throbbing urgency to this mythical, sylvan scene. After establishing itself as king of this musical spirit world, the bass is joined by John Guerin's drums and the song jumps from an abstract jazz feel into the breezy and melodic "Cotton Avenue," a down-to-earth song with the cool R&B feel of a Harlem juke-joint in the 1930s. Pastorius' bass is the only reminder of the realm visited in "Overture."

With barely a second to breathe, the musicians charge into the ego-world of insecurity on "Talk to Me." Joni attacks her guitar with a frantic desperation which is echoed in Jaco's glistening bass leads. "You can talk to me like a fool," she sings. "Shut me up and talk to me." It's a crazy, dizzy song—straight-forward and completely anti-introspective—filled with Joni's intriguing and rather odd humor.

"Jericho" slows things down again—and introduces for the the first time Weather Report's Wayne Shorter on spellbinding soprano sax. (Where's Joe Zawinal?) Not surprisingly, teaming him with Pastorius results in a bit of absolute magic, an intense rhythmic counterpoint that threatens to break loose into improvisation of the sort on "Overture." Even Joni's lyrics yearn for this sort of release: "Let all these dogs go runnin' free / the wild and gentle dogs / kennelled in me." Those dogs are unleashed on the next side.

"Paprika Plains," which takes up the entire second side, is, in many ways, the album's musical and thematic epicenter. It confronts the eagle/serpent, dream state/waking state dualities head on. Opening from the perspective of herself as a naive child, Joni uses the experience of North American Indians as a metaphor for a universal concern—the clash between the spiritual and the real, the holy and the blasphemous. Her piano and voice introduction, which has a slight show-tune feel to me, spells out the Indians' dilemma plainly: "But when the church got through / They traded their beads for bottles / Smashed-on Railway Avenues / And they cut off their braids / And lost some link with nature."

The bulk of the song is a huge instrumental exposition by Joni on piano accompanied by a full orchestra (arranged by Michael Gibbs). But this middle is not strictly instrumental, for the song's lyrics continue in the form of a long poem on the record jacket—an eloquent dreamscape mixing concrete and transparent imagery in a continuation of the Indian theme. The music is alternately sonorous and dissonant, lush and simple, smooth and choppy. Curiously, I found it all a bit overbearing until I heard it on a car radio not too long ago.

The instrumental passage completed, the opening melody reappears, only to give way to crashing drums and a two-minute, forty-five-second coda featuring Guerin, Pastorius, and Shorter. It is a peaceful, expansive close that lends the entire piece a strange sense of balance and coherence.

On side three we jump back to the world of surfaces with "Otis and Marlena," a scathing portrait of Miami Beach and the type of people attracted to it. "And the neon mercury stained / Miami sky / It's as red as meat / It's a cheap pink rose."

The song fades slowly, eerily into "The Tenth World," an all-percussion instrumental that sounds like a Haitian exorcism. It is clearly intended to serve as a physical means of re-entering a spiritual plane. I find seven minutes of this rhythmic frenzy about four minutes too long, but it does function as an effective bridge between "Otis and Marlena" and "Dreamland," which ends the side. In the latter song, Joni, with sultry vocal support from Chaka Khan, is backed only by a percussion ensemble; but this time, it is not furious abandon of the sort we hear on "The Tenth World," but an even, swinging beat.

Side four's "Don Juan's Reckless Daughter" offers the key, as I've said, to the duality theme that permeates the record. Whether you choose to interpret Joni's Don Juan as the brujo of the Castaneda books, the fabled lover or some God-head of her own creation is really not important: it all hinges on the serpent and the eagle.

"Off Night Backstreet" follows, a tale of bitter and jealous love as far removed from the eagle's "clarity" as "Talk to Me" on side one. The record ends beautifully with "The Silky Veils of Ardor," which features some shimmering Fahey-esque guitar work under a lovely, if not particularly melodic, vocal. And as if to bring the entire album into ambiguous focus she closes with the lines "It's just in dreams we fly / in my dreams we fly." You may be humming Fleetwood Mac's "Dreams" a year or two from now, but will it ever haunt you in the night?

BY LEONARD FEATHER

JONI MITCHELL MAKES
MINGUS SING

Legendary jazz musician Charles Mingus, knowing he was dying, approached Joni Mitchell in 1978 to collaborate on an album. Mingus came out in 1979 to mixed reviews. Leonard Feather, internationally renowned jazz critic, interviews Joni about her relationship with Charles Mingus and her development in the world of jazz.—SFL

Downbeat, September 6, 1979

The career of vocalist and songwriter Joni Mitchell has, within the last year, developed to emphasize her associations with jazz music, which have been evident at least since Tom Scott's L.A. Express joined her on *Court and Spark*. *Mingus*, her acclaimed collaboration with the late bassist/composer, and her Playboy Jazz Festival performance with Herbie Hancock, Don Alias, Gene Perla, and Randy Brecker are indicative of her latest direction. In conversation, Joni states her longtime involvement with jazz—the sound of Annie Ross is clearly discernible in some of Joni's phrasing, and sure enough, Lambert, Hendricks & Ross was an early favorite.

Born in McLeod, Alberta, Canada, Joni Mitchell enrolled at an art school in Alberta but soon drifted into folk singing. She took an increasing interest in songwriting, graduated from ukelele to acoustic guitar, and after working at coffeehouses in Toronto, moved to Detroit in 1966.

Her career moved into top gear after she signed with Reprise Records in 1967. During the years that followed, her own personal success as a singer was at times partially subjugated to the impact of others' versions of her songs ("Both Sides Now" provided a hit for Joni and a gold record for Judy Collins). Since 1972 Mitchell has been with Asylum Records.

A natural musician rather than a schooled one, over the years her close association with sophisticated musicians has led to an ever more sensitive awareness of the fundamentals of jazz.

Last year, it became known that she was embarking on an album in collaboration with the ailing Mingus, the sidemen including Wayne Shorter, Jaco Pastorius, Peter Erskine and Herbie Hancock.

By late April, the project had been finally mixed and the album was previewed at a private party. The interview below took place a few days later, when Mitchell still had not decided on a final title, which she discusses here.

The artwork consists of three paintings by Mitchell of Mingus. It was to this that I made reference in my opening comment.

Feather: I like what you put outside the album almost as much as what you put in . . . it's a beautiful cover.

Mitchell: Thank you. I like the cover myself. I've always done much more commercial covers—by that, I mean to distinguish it from my very personal, private painting. It's the first time I decided to put that out because it seemed to suit the music. The music is very painterly as well, I think, a lot of white canvas, and very brash, strokey interaction, especially on the things that were done with Wayne and Jaco, and Peter and Herbie.

F: Had you ever considered making that your career?

M: All my life I've painted. All through school it was my intention to go on to study art. It was a very academic culture that I came out of. Our parents had come up through the Depression, and insisted that we all have a very good education. I wasn't academically oriented and I was growing up just at the time before arts were included as a part of education. Four years later there were fully developed art departments and music departments in the high schools that I attended. But at that time I was kind of a freak.

F: Music education was very limited then, too.

M: Well, now, even though they've included that in the program, both the art and the music education are still limited. But [students] have access to a lot of fantastic equipment, and at least it is included in the curriculum. At that point in my education, when they discovered on an aptitude test that I had musical abilities, they wanted me to join a glee club, which was pretty corny music; it wasn't too challenging. So I didn't join.

F: Well, you couldn't learn the kind of music you later became involved with.

M: No; it was all exposure to people who moved me, that's how it came. It came really from the street, going into a club and hearing somebody hanging out with somebody. Not so much playing with people like jazz musicians, but just observing.

F: *What was the first exposure you had?*

M: When I was in high school—like I say, I wasn't too swift academically, but I did a lot of extracurricular drawing. I did backdrops for school plays, drawings of mathematicians for my math teacher and biology charts of life for my biology teacher. That was a way of appeasing them for being so disinterested in the academic aspect. One year I did a Christmas card for a fellow who was a school leader, and he gave me a present of some Miles Davis albums and about that time my only musical interest, actively, was in rock 'n' roll—Chuck Berry, and this was at the level of dance. I loved to dance. I think my time developed from that love. Going to two, three or as many dances as were available to go to a week.

Anyway, by my doing this card, he introduced me to some jazz. Then I heard, at a party, Lambert, Hendricks & Ross, *The Hottest New Sound in Jazz*, which at that time was out of issue up in that part of the country, in Canada. So I literally saved up and bought it at a bootleg price, and in a way I've always considered that album to be my Beatles because I learned every song off it. "Cloudburst" I couldn't sing, because of some of the very fast scatting on it; but I still to this day know every song on that album. I don't think there's another album that I know every song on, including my own!

I loved that album, the spirit of it. And like I say, it came at a time when rock 'n' roll was winding down just before the Beatles came along and revitalized it. And during that ebb that's when folk music came into its full power.

F: *What were the Miles Davis albums?*

M: *Sketches of Spain* . . . I must admit that it was much later that Miles really grabbed my attention . . . and *Nefertiti* and *In a Silent Way* became my all-time favorite records in just any field of music. They were my private music; that was what I loved to put on and listen to—for many years now. Somehow or other I kept that quite separate from my own music. I never thought of making that kind of music. I only thought of it as something sacred and unattainable. So this year was very exciting to play with the players that I did.

F: You did let your hair down one time when you did "Twisted."

M: Right—and "Centerpiece," I also did that. One by one I've been unearthing the songs from that Lambert, Hendricks & Ross album.

F: But there's no seeming relationship between the two worlds . . .

M: Which two worlds are you referring to?

F: The world of music you recorded and the jazz world.

M: All the time that I've been a musician, I've always been a bit of an odd-ball. When I was considered a folk musician, people would always tell me that I was playing the wrong chords, traditionally speaking. When I fell into a circle of rock 'n' roll musicians and began to look for a band, they told me I'd better get jazz musicians to play with me, because my rhythmic sense and my harmonic sense were more expansive. The voicings were broader; the songs were deceptively simple. And when a drummer wouldn't notice where the feel changed, or where the accent on the beat would change, and they would just march through it in the rock 'n' roll tradition, I would be very disappointed and say, "Didn't you notice there was a pressure point here," or "Here we change," and they just would tell me, "Joni, you better start playing with jazz musicians."

Then, when I began to play with studio jazz musicians, whose hearts were in jazz but who could play anything, they began to tell me that I wasn't playing the root of the chord. So all the way along, no matter who I played with, I seemed to be a bit of an oddball. I feel more natural in the company that I'm keeping now, because we talk more metaphorically about music. There's less talk and more play.

F: You've been associating with jazz studio musicians for how long?

M: Four years. I made *Court and Spark* five years ago.

F: Did that come about by design or by accident?

M: The songs were written and I was still looking for a band intact, rather than having to piece a band together myself. Prior to that album, I had done a few things with Tom Scott, mostly doubling of existing guitar lines. I wanted it to be a repetition or gilding of existing notes within my structure. So through him, I was introduced to that band. I went down to hear them at the Baked Potato in Studio City, and that's how all that came about.

They all found it extremely difficult at first, hearing the music just played and sung by one person; it sounded very frail and delicate, and there were some very eggshelly early sessions where they were afraid they would squash it, whereas I had all the confidence in the world that if they played strongly, I would play more strongly.

F: *So from that point on you worked with the L.A. Express?*

M: We worked together for a couple of years, in the studio and on the road.

F: *Did that expand your knowledge, being around them so much?*

M: Not really, not in an academic sense. It gave me the opportunity to play with a band and to discover what that was like. But I still was illiterate in that I not only couldn't read [music], but I didn't know—and don't to this day—what key I'm playing in, or the names of my chords. I don't know the numbers, letters, or the staff. I approach it very paintingly, metaphorically: so I rely on someone that I'm playing with, or the players themselves, to sketch out the chart of the changes. I would prefer that we all just jumped on it and really listened.

Miles always gave very little direction, as I understand. It was just "Play it. If you don't know the chord there, don't play there," and that system served him well. It was a natural editing system. It created a lot of space and a lot of tension, because everybody had to be incredibly alert and trust their ears. And I think that's maybe why I loved that music as much as I did, because it seemed very alert and very sensual and very unwritten.

F: *And you, in turn, trusted your own ears.*

M: I do trust my own ears. Even for things that seem too outside. For instance, sometimes I'm told that so-and-so in the band, if I hadn't already noticed, was playing outside the chord. I see that there's a harmonic dissonance created; but I also think that the line that he's created, the arc of it, bears some relationship to something else that's being played; therefore it's valid. So in my ignorance there's definitely a kind of bliss. I don't have to be concerned with some knowledge that irritates other people.

F: *"Outside" is only a comparative term, anyway.*

M: Outside the harmony . . . but still, as a painter, if the actual contour of the phrase is, like I say, related to an existing contour that someone is playing, then it has validity. Like, if you look at a painting, there seem to be some brush strokes that seem to be veering off, or the color may be dashing, but something in the shape or form of it relates to something that exists; therefore it's beautiful.

I see music very graphically in my head—in my own graph, not in the existing systemized graph—and I, in a way, analyze it or interpret it, or evaluate it in terms of a visual abstraction inside my mind's eye.

F: *Where did you first hear about Mingus?*

M: I remember some years ago, John Guerin played "Pork Pie Hat" for me, which is one of the songs that I've done on this new album; and it was that same version. But it was premature; he played it for me at a time when it kind of went in one ear and out the other. I probably said "hmm-hmm," and it wasn't until I began to learn the piece that I really saw the beauty of it.

Mingus, of course, was a legend. Folk and jazz in the cellars of New York were overlapping, so I'd heard of Mingus by name for some time. As a matter of fact, I'd heard that name as far back as when I was listening to Lambert, Hendricks & Ross in Canada. I was in high school then, but my friends in the university spoke of these legendary people. That was in the early '60s.

F: *When did you actually get to meet him?*

M: I got word through a friend of a friend that Charles had something in mind for me to do, and this came down the grapevine to me. Apparently he had tried through normal channels to get hold of me; but there's a very strong filtering system here, and for one reason or another it never reached me. So it came in this circular way, and I called him up to see what it was about, and at that time he had an idea to make a piece of music based on T. S. Eliot's *Quartet* and he wanted to do it with—this is how he described it—a full orchestra playing one kind of music, and overlaid on that would be bass and guitar playing another kind of music; over that there was to be a reader reading excerpts from *Quartet* in a very formal literary voice; and interspersed with that he wanted me to distill T. S. Eliot down into street language, and sing it mixed in with the reader.

It was an interesting idea; I like textures. I think of music in a textural collage way myself, so it fascinated me. I bought the book that contained the *Quartet* and read it; and I felt it was like turning a symphony into a tune. I could see the essence of what he was saying, but his expansion was like expanding a theme in the classical symphonic sense, and I just felt I couldn't do it. So I called Charles back and told him I couldn't do it, it seemed kind of like a sacrilege.

So some time went by and I got another call from him saying that he'd written six songs for me and he wanted me to sing them and write the words for them. That was April of last year, and I went out to visit him and I liked him immediately, and he was devilishly challenging.

He played me one piece of music—an older piece, I don't know the title of it— because we figured it was going to take eight songs to make an album: the six new ones and two old ones. So we began searching through this material, and he said, "This one has five different melodies," and I said, "And you want me to write five different sets of lyrics at once," and he said, "Yes."

He put it on and it was the fastest, boogieingest thing I'd ever heard, and it was impossible. So this was like a joke on me. He was testing and teasing me; but it was in good fun. I enjoyed the time I spent with him very much.

F: How sick was he then?

M: He was in a wheelchair. I never knew him when he was well, and I never heard him play; he was paralyzed then.

F: How much contact did you have, actually working together?

M: There were several visits to the house; the better part of an afternoon listening to old music, discussing the themes and his lyrical intent on the new melodies. Then he and Sue [Mingus] went to Mexico to a faith healer down there, and during the time they were in Mexico I went and spent ten days with them. By that time his speech had severely deteriorated. Every night he would say to me, "I want to talk to you about the music," and every day it would be too difficult. It was hard for him to speak.

So some of what he had to tell me remained a mystery. But Sue gave me a lot of tapes of interviews with him and they were thrilling to me, because so much of what he felt and described was so kindred to my own feelings; he articulated lessons that were laid on him by people like Fats Navarro and others. So he was definitely a teacher of mine.

F: *What in your work had attracted him to you and caused him to get in touch with you?*

M: Somebody played him some of my records. Now, this is a story that came to me—there's a piece of music of mine called "Paprika Plains" which was done in sections. The middle of it is about seven minutes of improvisational playing, which I had somebody else orchestrate for me. And then stuck on to each end of it is a song that I wrote later around it. It was improvised off of a theme; then I abandoned the theme and just left the improvisational part, which I cut together. It's a modern, technological way of composing.

It was recorded in January, and the piano was tuned many, many times, so by August, when I played the verses, which were born much later, the piano had slightly changed. So when it was orchestrated, it's in tune for a while, but then it hits that splice where it goes from the January piano to the August piano. With a fine ear you notice. So somebody was playing this piece for Charles, and Charles is a stickler for true pitch and time, and he kept saying, "It's out of tune, it's out of tune." But when the piece was over he said that I had a lot of balls!

So something about it—whatever it was he didn't like, he also saw some strength and certainly an adventuresome spirit, because I'd been pushing the limits of what constitutes a song for years; I keep trying to expand it—with an instrumental in the middle or with no known or pre-scribed length, but just as long as my own interest will hold out. And I presume that if it will hold my interest that long that it will at least hold the interest of a minority.

So, as near as I can tell, that was part of it, that he felt that I had a sense of adventure.

F: *Didn't you find it necessary in your later stages to finish off some of the music yourself?*

M: See, I can only work from inspiration. I have a certain amount of craft, granted, but I cannot work only from craft. A piece that is merely craft doesn't mean anything to me. It has to be inspired. Of the six melodies he gave me, two of them I never really could get into; they were too idiomatic in a way for me. They were modern enough for my own sense of what is modern—they were reminding me of something back there, and I couldn't find any new way I could transcend them. I had to just lock into them and do them and I just couldn't get inspired by two of them.

[Another] was extremely beautiful . . . but I couldn't get into it because the theme was very difficult. Charles referred me to a passage in his book, a long discourse between him and Fats Navarro about God. And it was his own metaphorical description of God and relationship to God. I couldn't just lift that literally and make it adhere to his melody. That threw me into my own confrontation with my own metaphors about God, and it boggled my mind; it just fried my brain. I somehow or other could not really figure that puzzle out. So those three never got finished.

The four that I did complete were all inspired: either I stumbled across pieces of the poetry in the street, or they came to me in mysterious ways—they were meant to be. But the other three melodies somebody else should write words to, because they're beautiful.

That left me with a song I had been writing before I met Charles, "The Wolf that Lives in Lindsey"—that strange piece of music, which I included because I felt that the wolves constituted part of Charles' musical concept about cacophony. There was some natural, beautiful cacophony; those wolves are singing in a chorus, hitting every note on the keyboard, but it's beyond dissonance, it transcends dissonance. So I thought it was kindred to Charles' way of thinking in that way.

The other song, "God Must Be a Boogie Man," is based on the first four pages of his book, and I tried to take those first four pages and use the meter and everything to the three of these melodies of his, but the words wouldn't adhere. So then I let them have their own syncopation and wrote my own melody to it. So that's very much his own self-description.

Then there's the documentary footage in the album, which I think is extraordinarily important due to the fact that Charles knew long before he became ill how he wanted his funeral to be carried out, what he did want and didn't want; I *had* to include that. And I love the spirit of the birthday song—which establishes the year he was born in; that's why I opened it that way.

F: *Was that a tape that just happened to be in his loft?*

M: Sue gave me that. She thought those things were important. And I also liked Sue's presence on the tape, because she is a wonderful woman—she was wonderful to Charles; she made that last time . . . she was very, very giving and great with him.

F: *You were saying at the party the other day that there were still some pleasures he was able to find in life, even at that late stage.*

M: Yes, he loved to eat, even though supposedly he was on a diet for his health; he liked to ride in a car—as a matter of fact, that was the only time he could sleep. Sue and a nurse and his son would load him up into the van and they would go off driving around and he would sleep peaceably in there; but he was an insomniac back at the house. So the ride in the car and the outings to the restaurant were highlights, something he really looked forward to.

F: *When was the last time you actually saw him or spoke to him?*

M: That would be in October. Sue told me something beautiful today. Now, Charles died at the age of 56 in Mexico; the following day he was cremated. That day 56 whales beached themselves on a coast of Mexico, and not knowing what to do with them, the people there burned them. So 56 whales were cremated the same day as Charles.

There was a lot of mojo in his life—there's a lot of mojo in my life, too. He was very wrapped up with natural phenomena. And that's why I think we all had a certain amount of faith in the possibility that he could actually beat it. I always addressed myself to that possibility. If I hadn't, I know the songs would have been much more directed at Charles, like "The Dry Cleaner from Des Moines" would have probably had a different lyric content, or "Sweet Sucker Dance." Because when it came down to the finished album, I thought, this is not a complete portrait of such a complex person; I wished then that every song had been dedicated to a certain aspect of his personality. Some addressed themselves directly; and indirectly they all had something that was kindred with his way.

F: *You mentioned that on some of the numbers, there were several different versions that had to be left out of the final album, that included a lot of interesting people such as Phil Woods, Gerry Mulligan, etc. How did that come about, and is there any possibility that those outtakes might eventually be used in some other context?*

M: They're in the can. If you laid them all out and said, okay, here's four versions of the same song, let's choose which one we like the best, you would find some people liked one version better than another and that no one would really agree. So, it came down to my decision and to my direction.

Charles and I differed musically; we shared things but differed in some ways. He had an aversion to electrical instruments and was very much a purist. And while I'm basically an acoustic player so I understand that, I never was prejudiced against electric instruments; I just don't have any mechanical aptitude. There are too many knobs for me, so I revert back to the simpler form. I know I'm sidestepping your question.

F: What I'm curious about is, did you make several versions just because you weren't satisfied with each one in turn, or you just wanted to experiment with different ways of approaching the same material?

M: Both of those things are true. The first sessions Charles was present at they were with Jeremy Lubbock, Don Alias, Gerry Mulligan; Stanley Clarke played at one of them. The groove was more there, it was closer to what Charlie wanted, they swung more, and Charlie was a stickler for them to swing. So in some ways they were stronger in that area. Alias is a great drummer; he can really play anything great. So they had a beautiful character to them. In some ways you could even say that I sang better, because the time was so solid.

But something happened, something was missing; to me, they could have been cut 20 years ago; they didn't contain something that we know now. And it was so abstract, and since I don't have the language, and owing to a sense of feminine inferiority that comes on me every once in a while when I'm in a position of leading men—every once in a while I get that, coupled with inferiority and illiteracy, you can understand that there can appear a complex from time to time. Especially when I'm looking for something that I can't articulate. There's an abstraction there. So I just kept cutting them over and over with different personnel and when we finally did these things that night, I realized what it was I was looking for—an integral relationship with the band where the band wasn't coupling up into a bass player and a drummer playing off each other, trading licks. That can happen in the best of bands, you know, where cliques develop internally within the band and people are playing for each other's pleasure, and the vocalist, while they are a leader of sorts, is kind of apart from what's going on behind them.

I didn't want this to happen, and on these dates I have here, they yanked the downbeat out from underneath me, so that suddenly the thing would be floating and I would be out there all alone—like hang gliding!

Especially Shorter—from playing with Miles, I guess—plays so beautifully, not off of a high linear line, not just matching tones, but he plays so brilliantly off of lyrics, because he has such a pictorial mind that he is talking. He's such a metaphorical player. I love the way he related to me. He especially made me feel like an integral band member. So we all seemed to be one organism on this music.

I think that's quite unique, even among the great jazz vocalists. They tend to be fronting a track; whereas in this music, we're all mimicking each other, we're shading the tail end of a phrase the way a tone . . . the tone has breath, people play breathy, even the percussion instruments seem to become breathy. If you look at it you'll see how entwined we are, and that, I thought, was a beautiful accomplishment and something special.

F: I got some of that feeling on my first listen; but I want to listen again. I don't know how many people listening for the first time will get the full impact.

M: I don't think so; I don't think you can. I've listened to it so many times, I've gone through so many changes about it, it's like quicksilver. It's very dependent on the mood you're in. It'll change on you like a chameleon. It requires many listenings, like good poetry; I think all good art has that quality. It just doesn't stand still, there's nothing static about it.

F: What do you expect from the album in terms of popular public reaction? Do you think it's commercial—not that that's the objective; but how commercial do you expect it to be?

M: I dare not have any expectations. If I have them, I probably would be disappointed, because I'm very pleased with it. So if I have any expectations, or hope, it would be that people would find it accessible. I think it is, but I know how intimidating great musicianship is to a lot of people; it can awe people and make them feel excluded rather than included; I hope that doesn't happen. I'm talking about within the context of the pop field, not within the context of the jazz idiom at all. I would be surprised if it wasn't well accepted in the jazz world, because it contains all the best elements of that music. It's very spontaneous, creative and fresh.

In the pop circles, I have no idea what will happen.

F: *I think a lot of it will be helped by just the fact that it's a Joni Mitchell album. Some of the millions of people who have bought your other albums will be a little more open-eared about it than they might normally be, just because it's you.*

M: Here's the thing that I intuitively felt. The earlier sessions, while they were more straight-ahead in the idiom, people in the pop field were more barricaded to that than they are to this, in that it was so idiomatic, it was blanket jazz to them. Whereas this is something else; you can't really say it's jazz or pop . . .

F: *It doesn't need to be classified. . . .*

M: It's not an obviously classified sound, and that will give it a greater chance to be explored. I think by the very nature of the fact that we're indicating everything rather than stating it completely, you'd think that would make it less accessible, but I think in a way it makes it more accessible.

F: *Do you have a title for the album yet?*

M: I have so many titles. Today it's called *A Chair in the Sky*. Although Sue objected to that title at one point and she had good reason for it, in that she didn't want Charles to be remembered as an invalid. But somehow that title seems to suit it the best. It has a lot of meanings for me—I first met Charles up in a Manhattan skyscraper in this chair, and he was a very commanding figure, because he just swallowed the chair up; it was like he was enthroned, very regal. I never looked at him so much like an invalid; it seemed like a regal position.

Charles saw a great importance in titling well, especially for nonlyrical music. He felt that that was where you got a chance to make your statement. As a matter of fact, on the projects, that's what he always asked me first: "What's the title of the song?" I always loved the *Hissing of Summer Lawns* title, but it was too oblique for most people. Take an afternoon like today when everybody has their sprinklers running—that's what it was about.

F: *Who is in the band that you're going out with now?*

M: Jaco Pastorius, Don Alias, Alex Acuna. It'll be two drums, bass, and two guitars—although we haven't set the guitarists yet.

F: *Do you expect on the tour to do most or some of the material out of this album?*

M: Some of it. "God Must Be a Boogie Man" I know we'll do; "Chair in the Sky"; "Pork Pie Hat" . . . but they'll be different, of course.

F: *Did Charles Mingus know anything about the choice of Jaco before you made it?*

M: We talked about personnel and the people he suggested, I didn't know any of them. I tried some sessions with people he suggested, but still, all the way along, in the back of my mind I had my favorites, and those are the people I ended up working with.

F: *Did you tell him about Jaco after you used him?*

M: No, we talked about him at an earlier stage—you have to understand he was very ill then, so I couldn't tell from his responses whether he knew Jaco's work or whether he liked it. I couldn't get any real feedback. All I knew was that he was very prejudiced against electrical instruments, but when he articulated his prejudices on a tape that I heard, Jaco transcends them all.

He felt that with an electrical instrument you couldn't get dynamics; that the dynamics were all done by pushing buttons and so on. But Jaco completely defies all that; he gets more dynamics than any bass player . . . he's phenomenal, he's an orchestra. He's a horn section, he's a string section, he's a French horn soloist—as a matter of fact, when you have a job for the bass player, you almost have to hire a bass player!

F: *Having gotten your feet wet in this area, do you have any comparable projects in mind?*

M: I'm not sure; I'd like to experiment more with rhythm eventually, if not on the next album. I might do a completely acoustic album, almost like a folk album, but harmonically it would be so different from folk music.

F: *All the great people have been against pigeonholing—Duke Ellington always was.*

M: It's so limiting. It casts you into a point of reference which is inaccurate. For the very sake of being accurate—which supposedly pigeonholing does—it in fact does the opposite. The great classical composers created songs.

F: *Which of the things you've done in the past, that have not enjoyed enormous commercial success, would you like to have seen enjoying it?*

M: Well, *Court and Spark* was commercially successful: it was a radical turning point from me being almost a solo artist to suddenly being there with the band, and it was very well received. Now, the next project was *The Hissing of Summer Lawns*, and it was again a departure, it was much jazzier, and it also marked a turning point for me as a lyricist, in that I began to write a more narrative and less personal song.

Critically speaking, that record received a tremendous amount of unnecessary hostility. It was voted the worst album of the year [*sic*] by *Rolling Stone*, when in fact it was quite a progressive work. I felt it was unjustly attacked; it was an album that took a long time to digest. People had to digest me coming from a different position as a storyteller.

Pigeonholes all seem funny to me. I feel like one of those lifer-educational types that just keeps going for letters after their name—I want the full hyphen: folk-rock-country-jazz-classical . . . so finally when you get all the hyphens in, maybe they'll drop them all, and get down to just some American music.

BY ED WARD

CHARLES, JONI AND THE CIRCLE GAME

A top-notch review of Joni's jazz album Mingus.*—SFL*

July 30, 1979

"There was once a word used—swing. Swing went in one direction, it was linear, and everything had to be played with an obvious pulse and that's very restrictive. But I use the term 'rotary perception.' If you get a mental picture of the beat existing within a circle, you're more free to improvise. People used to think the notes had to fall on the center of the beats in the bar at intervals like a metronome, with three or four men in the rhythm section accenting the same pulse. That's like parade music or dance music. But imagine a circle surrounding each beat—each guy can play his notes anywhere in that circle, and it gives him a feeling he has more space. The notes fall anywhere inside the circle, but the original feeling for the beat isn't changed. If one in the group loses confidence, somebody hits the beat again. The pulse is inside you. When you're playing with musicians who think this way you can do anything. Anybody can stop and let the others go on. It's called strolling. . . ."

—*Charles Mingus,* Beneath the Underdog

Joni Mitchell's new album, *Mingus*, is about a lot of different kinds of circles, from the closing of this cycle of Charles Mingus's incarnation (as his Vedantists would put it) to the ah-wooooos of the wolves in the Canadian forests. Since most of the record's production was overseen by Mingus, and he wrote most of the tunes, the musical circles he mentions above abound. But Mitchell has been playing with circles of her own on her last couple albums, playing with the circular placement of notes, improvising both rhythmically (along the horizontal line implied by Mingus's quote) and harmonically (along a vertical line).

This is nothing new within the jazz tradition, of course, but Joni Mitchell is only nominally part of that tradition, even after the release of this album. Which is not to put her down. Her tradition is a guitar-oriented, country-music-based one, while his is a piano-and-horn-oriented, blues-based one. Attempts to make a unified artistic statement out of the tension between these two traditions have been cropping up with increasing frequency in recent years, but it's usually been in the form of jazz going to rock. When a prerock style ("folk") approaches jazz in a thoughtful way, the results (John Martyn, Tim Buckley's later work) are usually so iconoclastic that popular success is unlikely, unless, as with Dan Hicks or David Grisman, the jazz era invoked is a bygone one.

And that is why *Mingus* is sure to be controversial. It works, but it works as a Joni Mitchell album largely composed by Charles Mingus, not as either the final specific bit of the Mingus legacy or as a generalized memorial or tribute album. It is a tribute, but in the very personal vocabulary of an idiosyncratic artist. It's even got one song, "The Wolf That

Lives in Lindsey," which doesn't seem to have anything to do with Mingus and sounds left over from one of her recent albums. Actually, it fits, but I'll get to that.

What we've got here is Joni Mitchell gently easing further into a territory she's been exploring for some time, and doing a much better job of it than on *Don Juan's Reckless Daughter*, because the guiding hand of Mingus is more assured than her own. She's not so much trying to become a jazz singer as trying to adapt her narrative/confessional style to the conventions of improvised jazz-vocal lyrics, where the placement of vowels and syllables and the creation of irregular internal rhyme-schemes are as important as, or more important than, the lyrical content itself. In other words, her model here is more Eddie Jefferson than Billie Holiday. Her framework is some tunes which were worked up by some more traditionally oriented jazz musicians (Eddie Gomez, Phil Woods, Gerry Mulligan, Dannie Richmond) under Mingus's direction, then handed over to a stone fusion band (Stanley Clarke, John McLaughlin, Jan Hammer) whose efforts were discarded, and finally interpreted by musicians who straddle the fence (Jaco Pastorius, Wayne Shorter, Herbie Hancock). The real acid test is where she takes a Mingus chestnut, "Goodbye Pork Pie Hat," and adds her lyrics. The band passes with straight A's, she sings nicely, and the lyric, a brave try, nearly succeeds even though it's just a bit over literal.

The only miss is "The Dry Cleaner from Des Moines," a fairly ordinary Mingus stroll blues that illustrates his point about circles better than anything else on the album, but which is sporadically marred by a clangorous, overwrought Pastorius brass arrangement that threatens to explode the whole piece. The other two new Mingus numbers are triumphs, especially "Chair in the Sky," a piece of lyricism that approaches Mingus's best. I envy those who heard its orchestral rendition in New York some weeks back. It makes use of the famed Mingus thorough-composition (or "extended form"), and Mitchell rides the swells of the vocal part expertly, displaying vocal technique and range I never knew she had. The tune of "Sweet Sucker Dance" is very close to that of "Chair," if a bit more amorphous, and this makes the performance perhaps a bit less satisfying, if that's not splitting hairs.

Wisely, the band on these tracks doesn't try to imitate Mingus, although it continues the Mingus tradition of making a small ensemble sound much larger than it is. Especially notable are Wayne Shorter's tiny, breathy punctuations, which come when they are least anticipated, really playing with those circles. Pastorius, surely the focus of much attention because he's the bass player, is, like Mingus in a large ensemble, most noticeable playing high-register bits that imply low-register pedal points, and manages to evoke his previous work with Mitchell while fulfilling Mingus's compositional requirements.

But like I said, when all is said and done, this is Joni Mitchell's album. The words are hers, her interpretation of Mingus's music and his world. Nowhere is this fact more evident than on "God Must Be a Boogie Man," which is nothing more than a rewrite of the first chapter of Mingus's autobiography set to music that sounds like an impression of the actual Mingus tunes on the album. And then there's "The Wolf that Lives in Lindsey," where it all comes together—the circular sense of tonality and pitch-placement she's been experimenting with, Mingus's circular sense of time rendered on her de-tuned guitar and Don Alias's congas, and the sort of gossipy lyric-writing she's been doing for the last couple of years. As for whether it has anything to do with a tribute to Mingus, listen to the chords those wolves are making and tell me that any musician with an interest in root tones wouldn't like to play behind *that*. (I find it interesting that Mitchell decided to use the wolves in the song because they were "in the right key"!)

Considering how many things could have gone wrong with this record, I'm very happy to see it succeed as well as it does. I could surely have done without the little snips of conversation sprinkled throughout, which get very annoying very fast, and I wish the air of sanctity that hovers over the album as a result was thinned out a little. Nevertheless, though Mingus fans may sniff and Mitchell fans likewise, people who don't let labels trap them can have a very good time exploring what's here to hear.

BY CARLA HALL

THE NEW JONI MITCHELL;
THE SONGBIRD OF WOODSTOCK
SOARS INTO JAZZ

A light take on Joni at the end of the '70s.—SFL

Washington Post, August 25, 1979

"Audiences have been great," said singer Joni Mitchell only minutes after she had finished a sold out concert at Merriweather Post Pavilion. "I tell you the letters I get are very encouraging. People say, 'We weren't with you three years ago, but now we're behind you.'"

She no longer is the girlish Joni Mitchell with long, straight blond hair and bangs, a folk heroine of sorts, composer of a generation's theme song, "Woodstock," and spinner of bittersweet tales about herself.

She rose to fame with that Woodstock generation, singing folk songs and ballads with clever lyrics, sometimes with a twist of rock 'n' roll.

But then she went from being a simple acoustic guitar soloist to a singer guitarist with a full band. She experimented with some jazz on her album, *The Hissing of Summer Lawns*. She added deep whining electric bass on a later album, *Hejira*. The changes alienated some fans, intrigued some new ones.

But she survived those changes and the changes in the musical tastes of the '70s.

Now, just a few months after the release of her most dramatically different album, *Mingus*, which is all jazz, she is in the middle of a six-week, 25-city tour—after a three-year hiatus. Certainly at the Merriweather Post Pavilion Wednesday and Thursday (the latter date sold out), the crowds were enthusiastic.

Minutes after Thursday night's final encore, a stunning, soulful, even mournful version of "Woodstock," she was guided off stage and into a waiting silver limousine, to be taken to Baltimore/Washington International Airport and her private Lear jet.

She settles into the back of the car cross-legged, and fluffs out her wavy shoulder-length hair, the curls now wilted in the humidity. "During 'Raised on Robbery' I felt like that clambake we had for dinner last night," she says, chuckling.

At 35, the on-stage Joni Mitchell has shed her once tentative, fawn-eyed look. It's been replaced by a mellow confidence. Years have softened the angularity of her face. The smile is more sensual. The eyes are a little tired. But the cheekbones, perfectly high and rounded, remain a trademark.

Lean, she wore an orange blouse and black silk pants with black satin high-heeled sandals. "I'm a clothes horse," she said, looking down. "I love fashion. The whole hippie thing was a relief in a way—we were all so fresh scrubbed and in jeans. I've always enjoyed clothes. But there was an inhibiting time, peer pressure. You couldn't dress up. Well, I succumbed to some of that. If anything I'm coming out now."

Mitchell's *Mingus* album combines her lyrics and the music of the great jazz bassist Charles Mingus, who died in January of Lou Gehrig's disease. Mitchell, at Mingus' request, met with him several times and wrote words to the music.

She spoke almost reverentially of Mingus during the concert. One of her favorite pieces was written for him, a funny song based on part of *God Must Be a Boogie Man*, Mingus' autobiography.

For her, the collaboration was a meeting of minds. Others feared the worst.

"Well, just the notion of a folksinger flirting with jazz is seen as presumptuous," she said, laughing ruefully, "rather than someone enthusiastically exploring her potential."

"Now, the criticism is lightening up. Even the reviews say that—that maybe some of the work done a few years ago was taken too harshly. When my engineer and I would work on a project, we'd say, 'Oh, they just don't understand what this is.' Now they do."

She says her audience is "very diverse. Some people like one period and don't like another. After the last two albums I have a small black audience, I have a small jazz audience."

"The tour is a pretty good mixture, mostly from the last five albums," she explained. She opened with "Big Yellow Taxi," but avoided some of the other old favorites. "I'm not looking forward to singing 'Help Me' or 'Both Sides, Now,'" she said. Especially 'Both Sides, Now.'

"I've heard it too often in supermarkets and elevators. I guess my first reaction when I hear it is a rush of pride. It's getting universal—almost to the 'Happy Birthday' stage. But I'm also critical of it when I hear it. They've usually reduced it to the lowest denominator."

Mitchell explained her changes in music as natural: "Most people in the business find a formula and stick to it. I would find that uninteresting."

Her current tour is about half finished. "I just felt like going out," she said with a shrug and giggle. "I think after this is over I'll go someplace with nice, blue salt water. I'll take a little vacation."

She has a house in Los Angeles and a loft in New York. For the past two years, she said, she has been living with Don Alias, her percussionist on the tour. Alias is a tall, well-built man with a warm smile who sits quietly in the back of the limousine with her.

"We've talked about getting married," she said. "I don't know. Kids? I don't know about that either."

She smiled softly. "I'm really strong as far as child-bearing goes. But it's a difficult time to bring children in the world." Mitchell was born in Alberta, Canada, and raised in Saskatoon, Saskatchewan. She went off to the Alberta College of Art in Calgary for one year, but started singing folk music in coffeehouses, and pursued music. She still paints, and some of her albums display her artwork.

"I go on jags," she said. "When I was in a writing block during *Mingus* I painted 14 canvases. Two are on the album cover. Sometimes I carry a sketchbook. And I've been doing some canvases in my New York loft. I'm always doing some extracurricular art project."

She also knits, and she proudly pulled out a simple, neatly done multicolored sweater. "Everytime I get on a plane now, I take along a bag of colored yarns. I'm making a sweater for Don now."

Mitchell said she enjoys working with the band touring with her—Alias, noted bassist Jaco Pastorius, Pat Metheny on guitar, Lyles May on keyboard, Michael Brecker on saxophone. "Herbie Hancock had wanted to do it," she said, referring to the jazz pianist who also recorded with her on *Mingus*, "but he had his own projects that he had to do."

Her settled feeling about the band is born out of repeated troubles in coordinating her own style with three of the other musicians with whom she has played.

"On this tour I feel like more of a band musician," she said. "I feel like an integral part of the band. They're great musicians and coincidentally, great jazz musicians. But I don't think of our music in terms of jazz or rock or fusion, I just think in terms of 'I wanna hire some musicians to do some work and play some music.'"

Mitchell said she sees her music becoming more rhythmic. "A lot of the older stuff we did tonight was more rhythmic. I would like to go in a more rhythmic direction . . . I see myself going toward epic poems. 'Song for Sharon' was an epic. I tend to think now in longer thoughts. 'Amelia' was an epic, too.

"Musically, I don't know where I'm going. I've flirted with pop classical. Gershwin was kind of my hero in that—the way he expanded into rhapsodies, but in a pop music context. 'Ludwig's Tune' and 'Down to You' are like that—pushing the strength of the song into even longer pieces. Some of those songs run 10 minutes long."

Outside the limousine, at the airport, a soft rain began to fall. Mitchell pulled on her shoes. "I'll know what my next album is as soon as it gets written. It might be acoustic guitar. It might be folk. I never know in advance."

She collected her jacket, knitted sweater and overstuffed purse, and headed for her airplane.

Part Four

A NERVY BROAD
1980–1991

BY VIC GARBARINI

JONI MITCHELL IS A NERVY BROAD

An excerpt from a joyous interview about patterns, love, Mingus, *spirituality, rhythm, Dylan, synchronicity, paradox, and waiting for the magic to happen.—SFL*

Musician, January 1983

Joni Mitchell is a nervy broad. That's what Charles Mingus said, and he should know. Dressing up like a black dude on her own album cover, out-of-tune orchestras on "Paprika Plains," Burundi drummers and synthesizers. Wayne Shorter soloing over a 12-string guitar . . . Check it out. 'Course, Charles had been dealing with nervy broads all his life, but this one was different. This one took risks not just to impress folks or for cheap thrills, but because her restless muse demanded it of her. What's more, she was usually able to pull off these stunts. And when her leaps of faith sometimes ended in belly flops, she invariably picked herself up and jumped right back in. Charles liked that. Liked it so much, in fact, that—knowing he was dying—he asked her to write lyrics for and record his last series of compositions. Some folks thought it was a pretty risky proposition for one of America's greatest black composers to leave his final legacy in the hands of a young white woman from Saskatchewan. Maybe it was, but that didn't seem to bother Charles. Artists, it seems, have a predilection for that kind of thing.

When *Court and Spark* was released eight years ago it was universally hailed as a near-miraculous synthesis of folk, pop rock and jazz (well, the L.A. lounge lizard variety, in any case). A careerist would have dug in and consolidated at that point, happy to mine a formula that had both critics and fans jumping for as long as the vein held out. But Joni Mitchell felt compelled to heed a different drummer—quite literally. Her next few albums followed a trajectory that took her farther and farther from the pop mainstream. Melody gave way to modality, conventional song structures were shattered, and the standard four-beats-to-the-bar pop format was lost in a stampede of African and Caribbean polyrhythms. Each new album attempted to stretch more boundaries, explore new compositional elements and rearrange old ones. *Hejira* eschewed the security of pop melodicism, opting instead for free-form verse shoved up against the beat. She kicked the remaining props out from under the rhythm section on *Don Juan's Reckless Daughter*, and finally broke free into traditional and hybrid jazz arrangements on *Mingus*.

Mitchell garnered little credit for introducing these fresh elements and innovations into popular music. In fact, she was often roundly castigated for even trying. That's what you get for debuting the Burundi beat back when Bow Wow Wow's Annabella was toddling off to kindergarten and David Byrne was signing up for art school. Or for attempting to work through musical, conceptual or spiritual puzzles under public scrutiny. Her latest release, *Wild Things Run Fast*, heralds Mitchell's reentry into the pop mainstream. You could call it the Concorde version of *Court and Spark*: supersonic production values, razor-edged guitars, streamlined hooks and melodies—all the nuances of vocal phrasing and rhythmic sophistication she picked up on her jazz pilgrimage applied to good ol' rock 'n' roll. In short, rock strategy enhanced by jazz tactics. *Wild Things* also signals a shift back to the first-person confessional style of her earlier work. And, as usual, the main action takes place in the arena of male/female relationships. Mitchell's ongoing fascination with documenting the cat-and-dog fights of modern lovers can be a bit much at times, but she effectively utilizes her own well-publicized romances over the years with musicians from David Crosby to Don Alias as a laboratory in which she can investigate and explore her chief fixation: paradox and duality. Shadows and light; love and hate; fire and ice; Don Juan's eagle of wisdom and snake of desire . . . unresolved contradictions honeycomb her work and conversation. Like a Zen master in front of a koan, Mitchell confronts paradox from every angle. Like the Indian cultures she feels a kinship with, she works more by intuition than through calculated design. For Mitchell, ordinary life is a semioticist's paradise, a place where coincidence and synchronicity can be the catalysts that reveal glimpses of a deeper pattern, a unity that underlies and ultimately resolves what appear on the surface to be irreconcilable opposites. In Mitchell's tales of incredible coincidences on steamy streets or chance encounters with affable drunks in hotel lobbies, vital pieces of the puzzle drop into place, and the whole is glimpsed.

Okay, I know what you're thinking: later for the artsy stuff . . . what's she really like? A fair question, and one that occupied my thoughts as I tossed down another Martinelli's Sparkling Cider, waiting for the good lady to arrive at her manager's Sunset Strip office. Obviously she was no longer the skittish, intense folk princess I'd first encountered at the Philadelphia Folk Festival fifteen years ago. Nor did I expect the glamorous Queen of Cool who, with a little help from a stellar crew of sidemen like Pat Metheny and Jaco Pastorius, had wowed the crowd at Forest Hills in 1979.

"Hi, got your letter!" says Mitchell cheerily as she sweeps through the door and plops into a director's chair. She's dressed in a smart gray skirt, white blouse and blue-and-white striped knee socks. The operative buzz words for the '82 model Mitchellmobile are elegant, open, secure and curious. And by elegant, I don't mean the ersatz *Cosmo* artiness of her album cover photos, but a natural, relaxed, earned sense of character and confidence, forged and tempered by struggle and suffering. After some small talk I ask why, two years after I sent it, she decided to answer my written request for an interview. "Oh, I liked your natural loose approach and the questions you raised about the creative process and inner growth. Sounded like we might have a decent conversation. I also like what you didn't want to ask me about." Such as? "My romances!"

As you'd soon discover, Joni speaks like she paints and composes. She's an ace storyteller, right out of the Homeric tradition, not so much describing or analyzing a situation as conjuring up visionary landscapes of cinematic power that take the listener vicariously through the event, like stepping into one of Don Juan's shamanistic visions. You emerge from the other side with the feeling that you've lived the event yourself and learned whatever lessons it inherently had to offer. Very exhilarating and a little spooky. But then, artists have a predilection for that kind of thing.

MUSICIAN: *After eight years of experimentation with jazz and polyrhythmic music, you've come back to rock 'n' roll. What caused you to take the leap in the first place, and why come back now?*

MITCHELL: Well, after *Court and Spark* I got fed up with four beats to the bar, and by the time I hit the Mingus project I was having the rhythm section play totally up in the air. Nobody was anchoring the music. I wanted everything floating around.

MUSICIAN: *Just a need to break up patterns and let go?*

MITCHELL: Yeah, I was trying to become the Jackson Pollock of music (laughs). I just wanted all the notes, everybody's part, to tangle. I wanted all the desks pushed out of rows, I wanted the military abolished, anything linear had to go. Then at a certain point I began to crave that order again. So doing this album was a natural reentry into it.

MUSICIAN: *How would you say your approach to rock has changed as a result of your jazz and experimental work?*

MITCHELL: For one thing, my phrasing against the beat changed radically. A rock singer usually sings tight up with the rhythm section. The rhythm section on the new album is still expressive even while they're anchoring, so if they come in on the downbeat I don't have to sing (heavily on the beat) "DOWN TO DAH RIV-AH BAY-BY." I can come in on the end if I want to, or cluster up anywhere—jazz phrasing—and still keep the rock groove going.

MUSICIAN: *Yeah, comparing this album to* Court and Spark, *it's apparent that you've learned how to bend and stretch the music to complement the lyrics and the emotional tone of each song. That first line of "Underneath the Streetlight" isn't about being in love, it is that exhilaration . . .*

MITCHELL: Yeah, you know how to get into that song? Just run down the street, throw out your arms, and shout "Yes, I do, I love you!" That should do it. I've been trying to do that with the music and lyrics for years, but I don't think it worked as well in the past because I wasn't as anchored to the rhythm. I was pushing it, kind of creating a certain friction against the rhythm. "Coyote," for instance, is a lot of stacking up. When I first started doing that years ago, there was a lot of criticism along the lines of "Hey, there's no melody, and it sounds like she's talking." In other words, the limitation of meter became oppressive, and wouldn't contain the poetry anymore, 'cause it wanted to go in a more blank-verse direction. I think now it's compromised, but not in a bad way, and that's why this album is more accessible than some of the other projects. It's still anchored to the beat, which is, for lack of a better word, the heartbeat of the people.

MUSICIAN: *Speaking of heartbeat, a number of the songs on the new album shift rhythms between chorus and verse. Did you have any models or precedents in mind when you were working with your rhythm section?*

MITCHELL: The Police. I love that band, and they were definitely a factor. My appreciation of their rhythmic hybrids and the positioning and sound of their drums was one of the main things calling out to me to make this a more rhythmic album. I was in the Caribbean last summer, and they used to play "De Do Do Do" at the disco. I love to dance, and anytime I heard it, boy, I didn't care if there was no one on the floor, I was going to dance to that thing because of those changes in rhythm. You get into one pattern for a while and then WHAM, you turn around and put a whole other pattern into it. My feet got me into that record.

MUSICIAN: *Yeah, considering how conservative radio is nowadays, I think the Police have done a real service in bringing reggae and Third World rhythms into the pop mainstream.*

MITCHELL: And hybridizing them, not just aping them or trying to sound authentically Caribbean, but coming up with a fresh approach. We did that with "Solid Love" on the new album. It's reggae in principle, and there are gaps between the bass lines, the repetitive figures with space between them. It begins to roll, like a reggae, but it's a hybrid and turns into something original again.

MUSICIAN: *It's a lot more nourishing than the musical junk food churned out by radio stations run by computers—or worse.*

MITCHELL: Yeah, radio's like the Catholic Church: you can only paint the saints, that's all we want to see. No more fishes, no more symbolism.

MUSICIAN: *Instead of inspiring or challenging you, they're going for the lowest common denominator, refeeding you yesterday's breakfast. Most of FM radio now sounds like Journey.*

MITCHELL: But Journey does do some good things on a sounds level. As a matter of fact, I learned some things about eq and sonic frequencies from their records that I applied in making my own album. You might think they're antiseptic or too this or that, but when they come on the radio, they have a sound that's outstanding. I began to notice a glitter or clarity to the sound of certain bands that I may not take inspiration from on a compositional, and certainly not on a lyrical, level. I spent a long time mixing this album. Our bass player Larry Klein, who's my boyfriend, is also a sound man. He's twenty-five and he's come up in an era that's more sound conscious than the previous wave. He stretched my ear in certain areas, like drum sounds, which we'd never fussed much with before.

MUSICIAN: *Who took responsibility for the overall production?*

Joni Mitchell and Odetta performing at the Bread and Roses Festival, 1978. Corbis/Roger Ressmeyer

MITCHELL: At the end there was myself, Larry Klein and Larry Hirsh. We were a perfectly balanced team in that I handled the treble aspects and placement of the vocal and horn sounds—"This should go over here because it'll pop if we put it over there." They handled the rhythm section sounds and certain things I couldn't hear. But I could hear that the snare had a certain quality, and its placement was related to what we'd liked on the Police albums. And I could hear that supersonic sheen on the Journey album. There's a place on our record where it sparkles so much that if you listen to it too long it'll make you nervous. After about an hour of mixing with certain eq on it, we were ready to snap at each other.

MUSICIAN: *Was there ever a point when you were out on a limb with some of your jazzier material when you asked yourself, "What the hell am I doing here?"*

MITCHELL: Oh, yeah, on the Mingus project. I remember sitting down with Charles at first and requesting some input as to the themes. "What does this melody you wrote for me mean to you," I asked. He looked at me wryly, like Rumpelstiltskin, and said, "These are the things I'm gonna miss." So I had to get inside his soul from all the way across the nation and write down what I thought he was gonna miss. That was the first song done, and he loved it. Next was "Pork Pie Hat," and he played me every version that had been recorded, over and over again, and I chose the one I like best to work from. The first step was to memorize that piece of music vocally, which was very complicated. It had one passage of trible tonguing (waggles tongue) BLBLBLBLBLBLBLBL. And I said, "You want me to write words to that?" and he smiled and said, YEAAAAAHHHHHHHH!" (laughs)

He gave me this melody, and I didn't know what kind of a theme to lay on it. He kept saying, "This guy was the sweeeetest guy," and he kept saying that over and over about Lester Young, who was gone, and it was given to me to write by a man who was about to go. And somehow or other, I felt that in the lyric—the lyric should contain both of them. So, the first verse was easy. But how to get out of this was a mystery, and the last verse wouldn't come. So one night, we're going uptown, my boyfriend and I, and we decided to get off the subway a block early. And we came out near a manhole with steam rising all around us, and about two blocks ahead of us was a group of black guys—pimps, by the look of their hats—circled around, kind of leaning over into a circle. It was this little bar with a canopy that went out to the curb. In the center of them are two boys, maybe nine years old or younger, doing this robot-like dance, a modern dance, and one guy in the ring slaps his knees and says, "Ahaaah, that looks like the end of tap dancing, for sure!" So we look up ahead, and in red script on the next bar down, in bright neon, it says "Charlie's." All of a sudden I get this vision, I look at that red script, I look at these two kids, and I think, "The generations. . . ." Here's two more kids coming up in the street—talented, drawing probably one of their first crowds, and it's . . . to me, it's like Charlie and Lester. That's enough magic for me, but the capper was when we looked up on the marquee that it was all taking place under. In big capital letters, it said "PORK PIE HAT BAR." All I had to do was rhyme it, and you had the last verse.

MUSICIAN: *I remember at your Forest Hills concert during the Mingus tour overhearing a couple of sixteen-year-old girls breathlessly discussing "this new album called* Mingus, *and he was this great jazz person, and Joni worked with him. " A critic friend with me got rather cynical about that, but I was quite touched to hear these kids talking about Mingus like he was Tom Petty or Bruce Springsteen.*

MITCHELL: The lovely thing is that while people of my own age jumped ship when I hit a certain pocket, these young kids, who maybe were presented with one of these records for their twelfth birthday, had come easily and open-mindedly all the way up through this whole progression without batting an eyelash. I find that personally very satisfying, no matter how silly it sounds to some New York intellectual. Even with the verbal simplification they gave, you can't beat the young enthusiasm and open-mindedness of something like that.

MUSICIAN: *Along the same lines, is it possible for an artist to make a statement that is rejected by his or her audience, and yet in fact be more in touch with what the audience itself is going through than they are?*

MITCHELL: Well, let's make an assumption here that an artist has a fine nervous system, okay? Now, there are also a lot of people with fine nervous systems, more sensitive spinal columns or whatever, who are not artists, who have no outlet of expression. I think the nuancy observations an artist makes are going to get picked up first by these sensitive people. Eventually they'll be picked up by people intellectually and then passed down through the culture . . .

MUSICIAN: *Trickle-down art. Supply side inspiration. I love it . . .*

MITCHELL: (laughs) There's a sensitivity lag. Some statements that are made by artists in their desire to look at the world in a fresh way have traditionally come up against a shocking reception. When Stravinsky first played, people jumped up out of their seats and booed and hissed. People were infuriated by even less dramatic changes, like Dylan going electric . . .

MUSICIAN: *. . . or Joni Mitchell going into jazz.*

MITCHELL: Sure. Rock 'n' roll was rock 'n' roll and jazz was jazz. and leaving one camp was a minor act of treason. It breaks down into all kinds of camps: your traditional jazz people who prefer bebop played acoustically and have a prejudice against all electronics. Charles was one of those who didn't like electronic music.

MUSICIAN: *What was his rationale?*

MITCHELL: He felt that on any acoustic axe the central quality of the line was more apparent between an artist and his instrument than in electronics. I disagreed with him. That was one of the battles we had in that I felt there was a new world of music opening up, regarding sounds, and that you had to play with electronic instruments and kind of warp them to get the individual tonality out of them.

MUSICIAN: *And yet people on that creative edge transcend stylistic and generic differences; they recognize a fellow spirit. After all, Charles reached out for you, didn't he?*

MITCHELL: Yeah. He liked . . . some things about me.

MUSICIAN: *Such as?*

MITCHELL: He thought I had a lot of nerve (laughs). He was critical of some things I was doing as well, but he was critical of his own work, too.

MUSICIAN: *What made him think you were nervy?*

MITCHELL: Two things: he thought I had a lot of nerve to be dressed up like a black dude on the cover of *Don Juan's Reckless Daughter*. He couldn't get over that. He was sort of thrilled by it. The other thing was the piece "Paprika Plains," which made him mad at one level, and kind of interested him on another. What happened was I hadn't played piano for a few years, and in January, just before making that album, I called up my producer and said, "Henry, we've got to go in the studio right now because for some inexplicable reason I'm playing piano better than I have any right to be. I can't hit a wrong note." What I'd done was give myself a freeing lesson and said to myself, "Everything resolves to C; no matter where you go you can't hit a wrong note, just go home to C." We went in the studio and cut this thing four times. It was a trance-like situation. The four improvisations we recorded all clocked in at between twenty-nine and thirty-one minutes, so my attention span each time was almost exactly the same. From those four performances I edited together a piece that was to become the bridge for "Paprika Plains," and months later I wrote a song in which I inserted this segment. In the meantime the piano had been retuned a number of times. Then I gave the piano piece with lyrics to an arranger who added strings. The strings begin in the January section of the piano piece, but when they hit the October part, the piano tuning has changed, so the strings have no chance to retune as they cross over. That really infuriated Charles. "The orchestra's out of tune . . . they're in tune, they're out of tune!" Well, that drove him crazy (laughs). So he thought I was a nervy broad.

MUSICIAN: *Speaking of nerve, do you usually trust your creative impulses, even if you can't explain them to others? Or to yourself, for that matter?*

MITCHELL: Oh, yeah, I work from intuition, so I'm always flying blind and looking to be thrilled. Waiting for the magic to happen. I think it's easier to recognize the truly spectacular from an intuitive position than from your intellect, which is linear, dealing only with knowledge of the past projected into the future.

MUSICIAN: *With all the attention we pay to the intellect in this society . . . .*

MITCHELL: . . . A vastly overrated instrument, the intellect. . . . I get bugged when people call me an intellectual (laughs).

MUSICIAN: *We know relatively little about developing those intuitive faculties, or learning how to deal with the stress of handling those energies when the magic does strike.*

MITCHELL: Sure. The Western world doesn't know anything about the need to prepare yourself for dealing with creativity or the time you have to put in an apprenticeship. Back on the coffeehouse circuit I loved being a musician, I was a real ham for it. But the moment I hit the big stage, and heard people suck in their breath at the mention of my name, it hit me . . . and there were years and years of maladjustment to contend with. My own apprenticeship, finding my balance, took eight years. The battles I have with it now are minor compared with those.

MUSICIAN: *Was there a clash between your ego and your creative nature over who was going to take credit for those goodies?*

MITCHELL: Are you kidding?! I used to go in the dressing room after a show and just . . . *cry*. People were just discovering you, so you received this radiant enthusiasm and you'd think, "What are they applauding for, that was *horrible* what I just did out there." There was emotional deception, there was technical failure. I couldn't get into this song and they didn't know the difference. There's a danger of becoming contemptuous of your audience at that point.

MUSICIAN: *If they couldn't seem to differentiate between good and bad performances, what do you feel they were responding to?*

MITCHELL: There's a story about a clown that kind of sums it all up for me. I think it's Henry Miller, but I'm not sure. Now pay attention. Anyway, he's the greatest clown in the world, and one night when he's at the climax of his act he forgets his part, he just has this blank spell. It seems interminably long, the audience are on the edge of their seats, and just at the tension point where they're gonna boo him, all of a sudden he regains it. The audience goes crazy! He's never seen such applause. Next night he comes to the same place and seems to be forgetting what to do. He draws it out, draws it out, the audience leans forward, and just then he remembers the part and the audience again goes nuts. So he keeps this up for a while, and one day he wakes up and finds it repulsive that they don't know that he's faking, that he's manipulating them like that. He can't bear himself for doing it, so he quits. Finally, he winds up as an elephant boy in another circus, and one night the head clown takes sick. So our hero volunteers to step in, and he does the guy's part, and from the audience comes the biggest roar he's ever heard. The sick clown in the back room hears this and realizes that this replacement who's never done his routine before is getting more applause than he ever did. It breaks his heart, and he dies. The burden of hearing about this is too much for our hero, so he quits the circus and wanders around as a bum, sleeping in parks. One day he senses that it's his day to die. Coming down the walk is a cop, slapping a billy club on his leg. So he goes into his original routine and he gets up to that point and seems to forget the part, and he pulls the tension out and then regains it. The cop goes into absolute hysterics, just laughs and laughs. And the clown has this great contented feeling, and with that feeling he dies. So there you have the old yin and yang of it (laughs) . . . kinda subtle.

MUSICIAN: *Did you come to a moment when you realized you had to withdraw, to let go of it all to keep your sanity?*

MITCHELL: In the early '70s I just quit. I built a retreat up in the Canadian bush and swore I was never coming back. I built a house and wrote *For the Roses* during that time, so my little retreat was not complete (laughs). But I became a hermit. I felt extremely maladjusted about . . . the contrasts that were heaped on me. It was just too much input.

MUSICIAN: *So you couldn't trust either the positive or the negative feedback you were getting?*

MITCHELL: Yeah, it was as if (sings like Dylan) "People just got UGLIER and I had no sense of TIME!" (laughs)

MUSICIAN: *Could you find a place in yourself where you could sort things out?*

MITCHELL: One day about a year after I started my retreat in Canada I went out swimming. I jumped off a rock into this dark emerald green water with yellow kelp in it and purple starfish at the bottom. It was very beautiful, and as I broke up to the surface of the water, which was black and reflective, I started laughing. Joy had just suddenly come over me, you know? And I remember that as a turning point. First feeling like a loony because I was out there laughing all by myself in this beautiful environment (laughs). And then, right on top of it, was the realization that whatever my social burdens were, my inner happiness was still intact.

MUSICIAN: *John Lennon spoke of going through the same process in his last interview. He'd gotten in his own way, and finally Yoko sent him alone to Hong Kong, where it all came back to him while sitting in a bathtub. When he finally let go, he found he had it all again. He found that creative center again.*

MITCHELL: See, during my problems the creative spot never left me. I'm just hyper-creative. I'll create no matter what situation I'm in. If I have no tools, I'll dance. That doesn't go. My problem is my tremendous personal

Herbie Hancock and Joni Mitchell, 1978. © Corbis/Roger Ressmeyer

and social self-consciousness, which over the years has lessened and lessened and is now quite nicely balanced, I think. There's a gently undulating pattern between low and high self-esteem, which I think creates the proper tension.

MUSICIAN: Very early on you documented your personal struggles and conflicts in your music. But around the time of The Hissing of Summer Lawns *you shifted your perspective from a sort of confessional stance to that of an outside observer, commenting on what you saw happening around you. Why the shift?*

MITCHELL: Well, first of all, the pop star is very self-promotional. You know, "I'm DA GREATEST LOVER, BAYBEEEEE!" The nature of the beast is to present yourself in the early years as some kind of teen idol. Initially I wrote those extremely personal songs like "Marcie" as a response to the big roars from the audience. I would stand up there receiving all this massed adulation and affection and think, "What are you all doing, you don't even know me." Affection like that usually doesn't come without some kind of intimacy, like in a one-on-one relationship. So I thought, you better know who you're grinning at up here, and I began to unveil more and more of my inner conflicts and feelings. Then, after about four years . . . I guess it's just the nature of the press, having built you up, they feel it's time to tear you down. So I began to receive a lot of unfavorable attention. At the same time it became harder and harder to sing these intimate songs at rock festivals. The bigger the audience I drew, the more honest I wanted to be (laughs).

MUSICIAN: *Could you sense when real contact and communication was taking place onstage, when something was connecting? And was there anything you could do to help bring on or deepen that contact?*

MITCHELL: Oddly enough, there were a lot of times onstage when my errors were icebreakers. For instance, I'd flat-out forget a piece onstage, or I couldn't get into a song, so I'd start another one. That would be a turning point many a night. I would be oblivious to all this, but (manager) Elliot (Roberts) would tell me later that it had humanized the show. He said it actually made people feel more comfortable and heightened their enjoyment. That was a long time ago, mind you. You couldn't do that playing with a band, because you'd wind up with five embarrassed people.

MUSICIAN: *In a sense those errors broke a pattern and created an opening for something special to enter. Do you find that because your songs are tied to a narrative format whose structure doesn't alter much that it's harder for that magic to happen—harder than for, say, Mingus or [Jimi] Hendrix, who had large pockets of improvisational material with a lot of openings for something to enter.*

MITCHELL: Well, rather than talking generally, let me give you an example. On *Don Juan's Reckless Daughter* there's a song called "The Wolf That Lives in Lindsey." It was a live duet between Don Alias and myself; it's a strange piece of music, in that it's an example of a song that has a structure that I had completely ignored. I dropped beats, I added beats, there's bars of 3/4 that are in there, and there's all kinds of abbreviated signatures. Don was thrown into a highly alert position as a drummer, to be able to follow this thing, which was not maintaining a groove, just bursts of rhythmic passages. It was very spontaneous. And, when the thing was over, we figured that magic had, in fact, occurred. As raw as it was, and as technically peculiar as it was, you couldn't beat it for spirit. And I turned to Henry [Lewy, engineer] and said, "You know what we need on this now? We need wolves and water gongs." That was on a Wednesday night. So he was going to make it a project over the weekend to look through the A&M library of sound effects, and we were going to get some wolves.

So, anyway, that weekend I had company coming from Texas, and I had company coming from Canada at the same time. And simultaneously I was supposed to be at the Bread & Roses Festival. When my guests arrived, coming already from long distances, I had to tell them, "We're moving now!" And we all went to this festival in San Francisco. Things kinda got screwed up and there were some vibes around the whole situation, which I won't go into, that made me very introspective. And I noticed at dinner that night, that my introspection was also making the table introspective. So, I thought, "I don't want to be here in this mood with these people, I'm influencing their mood," and so I excused myself. I had told a friend of mine, Tim Hardin, that I was gonna meet him back at the hotel. So I get to the hotel desk, and I say to a very uptight desk clerk, you know, "Would you please give me Mr. Hardin's room?" And he replied, "Can't you see I'm busy?" He was *really* uptight. The lobby of the hotel was gigantic, and suddenly, across the hall there came a drunk, singing "Why Do Fools Fall in Love?," stumbling across the lobby snapping his fingers, right? I had nothing but time on my hands, so I perked up, because suddenly there was externally something interesting (laughs), and I was drawn across the hall, and I linked up with him, and we came back across the hall, singing "Why Do Fools Fall in Love?" We ended up standing by the desk, with this uptight guy in the background, and the next thing I knew, we had drawn in two more singers who turned out to be the Persuasions. Well, when we stopped singing, everybody was in great spirits, we all laughed, you know, we patted each other on the back, and we shook hands. "So now," I say to the guy, "Would you give me Mr. Hardin's room," and somebody in the crowd yells, "Oh, Hardin's in the bar." So I go into the bar, there's a kind of loungey jazz band playing, and Hardin is pissed out of his mind, and he comes dancing towards me through this crowded room here, singing to the band, "Hello, Joni," and doing improvisational lyrics. So I start dancing towards him, singing "Hello, Timmy! So good to see you!" The bartender says, "What would you like?" And I sing to him, "One white wine," and the bartender raises his hand in the air, and sings back, "One white wine." And the next thing, the whole room was engaged in this spontaneous Broadway show. Anyway, the story hasn't come to an end yet. Now, we're all in very high spirits. We discover that there's a party on the third floor. We go up to this room, and all the way up the hallway—you know, Timmy and I are hamming it up, just being goofy. We get into the room, and suddenly, the same guy that was drunk in the lobby singing "Why Do Fools Fall in Love?" comes up to me and says, "I have a tape of some wolves." And I say to him, not even realizing how profound it is, "Oh, I'm looking for a tape of some wolves. I'll write down my address and you send it to me." He said, "No, I mean, I've got it *on* me." So I said, "Okay," and he produced this box of tapes, all homemade with labels on them, and we thumbed through it. It was all African animal sound effects. Well, the very last entry was wolves. So he loaned me his tape recorder, I put the tape on, and it was a cycle of a wolf—it starts off with the lead wolf, and then you hear yipping of pups and female voices, you know? And then he goes, "Aaaooo-aaooh-ahh." Like, the same yelp, but one note up higher in the scale. And then the yipping of the pups, and the females. And the thing was looped about four times. Well, the first time I did "The Wolf That Lives in Lindsey," I just hit the button right at the beginning, picked up the guitar, and uncannily, *it was the perfect key.* The way the loop was designed, if you started it at the top of the tape and went all the way to the end, it fit the structure perfectly. So anyway, the next night when I went to the concert, my friend Joel Bernstein hooked the tape up and for an encore, I came out and we did this song and we blasted the wolves, mixed them in with the song, and the audience—when I was finished singing, some clapped, but most of them howled me back on for another encore. So you see, there's still ways to get spontaneity into a show.

MUSICIAN: *I guess so. If you had to point to a particular album that realized as much as possible what you were aiming for at a particular time and place, where you thought, "Yeah, that's as honest and clear as it's come through," what would it be?*

MITCHELL: The purest one of all, of course, is *Blue.* At the time I was absolutely transparent, like cellophane. If you looked at me, I would weep. We had to lock the doors to make that album. Nobody was allowed in. Socially, I was an absolute wreck. Imagine yourself stripped of all defenses . . . going to a party! (laughs) Not only did I have no defenses, but other people's defenses were alternately transparent, which made me very sad . . . or people really tend to aggress on you when you're weak. You know what it was exactly like? It was like being in an aquarium with big fish coming at you and they weren't saying anything, and sometimes the sound would shut off. It was just like that scene in *All That Jazz* when suddenly the heartbeat becomes dominant.

MUSICIAN: *But there was a positive aspect to it . . . ?*

MITCHELL: Oh, that would be a beautiful space if it wasn't so scary. If you could just magically wipe out the fear. There's nothing there but . . . but what is there. Having no defense, you have no ability to . . . you have no pretense, which you need.

MUSICIAN: *You need it as a buffer. Like deflector shields.*

MITCHELL: Well, that's what happened. There was no social personality, but still a strong inner life.

MUSICIAN: *That can be an awfully painful state . . .*

MITCHELL: But it produced that beautiful album. There is not a false note on that album. I love that record more than any of them, really . . . and I'll never be that pure again (laughs).

MUSICIAN: *Don't worry, someday you'll be a virgin again.*

MITCHELL: Sure! (cracking up)

MUSICIAN: *No, I'm half serious. It reminds me of something Robert Fripp once wrote for us, about how you can't regain your innocence, but you can learn to act with innocence and reenter that world, and to touch that place without having to shatter the personality.*

MITCHELL: Yeah, I'm spiritually very promiscuous. I've been Shoko Buku'd, I have a TM mantra. I've been to the mountain, done my hermitage, my self-confrontation pockets. I've hung with Zen Buddhist priests, and all of them have opened some little pocket. I've had my fair share of pushes in the right direction. I *desire* it, though, and that's the key. I'm sort of headed in that direction, but I backslide.

MUSICIAN: Can you see your inner growth reflected in the evolution of your music?

MITCHELL: Basically, I'm a sensual primary, a compulsive, creative person. So, yeah, I can see my growth in my harmonic sense, for instance, although I still like dissonance in music, which is not enlightened chord structure. But that dissonance is very full of human travail. I still like conflict in poetry, I'm still in the flames. I guess I'm just a . . . a . . .

MUSICIAN: . . . a teenager in love? (Joni laughs) Speaking of which, is there a certain sensibility connected with growing up in western Canada that you share with Neil Young?

MITCHELL: I feel very kindred to Neil, yeah. We're caught between two cultures—we're neither-nor. We still salute the Queen up there, though Canada's becoming more independent lately. We grew up in the pre-TV era, and at that time radio was happening. There was more of an English influence then, a lot of BBC humor. We went to J. Arthur Rank movies on the corner, Dr. Seeley, that whole series. So we had an infusion of British comedy, which is a different sensibility than American humor.

MUSICIAN: Do you feel that Americans sometimes miss the humor in your work?

MITCHELL: Yeah, people sometimes aren't sure that they can laugh at my stuff. "Coyote" has a lot of that dry humor that can get by people, not jokes per se, but . . . . Okay, now if I had a voice like Donald Fagen there'd be no problem. He's got that irony, that black, dry kind of humor that I call a Canadian sensibility. His voice can convey that even though he's not Canadian. Mine had this high (in a high register) earnest kind of melancholic quality that doesn't project a lot of humor unless I break into a Bugs Bunny voice on certain lines and really nail 'em. Like, (à la Bugs) "Now it's gettin' on time to close." Or if I dramatize a character within the context of a song, people will laugh . . . I don't know what I'm talking about! Do you know what I'm talking about?

MUSICIAN: Sure, you've just exposed your essential wabbit nature to the American people. And we understand.

MITCHELL: (laughs) But getting back to Neil. He and I have uncanny similarities of background. We both come off the Canadian prairies; we were both struck down by polio in the same epidemic; both in the back, in the precious spine, and in the right leg. That's a great will-forger, you know. There's a big struggle involved with walking around after that. When you're struck down early in your childhood with crippling diseases and have some of the background problems he did, you've got a lot of peer group disadvantage from an early age. Maybe that gives him a tail-wind.

MUSICIAN: *If there's one recurring theme that runs through your work, it's your obsession with duality and dichotomy. Shadows and light, fire and ice, the eagle and the snake, love that's hopeless and inspired. Those oppositions form the core of almost every song . . .*

MITCHELL: Well, if you take your intellect as far as it will go, you run smack-dab into paradox.

MUSICIAN: *And then what do you do?*

MITCHELL: Then you forget about it! (laughs)

MUSICIAN: *Okay, maybe you don't try to think your way through them, 'cause that's not possible. But you're constantly placing yourself in front of them. It's especially apparent in your songs about struggling with male-female polarizations in relationships.*

MITCHELL: In spite of all my yelling at my lovers in public (laughs), I've received a lot of affection in my time. People have been as good to me as they could, but . . . yeah, I guess it is all about compatible madnesses. There are pockets where people flat out don't understand each other, they come to impasses. And they stubbornly hold to one side or another, conflicting points of view. So, yeah, those paradoxes are dramatized in love relationships. All along I guess I've been trying to figure out (sings) "What is this thing called love . . . this crazy thing called love?"

MUSICIAN: *The new album seems to be an attempt to come to grips with just that question. It impressed me as being a cycle about love that starts with the youthful sentimentality of "Chinese Café," then advances into emotional adolescence with "Man to Man" and "Ladies Man," where you're the naive victim. Then there's "Solid Love, " which is a step up, a genuine contact with someone, not just the old I-need-you-to-comple-ment-my-neurosis situation. "Underneath the Streetlight" is another gutsy affirmation, a commitment and recognition of a real soul-to-soul contact. Finally, there's "Love," the piece you borrowed from Corinthians, and the last song on the album. It's like a glimpse of the goal, the higher egoless, transcendent level of love, beyond conflicts and paradoxes: the summation of everything you've been striving for all these years.*

MITCHELL: Yeah! It is! I never really saw that when I was putting the album together, but in hearing you say it, I can see what you see, and it has validity to me. That thing from Corinthians *is* on another level. I'm not talking about hippie sloganeering there, I'm talking about the real shit. There's a qualitative feeling to that kind of love that's beyond the bounds of sexual attachment. I didn't write that, though. I stole it from the Bible (laughs). I appreciated it, then I presented it.

MUSICIAN: But as with the "Pork Pie Hat" story and the wolves song, you recognized the deeper pattern that your artistic sensibilities were cre-ating with the album. Something in you knew that had to be the last song on the album, the summation.

MITCHELL: Right, and that was magical, that recognition. Magic does-n't have anything to do with intellect, which is linear. Intuition appears to be more chaotic, even stupid sometimes . . .

MUSICIAN: But it can pass through dichotomies and reach something higher.

MITCHELL: Right, intuition cuts through all that. Intellect comes in paragraphs, ya-da-ya-da-ya-da, and intuition comes ZAP!, like a bolt of lightning. It comes as a pill, and then has to be translated from an impulse into language by the intellect.

MUSICIAN: When you reach the end of your rope in front of some para-dox, you suddenly see the deeper pattern, and know where the pieces fit.

MITCHELL: That's it. The magical moment comes at the point of despair, where you say, "I can't do this!" At the peak of my frustration, I meet a guy singing in the hotel lobby, or see those tap dancing kids in front of that bar. When all intellectual options have been exhausted and there's no way out, suddenly something cracks open and takes you through to the other side. Finding that song and knowing to put it at the end of the album was the same as stumbling on that drunk guy with the wolves tape. It was the missing piece. The last verse. As you said, most of the other songs were about conflict or paradox, but that song was the resolution. The missing piece. That last verse.

BY ROSEMARY PASSANTINO

JONI MITCHELL: DOG EAT DOG

In an interview from 1994, Joni says, "With Dog Eat Dog, *the press went to sleep en masse: Ronnie Reagan could do no wrong. It took a few years for the press to wake up. This Japanese interviewer said to me, "Joni, you used to be a poet and now you're a journalist." And I said, 'That's because America is a land of ostriches and somebody's gotta be Paul Revere.'"*
A review of Dog Eat Dog.—*SFL*

High Fidelity, January 1986

Joni Mitchell, Larry Klein, Mike Shipley, and Thomas Dolby, prods. Geffen GHS 24074.

Tuneful, enticing, politically correct, Joni Mitchell's fourteenth album moves in subtly surprising ways. Formulated by Mitchell and a supporting cast of technowizards, the LP's arrangements—from the brisk, polyrhythmic syncopations of "Fiction" to the looping clatter of a cigarette machine in "Smokin' (*Empty, Try Another*)"—glisten with a bracing, mechanical sheen. But the cool precision of sequential Fairlight samples and whip-track percussion patterns is tempered by warm, deftly layered jazz and folk accompaniment, like the drowsy piano and shakahachi drum haunting "Ethiopia," the serendipitous sax of "Lucky Girl," or the gliding harmony Michael McDonald lends to "Good Friends." These novel aural configurations seldom fail to allure.

In seven out of the album's nine full songs, Mitchell's unwavering liberal conscience compels her to take on everything from the disorienting effects of media saturation to tax-evading evangelists who preach war in God's name. Her proselytizing is undoubtedly sincere, but her lyrics, especially in "Fiction," "The Three Great Stimulants," and "Tax Free," are uncharacteristically pedestrian, even tiresome. She gets across the same conviction with clever, austere writing and clipped-punch delivery on "Shiny Toys," a droll electronic samba that playfully indicts yuppie materialism. "Good Friends" and "Lucky Girl" are more highlighted and self-reflective. Even these, however, avoid examining Mitchell's recent transition from wandering romantic to married woman [to bassist Larry Klein], an exposé many of her devotees may rightfully expect.

BY IAIN BLAIR

JONI MITCHELL—LUCKY GIRL

"It was . . . the hardest record I've ever made, for a lot of reasons," says Joni. *"There's a lot of blood on those tracks." Joni talks with Iain Blair about creating* Dog Eat Dog. *(Note: Great story at the end about Joni's visit with Georgia O'Keefe.)—SFL*

Los Angeles Herald, March 9, 1986

With her long blond locks falling naturally over a stylish suit, Joni Mitchell sits in her manager's office on a cool California afternoon, looking happy and relaxed. While she chats, she chain-smokes.

"It is a bad habit, but it's not a nervous one," she insists. "I just like to have something in my hands." She laughs mischievously. For someone with such a "serious artist" reputation, Joni Mitchell's speech is surprisingly well peppered with laughter and jokey asides. She hoots when asked about her involvement with Northern Lights for Africa, the Canadian version of Band Aid that teamed her with the likes of Bryan Adams, Neil Young and Oscar Peterson.

"I know it sounds ridiculous, but I was literally starving when we did the session. Pretty ironic, considering the subject matter. My yoga teacher—this is all California nonsense—had sent me to a psychic dietitian who, while rubbing her chin and swinging her arm around in a circle, had diagnosed a lot of food allergies. The result was that I was hardly allowed to eat anything. So by the time I arrived with an apple and a rice patty, my poor stomach was making all these strange noises. And then we

Hoyt Axton, Stephen Stills and Joni Mitchell, 1978. © Corbis/Roger Ressmeyer

get in the studio and the engineer says he can't record 'cause he's picking up some weird rumbling sound from my direction."

Mitchell has regained a few pounds since then and seems in no immediate danger of fading away. On the contrary, the normally reclusive artist is now eager to talk on just about any topic, including her most recent album, *Dog Eat Dog*.

"It's definitely different from anything I've ever done before," she says. "It was also the hardest record I've ever made for a number of reasons. There's a lot of blood on those tracks. These are dangerous times, and I suddenly felt a sense of responsibility to speak up now or forever hold my peace."

For anyone at all familiar with Mitchell's work during the past 20 years or so, from her early folk days through her collaboration with jazz great Charles Mingus, this, her 14th LP, may indeed come as something of a surprise. Its tone is angry and overtly political—a far cry from her last album, the ultraromantic *Wild Things Run Fast*.

"Yes, well, it's certainly not what most people expect from me," she concedes. "I'm talking about everything from the insane arms race to the current attempts to censor lyrics by various extreme rightwingers. Basically, I feel that a lot of strides were made in this country during the '60s—equal rights, feminism, freedom of speech, etc.—but under Reagan's new conservatism, much of that's being eroded and undone.

"For instance," she continues, "I think all these censorship attempts are really dangerous. I hate to see the country backsliding into extremism, and that's exactly what's happening today, sadly. The rock 'n' roll lyric issue is just the tip of the iceberg."

Songs from her album, including the title track and "Ethiopia," don't pull any punches in addressing some of Mitchell's newly voiced public concerns. A song called "Tax Free" features Rod Steiger as a flamboyant Moral Majority-style evangelist advocating the invasion of Cuba. Her jaundiced view of the current state of affairs is explored in "The Three Great Stimulants"—not, as you might expect, sex, drugs, and rock 'n' roll, but rather "artifice, brutality, and innocence."

"Innocence has always been a stimulant," she says, "especially when a culture is entering a decadent period. You get kiddie porn, the cult of the youth, an obsession with youth, in fact, and stuff like face-lifts—yech!" She wrinkles up her own 42-year-old natural features in disgust.

The gloomy side of the album is tempered, however, by her old-style, personal insights in songs such as "Good Friends," an uptempo duet with ex-Doobie Michael McDonald, and the appealing "Lucky Girl," whose self-described "happy Hollywood ending" unashamedly crows over Mitchell's marriage to her bassist and coproducer, Larry Klein.

It is her second marriage. Her first, to Detroit musician Chuck Mitchell, took place in the mid-'60s and ended in divorce within a couple of years. "We just gradually drifted apart," she says. "This time round it's a lot different.

"We get on really great," she says of her life with Klein, "and married life is certainly agreeing with me. Of course, when you live together and work together all the time, there's the inevitable tensions and silly little arguments, but I think we're very good for each other. It helps that we're both in the same business. Being a musician as well, he understands us temperamental 'artistes.' I mean, if I had to go off on the road by myself all the time, I'd get very lonely and a bit crazy probably."

Their last tour took them out on the road for more than nine months, "which can be pretty daunting," Mitchell admits, "but I really enjoyed myself. It was like one big happy family and very integrated. Everyone got on well together, which is important in these situations. When I tour this year, I want to go on the road with pretty much the same band.

"Larry's given me a very stable home life," she sums up with a smile. "I've been very busy just living for the past three years or so. People tend to say, 'Oh, you've been laying low—we haven't seen your photo in the papers much.' But the thing is, to be a writer, you need to be slightly invisible, and you need to live and go where ordinary people are. To be 'a star' means that no longer are you the watcher; you're the watched. And when you're being watched it's very hard to create. I'm more of a watcher."

She finally re-entered the public eye with *Dog Eat Dog*. During the production of the album she took tight control over the studio sessions, leading to "a definite clash of temperament" with British electropopster Thomas Dolby, who had been called in as a technical adviser.

"Well, I'm very fond of him, but man!" She pauses carefully, as if reliving the frustration. "He was very quiet—and stubborn—and when we disagreed, we'd have these discussions and he'd say, 'Well, I'm not getting anything out of these adult talks, Joan,' and then I'd say, 'Well then, neither am I,' and we'd be stalemated.

"I'm basically unproducible," she explains with a sigh, "and used to letting my albums take their own eccentric course, for better or worse, making my own mistakes. But this time, in order to make the technological leap, I needed assistance. And that's why Thomas was called in.

"The problem was that in all my records, the structure of any song is usually laid down by acoustic guitar or piano first, and then I bring in other players and just give them the freedom to blow and countermelody against that. Sometimes I edit them, sometimes I just take their parts and move 'em around. So basically, I gather all this material and then collage it in afterwards.

"The advantage is that it keeps spirits up in the studio and saves me from having to give a lot of verbal instruction. That's the way I'm used to working, so when Thomas came in and immediately started building and building tracks, it just drove me crazy," says the singer. "I'd say, 'You know why you were hired, to set up sounds on the computer, so please get off the keyboards and let me play.' Sometimes it would just fall on deaf ears, and we never used those tracks 'cause I just can't work that way, and I couldn't give over that much territory."

In the end, she didn't have to. She stuck to her guns and made her own decisions. "I felt very mixed up about it, I must confess," she says. "On one level, I thought, perhaps I'm not being very cooperative about it, but on the other I thought, no, this is composition, and if my structure is radically altered at the beginning, I don't want to be interior-decorated out of my own music. I've always had the luxury of making my own mistakes, and that's something important to protect."

Now that *Dog Eat Dog* is finished and in the stores, Mitchell is gearing up for a six-month tour to promote the record, beginning this summer—"if they can drag me away from my easel," she laughs.

"Painting's become a bigger and bigger part of my life, especially over the past five years," she says. "In fact, I've painted more in the last three years than in my entire life—and I've been painting all my life. People don't know it, but I only became interested in music much later."

Her commitment to painting is so strong that it has occasionally threatened her music career. "You know, when it came to signing my current record deal, I almost quit then. I mean, I'd been at it since the mid-'60s and I suddenly felt it was time to stop and just pursue my painting, which was going quite well. When we toured in '83, they actually had to threaten me to put my paints away and go into rehearsals. I'd much rather have stayed home and continued painting. Although once I got into it and then out on the road again it was okay.

"But the moment I got back home again, I went straight into the thick of the pigments again."

The singer says she has been particularly influenced by the painter Georgia O'Keefe, whom she visited at her home in New Mexico a few years ago. "The whole trip was very inspirational," Mitchell explains. "I started painting like mad the moment I got home again.

"I was working on my Mingus album at the time," she recalls, "and I went to visit her and ended up staying for five days. She was a pretty fascinating character and quite superstitious. I remember when I arrived at her front door, she opened it before saying anything to me, turned to her housekeeper and commented, 'Did you see what time she arrived at?' Apparently the sun had just set behind the mountains at that precise moment, and to Georgia it was a very good omen.

"So my timing was good, I guess," she laughs. "Anyway, we had dinner. Everything was home cooked and delicious, and I had the distinct feeling she was checking me out. The funny thing was I'd bought all these Indian things—ankle bells and rattles—in Santa Fe on my way there. I was just dying to go up to my room and try them on. But I didn't want to appear rude and just leave her there, and she kept chatting away. But in the end I thought, what the hell, so I put them all on and then let out a few chants and leapt around the room. She just stood there leaning on her cane, staring at me, saying, 'You're a pretty curious visitor.'"

Early the next day, O'Keefe woke her up early for a long walk in the country. "She was amazingly energetic for a woman in her 90s," Mitchell marvels. "She's racing along this road, and of course I'm chain-smoking all the way, trying to keep up with her. She suddenly stops and says, 'You shouldn't smoke.'

"Her housekeeper, Juan, said in surprise, 'Georgia, you don't usually tell people what they should do.' And Georgia turned to me and said sternly, 'Well, you should live.'

"Of course, I'm still smoking."

BY PHIL SUTCLIFFE

JONI MITCHELL

In the wake of Chalk Mark in a Rain Storm, *Joni looks back on the 1980s and the early days of her career. The many highlights include a danger diffused at the Isle of Wight concert, the drug scene of the late '60s and '70s, how Joni ripped off cops for amusement, and an edgy meeting with aging bluesman Furry Lewis. —SFL*

Q, May 1988

On the office wall, in elegantly lit monochrome and framed, Joni Mitchell's husband, Larry Klein, bends down fondly to bury his face in the hair at the nape of her neck and wraps his arms around her. Nestling against him, she in turn affectionately hugs a bright-eyed cat. A picture of love and fulfillment—at last, you might fairly say.

There is recent evidence too of her public life: copies of *Chalk Mark in a Rain Storm,* her fifteenth album in 25 years, the last 16 of which have seen her veering away from her early folk roots into a sequence of experiments and unpredictable collaborations which are evolving still: with Crosby, Stills & Nash, jazz virtuosos black and white—Charlie Mingus

A Nervy Broad
139

and Jaco Pastorius, soul singers black and white—Lionel Richie and Michael McDonald. She's even been working with Prince, a devotee of her 1975 LP *The Hissing of Summer Lawns*, though nothing has emerged yet.

Now, though, after working for a couple of years in nine British and American studios, she has completed her most elaborate cooperative venture.

The *Chalk Mark* cast includes Peter Gabriel, ex-Eagle Don Henley, old outlaw Willie Nelson, Hopi Indian Iron Eyes Cody, Wendy Melvoin and Lisa Coleman from Prince's Revolution, Tom Petty and, perhaps least likely of all, Billy Idol ("I saw him at the Grammies, thought he was fantastic, rang him and told him I wanted him to sing with me"). And the result is a wonderfully original album, her most compelling compositions for years molded, as ever, by her remarkable ear for arrangement.

The picture of wedded bliss hangs on the wall of her manager Peter Asher's office in Los Angeles, between Sunset and Santa Monica boulevards. There have been rumours that Joni is "under the weather," but she arrives, half an hour late after a 15-minute drive from her home in Bel Air, apparently in the pink, at ease and expansive whichever way the interview turns. We perch on either side of a glass and chrome desk like job applicant and employer. Someone looks in to toss her a pack of Camels.

Joni Mitchell laughs a lot, from the lower end of her range. When she tells a funny story she makes big, comic gestures with her arms. She's 44 now, but there's still something enduringly innocent about her. Her mild accent turns "out" into "oat" and "docile" into "dossl." Talking, as in writing, she takes care with words and relishes what she calls "a well-contoured phrase." Though names and numbers escape her, she has almost total recall of what she saw and what she felt at any particular moment. She can even remember what she was *wearing* at every crisis point in her life.

—

Q: *A media picture of you has emerged from about '69. You were living with Graham Nash and apparently keeping virtual open house to the press.*

A: You have to put it in the context of those times. Back then, we, the musical . . . heroes, for lack of a better word, didn't feel very separated from our audiences. We were all hippies. It's not like now, where the musical stars have become like the movie stars of the era before us—transformed by luminous images. We felt we were all in this together. I know I didn't feel separate from the press—which was a mistake. Oh yeah, you must maintain some privacy. I mean, I like my place to be cozy. I like cats. They give the home a heartbeat—in lieu of children. I don't have children. I see home as a sanctuary with a tea kettle rocking and good conversation.

Q: What did you feel at the time, then, about that public scrutiny via the media?

A: Oh, I couldn't stand it. All that exploitation and posturing, the gasping at the mention of your name, the pursuit by photographers and phenomenon-seekers . . . you get that shot of adrenalin and it's fight or flight. I chose flight many a time.

Q: Hard to do on stage; you're not supposed to . . .

A: The first time I stood my ground was in front of half a million people at the Isle of Wight. What happened was this. It was a hostile audience to begin with. A handful of French rabble-rousers had stirred the people up to feel that we, the performers, had sold out because we arrived in fancy cars—Neil and I had rented an old red Rolls, the driver had to sit outside, a real horseless carriage. Backstage there was all this international capital—bowls of money, open coffers.

Some acts canceled, so there was a dead space of about an hour. No one would go on. But in a spirit of cooperation, knowing it was death, I said, OK, I'll go out there.

In the second number a guy in about the fifth row, flipped out on acid, comes squirting up and lets out a banshee yell, guttural, demented, devils at his heels. It's as if a whale came out of the water, the waves, the energy from him spreads to the back so fast. Now the whole thing is *undulating*. I go and sit at the piano and this guy I knew from the caves at Matala, Yogi Joe, he taught me my first yoga lesson, he leaps up on stage. He gives me the Victory sign, he sits at my feet and starts to play the congas with terrible time. He looks up at me and says, "Spirit of Matala, Joni!" I bend down off-mike and say, "This is *entirely* inappropriate, Joe." It was "Woodstock," of all the songs to be singing, because this was so different—it was a war zone out there.

At the end of "Woodstock" Yogi Joe springs up, grabs the microphone and yells, "It's desolation row and we're all doomed!" or some-thing to this effect. A couple of guards grab him. The crowd then stand up and scream, "They've got one of ours!" And they're moving forward.

Now, what would you do? I've run for much less than that. But I thought, I can't, I have to stand up. The place I drew my strength from was very bizarre. I had been to a Hopi snake dance ceremony—it's a very high ceremony to bring rain to their runty corn crops. They dance with live snakes, and there was one that stood up on the end of its tail and launched itself like a javelin right into the audience. The people scattered, but the musicians, the antelope-priest drummers, never missed a beat. Their earnestness, their sincerity, their need to bring rain, was unaffected. They kept the groove.

So, with my chin quivering, fighting back tears and the impulse to run, I said "I was at a Hopi snake dance a couple of weeks ago and there were tourists who acted like Indians and Indians who acted like tourists—you're just a bunch of tourists. Some of us have our lives involved in this music. Show some respect." And the beast lay down. The beast lay down.

Q: Did you and your friends live communally?

A: No, not really. There was a community of musicians, but we didn't all live under the same roof and alternate duties or anything.

Q: You wouldn't have wanted that?

A: I'm too much of a loner. I was too much on the fringes of everything.

Q: But all your personal relationships centered around the "community of musicians"?

A: They usually began as friendships, burst in flame (laughs), and contin-ued after the fact as friendships.

Q: Did the whole hippy cultural and social period feel natural to you?

A: No, never, because it was a *style*, you know, lay off the scissors and you were a hippy.

Q: In your group of friends there was closeness, but was there also com-petition, rivalry?

Joni Mitchell painting, 1984. © Corbis/Henry Diltz

A: Uh-huh. It doesn't suit my body, though. I short circuit. It feels tense and, uh, vulgar. I was passive in my twenties, very manipulable. I was opinionated, mind you, but . . . I had a desire to be agreeable and cooperative and you can take that desire and move a person around.

Q: *Did you get moved to where you didn't want to be?*

A: In some cases. Woodstock, for instance. We were all standing in the airport, CSN and myself, and it was agreed by the managers, David Geffen and Elliot Roberts, that I should not go because it would be difficult to get me out of there and back to New York for a television show that Monday night. If it happened now, I think I would have given them a good argument because it kind of broke my heart. But I was the girl in the family. "Daddy" said I couldn't go.

Q: Where did drugs figure for you?

A: I was late to try everything. I was so overprotected within this stable. When Crosby, Stills, Nash & Young did their first album, all I knew was suddenly all their personalities were changing. Graham was getting thin: he wouldn't eat and he stayed up all night. I didn't know any of them was doing drugs. They would hide them and whisper when I was around.

Q: But you eventually tried them?

A: Oh yeah, I tried everything. Well, I never tried heroin because I thought, "What's the point? The worst that could happen would be you'd like it." But altered consciousness is completely tempting to a writer. I did some good writing, I think, on cocaine—"Song for Sharon" (*Hejira*)—but it kills your heart, takes all your energy, puts it up in your brain and gives you the arrogance that, you know, ruined Jaco Pastorius. (After destitute years of drink and drug problems the former Weather Report and Mitchell band bassist died last September after being beaten up outside a Florida club.) I watched it ruin a lot of people.

Q: Were you aware of being "the spokeswoman for a generation"?

A: You mean via the song "Woodstock?" If I was a spokesperson, nobody heard me, so big deal.

———

In 1975 Joni Mitchell took a typically peripheral part in the great rock 'n' roll gang show, The Rolling Thunder Review, which featured [Bob] Dylan, [Joan] Baez, [Roger] McGuinn and friends. But she was preparing to make her own splash with an album which can now be seen as the axis of her career. *The Hissing of Summer Lawns* came out in the autumn, and its smoky, langorous, jazz tension provoked her first critical pasting, in America at least. She had been revered, "the Goddess of song" no less. Now she stank the place out. The crime seems to have been, as with Dylan a decade earlier, that she had deserted folk and, thus, all the associated purities she had represented.

Some small consolation was that it did strike a chord in Britain. In case anyone was going to miss the point of it all, she drew a diagram. Her cover painting showed Amazon tribesmen bearing a giant snake, approaching the outskirts of a cityscape incorporating LA and New York—with the Mitchell homestead bottom left.

She had taken a theme outside love lost and found and worked it to the limits of her imagination and intellect to build a whole album. Offsetting black and white, the jungle and the city, she had a muscular metaphor for the big idea that was eating her—how the orderly and the wild fight it out beneath the skin of everyone. Burundi drums thundering through "The Jungle Line" or sprinklers hissing like snakes. . . . She had her subject, the animal/human/animal. She had her musical field to explore, at last discovering how she might connect with the black and white blending she had loved so much on her old Lambert, Hendricks & Ross LP. (She covered their "Twisted" on *Court and Spark* and "Centerpiece" on *The Hissing of Summer Lawns*.) It wasn't that she took a vow against "personal" songs from then on, but they were no longer a trap to her.

Her next, *Hejira*, was written almost entirely on the road, in the [Jack] Kerouac sense. She was cooling her heels on the beach at Neil Young's house one day when some friends came by and said they fancied driving across the country. They climbed into her car and did it. Among other things, *Hejira* actually bade farewell to another lover— presumably [John] Guerin, whom she left that year—but "Furry Sings the Blues," a reflection on her encounter with ancient bluesman Furry Lewis, was the piece which attracted controversial attention.

Then, astonishingly, she turned up in blackface on the cover of her next, *Don Juan's Reckless Daughter*, a yet more ambitiously jazzy double set, with the late bass virtuoso Jaco Pastorius a forceful presence. While it took her further away from a mainstream audience, Charlie Mingus, a jazz immortal composer, acoustic bass player and band leader, listened and liked it. He contacted her through the grapevine with a proposal that they work together on T. S. Eliot's *Four Quartets*. If she could trim the texts down a bit ready for singing, he would write a score for full orchestra. Joni read the thing and, regretfully, cried off. But Mingus was persistent. In April '78, already crippled by a rare, paralyzing disease, he produced what proved to be his last six compositions and told her their provisional title was *Joni I–VI*.

It was a great gamble. She had never collaborated with anyone to this degree before, and Mingus's music was very difficult, but how could she resist? She spent time with him in Mexico while he consulted a faith healer. The dying of a great man hung over her work, challenging her ingenuity and her artistic integrity. She gave up on a couple of the pieces. She tried his signature tune, "Goodbye Porkpie Hat," instead and it took three months to get a lyric. Finally, she found she had recorded up to four separate cuts of every track, and, although she knew Mingus hated amplified instruments, she chose the electric versions because she felt they were best.

In her touching sleevenote she sees herself "dog paddling around in the currents of black classical music." Referring to the two tunes she had to leave out altogether, Joni said they were "too idiomatic" for her. Ironically, this was exactly how the entire album would sound to her fans.

No such nice considerations, though, for Joe Smith, chairman of Elektra/Asylum. On surveying the plush gatefold sleeve and listening to the music therein he made a conference phone call to his promotion men nationwide. "I'm having a contest for them on sales of *Mingus*," he explained afterwards. "First prize is they get to keep their jobs!"

—

Q: Your most controversial work in the second half of the '70s came from your unusual approaches to black music from "The Jungle Line" and on to Mingus. *In between there was "Furry Sings the Blues." How did that song come about?*

A: I had been out on Rolling Thunder and for my own amusement on that tour I had taken to ripping off cops. I would use my wits and try and get a piece of cop paraphernalia off 'em—I got hats and jackets and tie-clips and badges. One time I chased a cop and he wouldn't give me anything, so I said, "What if I get a gang and we pin you up against a wall and you tell your superior you were outnumbered?" He was real deadpan. This smile came over just one corner of his mouth and he said, "Go get your gang." It was really a charming game. I would introduce myself as Mademoiselle Oink, the liaison officer between rock 'n' roll and the cops.

So when we got to Memphis on my own tour I hit on this cop, and he agreed we would trade a badge for a record. Then he said we should go and see old Beal Street, which used to be the heart of blues music in the town. Well, it was an amazing vision, like a Western ghost town three blocks long. Shards of wreckage all around, cranes with wrecking balls still standing there. Two pawn shops were functioning, and there was a modern movie theater with a double bill of black machine-gun movies—next to a statue of W. C. Handy, a trumpet player of the jazz era. We came down the street, and, if I'm not embellishing, a tumbleweed drifted across in front of the car—it seems to me it did.

Standing in front of one of the pawn shops was a guy in a purplish-blue shirt, bright blue blazer with brass buttons on it, bald, smokin' a stogie. He looks at me and says, "You Joni Mitchell?" I think, "Culturally this is impossible. This guy should not know my name." However, I had heard that Furry Lewis lived in Memphis, so I mentioned it to the pawn-broker. He says, "Oh sure, he's a friend of mine. Meet me here tonight and we'll go over and see him. Bring a bottle of Jack Daniels and a carton of Pall Mall cigarettes."

Furry was in his eighties or nineties and senile at this point. Lived in a little shanty in the ghetto there. It was quite a nice visit until I said to him—meaning to be close to him, meaning "We have this in common"—"I play in open tunings too." Now, I dunno, people must have ridiculed him about it or something, because he leaned upon the bed and said (*hoarse old voice*), "Ah kin play in Spanish tonnin'." Real defensive. Somehow or other I insulted him. From then on it was downhill. He just said, "I don't like her," as I wrote in the song.

Q: What do you feel about this whole episode?

A: I'm too sensitive. I'm likely to feel shitty over things that would just roll off another back. I would like to be appropriate. I would like to be fine-tuned to the point where my instincts are working well, where everything is in alignment. But to say, I play in open tunings too—this is not an insulting remark (*laughs*)! You can't control these things.

Q: And how do you see the experience with Charlie Mingus now?

A: The musicianship on that album is at a very high level and I'm proud of it. But it's obscure. It hammered the nail into my coffin which said: Joni is dead on pop radio, she's a jazzer. I would do it again in a minute, though, that project. To have the experience of collaborating with such an ususual character and a fine jazz musician. Definitely.

Q: Was Mingus's being black a big part of it for you?

A: No, *my* blackness was a part of it actually, because I appeared on the cover of *Don Juan's Reckless Daughter* as a black man. Charles thought I had a lot of audacity to do that, and that was one of the reasons he sent for me.

Q: His response seems unusual. The old "nigger minstrel" blacking-up business is normally taken as racist. Why did you do that?

A: There's a whole history that led up to that action. The first seed was on Rolling Thunder. Bobby [Bob Dylan] and Joan Baez were in whiteface and they were going to rescue Hurricane Carter. I had talked to Hurricane on the phone several times, and I was *alone* in perceiving that he was a violent person and an opportunist. I thought, Oh my God, we're a bunch of white patsy liberals. This is a bad person. He's fakin' it.

So when we got to the last show, which was at Madison Square Garden, Joan Baez asked me to introduce Muhammad Ali. I was in a particularly cynical mood—it had been a difficult excursion. I said, Fine, what I'll say is—and I never would've—I'll say, We're here tonight on behalf of one jive-ass nigger who could have been champion of the world, and I'd like to introduce you to another one who is. She stared at me and immediately removed me from this introductory role. I thought then, I should go on in blackface tonight. Anyway, Hurricane was released and the next day he brutally beat up this woman. . . .

So there came Halloween, and I was walking down Hollywood Boulevard. There were a lot of people out on the street wearing wigs and paint and masks, and I was thinking, What can I do for a costume? Then a black guy walked by me with a New York diddybop kind of step, and he said in the most wonderful way (*croons*), "Lookin' good, sister, lookin' gooood." His spirit was infectious and I thought, I'll go as him. I bought the makeup, the wig, the sideburns, I went into a sleazy menswear [store] and bought a sleazy hat and a sleazy suit, and that night I went to a Halloween party and nobody knew it was me, nobody.

The art she professed herself most worried about at the start of the '80s was "growing old gracefully." Further, with mock melodrama, she inquired of a journalist, "Is my maternity to amount to a lot of black plastic?" She had drifted a long way from center stage. Like *Miles of Aisles*, the *Shadows and Light* live double, her last recording with Pastorius, seemed to have drawn a line. Then she went to ground for a while.

Wild Thing Run Fast, in '82, featured Guerin on drums—she's terrific at staying friends with former lovers—and her new husband, Larry Klein, on bass. It took a potshot at a single hit with a spunky remake of Leiber and Stoller's "(You're So Square) Baby I Don't Care." In Lionel Ritchie [*sic*] it introduced the first of what, on her last three albums, has become a parade of unlikely guest duetists. It was very good—she really has never made a clinker—and sold moderately.

The same applied to her next, *Dog Eat Dog*, three years later. While shifting further towards the adult rock consensus it was literate as ever, sharply satirical about fang-and-claw consumerism and the seedy side of pop's efforts for Ethiopia. Joni found new Madonna and Stevie Nicks areas in her voice and, while English new-tech wizard Thomas Dolby's production work didn't make much impression, two straight ahead songs with music by Klein—"Fiction" and "Tax Free"—hinted that she might be examining the possibilities of stadium rock.

In the middle of recording, she broke with Elliott Roberts after 17 years. For a few weeks she tried to look after herself as she had done back in the coffeehouse days, but, when she realized it meant the phone never stopped ringing, she turned to her old friend Peter Asher, actress Jane's brother and very late of '60s chart duo Peter & Gordon, not to mention longtime manager of James Taylor and Linda Ronstadt.

No magic wand to hand, though. "I loved *Dog Eat Dog*," he says. "Other people didn't. Of course, Joni was disappointed when it didn't do well. The thing is, every artist has a reluctance to accept that basically, not enough people liked the record. Then anyone who's around gets blamed, which is usually the record company.

"But Joni doesn't have any of this even vaguely on her mind, not for an instant. In the studio her objectives are solely artistic. And I don't say that is a virtue. She doesn't even *think* of pleasing the public. In that sense she's lucky she's as popular as she is. At least, around the world, she still does half a million every time. No danger of Geffen losing money on her—and even if an album didn't get its costs back, another label would sign her right away because of her reputation and creativity."

It turns out that *Chalk Mark in a Rain Storm*, her latest, is a wonderful album. Apart from the intriguing and varied list of duetists detailed earlier, the songs show off her full scope quite beautifully (there's even a nostalgic variant on folk standard "Corrina Corrina"). The depth of reflection she is putting into her work now emerges in two songs which reach back over 20 years to events touched on elsewhere in this interview. Those Hopi antelope-priest drummers who inspired her at the Isle of

Wight are on her mind again in "Lakota," a protest against government attempts to take the tribe's land for uranium mining. And Fort Bragg, the army camp where that besotted captain sold her a favorite guitar, is recalled in "The Beat of Black Wings"—it was there, she explains, that she met the song's central character, the Viet Vet, Killer Kyle.

"He was there. Fort Bragg was an interesting place. It gave me a balanced view because everyone I knew was, you know, dodging the Vietnam draft like crazy, pleading insanity and homosexuality, anything. The boys down there were Southerners for the most part: they all believed in America, mom, apple pie and the War. They were not at all bohemian.

"There were some soldiers there who hadn't been to the War yet, and then you had the damaged coming back—Killer Kyle was such a person. He was in the Airborne Division, a paratrooper medic. Terrible experiences, hell on earth, you know? I came offstage one night—I can remember what I was wearing, the whole incident was so vivid: an old '40s purple silk velvet evening gown and my hair plaited up on my head with some roses in it. I looked like an old Sarah Bernhardt poster.

"I went into the dressing room and Killer was there, red-in-the-face angry, his fists clenched, in his neck the veins were standing out—it was kind of frightening. He said to me in a thick Southern accent (*which she doesn't mimic*), 'You've got a lotta nerve, sister, standing up there and singing about love, because there ain't no love and I'm gonna tell you where love went.' He ended up crying and shaking. The song doesn't exactly depict what he told me, though. What he told me doesn't make a song."

Q: Did you start the '80s thinking "I have a problem here"?

A: I started the '80s by going to a party—at Stephen Bishop's—with the theme "Be nice to the '80s and the '80s will be nice to you." Everyone realized at the brink of it that it was going to be a hideous era. I had this car, my beloved '69 Bluebird, and I was on my way, driving past Tower Records on Sunset, it was that royal blue time of night, just before it goes black. I stopped and ran into the store because I just had to listen to a Jimmy Cliff record, *The Bongo Man Has Come*. But when I came out there was the empty slot where my car had been. Never saw it again. I loved that Bluebird.

Anyway, that's how the '80s were ushered in for me, and it was all downhill from there. The government ripped me off—I was one of just 12 people in the entire country who were forced to pay a new tax on a record at the point you hand it over to the record company. Twelve people! What kind of justice is there in this thing? I'm still fighting it. Then my housekeeper decided to sue me for $5 million.

Q: *What did you do to her?*

A: I kicked her in the shin because she was ripping me off. She was a Guatemalan and I'd paid for her to go home twice, and the second time she didn't even go, she went to Europe, so she'd been lying. Finally, I kicked her in the shins. But I can't do that as a public person. She went to the criminal court, and they threw it out because it's just laughable. But she's still after me, though she's on her fifth lawyer. Then I had trouble with the record company, which we don't wanna get into, OK, because I'm still there.

Q: *They wanted you to sell more records, I expect.*

A: No, no. Anyway, it's like the Antichrist is running things in this era.

Q: *Why did you split with Elliot Roberts?*

A: He needs a manager (*laughter*). We're still good friends. I don't really want to get into that.

Q: *Why did you decide to get married at last?*

A: Because Larry's such a wonderful person and I just love him.

Q: *And you've become marriable?*

A: Exactly. I've settled down.

Q: *Have you ever been out with a nonmusician?*

A: Since my youth . . . not really. I'm drawn to talent. I've been out with a painter. Always in the arts, though.

Q: How do you spend your time now, outside of music?

A: I'm so artsy, you know. When I'm not doing music I'm painting, I'm writing poetry. We enjoy home life. It's fairly simple really; we enjoy movies. I love card games, video games, backgammon . . . I don't go to the supermarket because I hired a cook, but up till then I did. I don't lead a tremendously sheltered life. We frequent a little restaurant in our neighborhood almost every day. Most of our best friends are not in the Hollywood firmament.

Q: Does it matter to you that this album is a hit?

A: I could use a hit, yeah. On the last two records the production, the layering of keyboards, was an expensive process, and I gotta sell more records to recoup, just to break even.

BY STEPHEN HOLDEN

JONI MITCHELL FINDS THE PEACE OF MIDDLE AGE

"You wake up one day and suddenly realize that your youth is behind you, even though you're still young at heart," says Joni Mitchell, in this piece by Stephen Holden. Joni celebrates middle age—and resigns herself to it—with her latest, Night Ride Home.*—SFL*

New York Times, March 17, 1991

"Oh I am not old / I'm told / But I am not young," Joni Mitchell sings in "Nothing Can Be Done," from her new album, *Night Ride Home.* The song, which has lyrics by the 47-year old singer-songwriter and music by her 34-year-old husband, Larry Klein, addresses a subject that is virtually taboo in the youth-obsessed world of pop music—middle-age resignation.

"Must I surrender with grace / The things that I loved when I was younger?" she asks. "What do I do here with this hunger?" Ms. Mitchell's stoic reply to her own question, repeated almost like a mantra throughout the song, is simply: "Nothing can be done."

"I'm 47, and I guess I've come through my middle-age crazies, which are as predictable as the terrible twos," Ms. Mitchell reflected in a recent interview from Los Angeles, where she lives with her husband of eight years. (She met Mr. Klein, a bassist and producer, while working on her 1982 album *Wild Things Run Fast*.)

"You wake up one day and suddenly realize that your youth is behind you, even though you're still young at heart. You've got to get through this lament for what was. The song was based partly on 'The Desiderata,' which says, 'Surrender gracefully the things of youth.' When I play the song for my middle-aged friends, they either won't look at it or they look at it and weep."

———

The new album (Geffen GEFD 23402; all three formats), with its wistful backward gazes and twinges of longing for new adventure, is serene compared to Ms. Mitchell's 1970s albums, *Blue*, *For the Roses*, *Court and Spark* and *Hejira*. Her confessional lyrics on those recordings set the standards for personal honesty and poetic grace in what was labeled the singer-songwriter genre.

When that genre fell out of fashion at the end of the decade, Ms. Mitchell explored other musical realms, and her album sales dipped from more than a million to under 500,000.

Indeed, her musical innovations remain undervalued. In 1979, six years before Sting began exploring jazz instrumentation in mainstream pop, Ms. Mitchell collaborated with the late jazz composer Charles Mingus. The following year she released a concert album, *Shadows of Light*, [*sic*] featuring such eminent young jazz players as Pat Metheny, Michael Brecker and Jaco Pastorius. A decade before Paul Simon's African pop album *Graceland*, Ms. Mitchell had recorded "The Jungle Line," a song for voice and percussion made with the warrior drums of Burundi.

The 1980s found her experimenting with cinematic textures and scenarios. The political album *Dog Eat Dog* (1985) featured Rod Steiger on one cut portraying a Jimmy Swaggart–like television evangelist. Characters also appeared in some of the aural collages on *Chalk Mark in a Rain Storm* (1988), which editorialized against the materialistic values of that decade.

Like most of her peers, including Bob Dylan, Neil Young, Joan Baez and Crosby, Stills and Nash, Ms. Mitchell is still signed to a major label but is no longer a best-selling artist. At the same time, she is an avidly admired cult figure. Prince, of all people, has cited her as a major influence. For the last several years, the performance artist John Kelly has been doing an eerie, worshipful impersonation of Ms. Mitchell as a brooding, flaxen-haired ingenue. "The Joni Mitchell Project" —a revue of her songs with a format similar to that of "Jacques Brel Is Alive and Well and Living in Paris"—won critical acclaim last November at the Los Angeles Theater Center. It played for three months, and is scheduled to open in the fall at the Berkeley Repertory Theater.

Night Ride Home, Ms. Mitchell's 16th album, is also a kind of retrospective. With its spare, ringing guitar textures and introspective lyrics, it is closer in spirit to her '70s albums than anything she has released in more than a decade. But where the songs on her confessional masterpieces of the '70s were scorched with erotic passion and yearnings, *Night Ride Home* takes a longer, cooler view of life and love. Its songs jump back and forth in time to form a sort of dialogue that Ms. Mitchell describes as taking place "between the present, my youth and the year zero in the Christian calendar."

The most farsighted number is her reworking of William Butler Yeats's "Second Coming," which she has retitled "Slouching Toward Bethlehem," in acknowledgment, she says, of the Joan Didion essay. Although most of the lines have been changed slightly to make the words sit comfortably with Ms. Mitchell's flowing folk-pop melody, the song remains essentially true to the poem's spirit and tone. The most significant adjustment was to alter Yeats's lines "The best lack all conviction, while the worst / Are full of passionate intensity." Her adaptation reads: "The best lack conviction / Given some time to think / And the worst are full of passion / Without mercy."

Ms. Mitchell changed it because "I kept thinking where the reverse applied. I couldn't see passion as a bad thing."

The album's most open-hearted songs reminisce about childhood and adolescence. "Cherokee Louise" describes the plight of a childhood friend who is sexually abused by her foster father and hides in a railway tunnel. In "Come in From the Cold," whose seductive Latin beat echoes '60s hits like "Save the Last Dance for Me," Ms. Mitchell looks back to her adolescence in the sexually repressed '50s, when "we had to dance, a foot apart, and they hawk-eyed us from the sidelines."

In a lyric that moves forward from the late '50s, the singer describes a change of personal philosophy from one of romantic idealism ('We had hope / The world held promise") to deep skepticism ("But then absurdity came over me / And I longed to lose control").

Joni Mitchell—the woman who exalted the hippie culture of 20 years ago in the counter-cultural anthem "Woodstock"—is not especially sentimental about the 60's. One night recently, at a post-concert dinner party at which she, Sting, Bruce Springsteen and Don Henley shared a table, a young man approached and started waxing romantic about the '60s.

"I told him, 'Don't be romantic about it—we failed,'" she recalled. "And he said, 'Well, at least you tried.' And I said, 'But we didn't try hard enough. We didn't learn from history. If any progress is to be made, we must show you how we failed.'"

In tracing her own artistic growth in the past 20 years, Ms. Mitchell uses metaphors drawn from American Indian mythology, in which the four points of the compass represent different ways of perceiving the world.

"At the time of *Blue*, I was very west, which is emotion, and as a result I couldn't communicate with the northeast, which is more rational and business oriented," she said. "I had no defenses. I would look at the business people and burst into tears. They had to lock me up to make that record. There's a purity in *Blue* that comes from an almost nothing-left-to-lose attitude. After that I had to grow some claws to survive, which means I had to develop my northeast and become more emotionally detached."

Ms. Mitchell has also developed a second career as a painter and has exhibited in Europe and Japan. Because she has no formal musical training, she often employs a visual artist's vocabulary when talking about music.

"I know none of the numerics of music," she explained. "I see music as fluid architecture. For me, the chords are colors that you stir into mutant shades, as in painting."

The sounds that have had the greatest impact on her, she said, have come from every corner of the musical map.

"The first record I ever bought was the theme from the movie *The Story of Three Loves,* the 18th variation from Rachmaninoff's *Rhapsody on a Theme by Paganini.* I flipped for it. The second was Edith Piaf singing 'The Three Bells.' My major influence as a singer was Edith Piaf.

"I came through folk music simply because it was easy to get into it," she continued. "You could play for three months and become a professional. In high school I was always writing poetry, but I never thought that poetry and song could be the same thing until Bob Dylan came along. The song that did it for me was 'Positively Fourth Street.' I owe much to Bobby for that."

Even though *Night Ride Home* has garnered more critical praise than any album Ms. Mitchell has released in years, she does not expect it to bring back the kind of mass adulation she enjoyed in the 1970s. Nor does she desire that kind of fame.

"I had a flirtation with the big roar at one point," she said. "And I didn't like getting to a place where my audience was bigger than those who understood what I was saying."

"The question now is whether people can enjoy the singing of a middle-aged woman, even though the consensus is that if you don't evoke your dreams, you're in trouble. Would they truly enjoy it more if my jawline were tighter? My husband is younger than me, and he's not afraid of the wrinkles or the natural sagging of my jawline. What I'd like to do is experiment and create roles for myself. Maybe I could become a character singer like Willie Nelson."

Part Five

CHARISMATIC SIREN . . .
DOOM-LADEN SEER
1992–1999

Joni Mitchell and Larry Klein, 1984. © Corbis/Henry Diltz

BY CHARLOTTE GREIG

THE CHARISMATIC SIREN GIVES WAY TO THE DOOM-LADEN SEER

The two Grammys garnered for Turbulent Indigo *started an avalanche of long-deserved accolades for Joni Mitchell. The following is an interesting review—but for this album, an uncharacteristically negative one—from the British magazine* Mojo.*—SFL*

Mojo, November 1994

It would be easy to claim that the title says it all. Where once there was *Blue*, short, sweet and to the point, now there is *Turbulent Indigo*, overwrought and ambiguous. But that wouldn't be the whole story. *Indigo* is not among Mitchell's best work, but then at half-power she still leaves most of her successors in the dust. Musically she is, as ever, completely self-assured; whatever the complexities of the songs—and some of them meander along like a drunk zigzagging home, throwing punches and hazy philosophical clichés at the air—her poise remains exquisite. She never falters, though she's careful not to venture too far from the elegant folk-jazz formula established on *Hejira* and so successfully revisited on her last album, *Night Ride Home*. The trouble comes from the lyrics. It's not that she's lost her facility for language or her acrobatic way with a rhyming scheme; the problem is with what she has to say. *Turbulent Indigo* sees Mitchell trading in her persona as charismatic siren for a new role as doom-laden seer. No more navel gazing, it's time to set the world to rights. Which is unfortunate, because the new politically responsible Joni Mitchell is verbose, morose and exceedingly bad company.

Not that she was ever exactly likeable, but you couldn't help but admire her free spirit. Her mercurial, if self-absorbed, reflections charmed a generation in the '70s, and that, along with her immense musicality, let her get away with adopting the role of spoilt minx in songs like "Free Man in Paris." But in the '90s the charm is wearing thin, because the current, environmentally friendly, caring'n'sharing Mitchell seems to have swapped self-obsession for self-righteousness. If she wasn't so good musically her lyrical indiscretions would matter less; but *Turbulent Indigo* is full of distressingly banal reflections and literary references that don't measure up to the sophistication of their settings.

That said, the album starts on a high note, a beautifully judged vignette called "Sunny Sunday" about a bored rich girl with a gun. But then comes "Sex Kills," and suddenly crass literalism is the order of the day, as an unpleasant and outmoded screeching guitar accompanies Joni's dinner-party musings on the ills of the world—"doctors's bills," "traffic," "rapists," "little kids packing guns to school," not to mention "lawyers" who haven't been this popular since Robespierre slaughtered half of France" (sorry?). Finally she spots a Cadillac with the [license] plate JUSTICE and wonders "Is justice just ice?" Well, who can say?

The rest wanders between the poles established by the first two tracks. On the credit side is an engaging version of James Brown's "How Do You Stop," with Seal on backing vocals. "Last Chance Lost" and "Yvette in English" hark back pleasantly enough to the romanticism of *Court and Spark*. And there's the epic "Magdalene Laundries," in which she conjures up a claustrophobic female world, with unmarried pregnant girls, prostitutes and destitutes all scrubbing away in a steamy religious allegory of "dreamless drudgery." This is Mitchell at her eccentric best, painting pictures of imaginary worlds that are nevertheless familiar, stuffed as they are with iconic resonance.

On the down side are state-of-the-planet moans like the trite "Borderline" and a dull anti-rape number called "Not to Blame." On the title track, Mitchell complains that people don't understand what great artists like her and Van Gogh have to endure, what with living in turbulent indigo and all—but having been so thoroughly patronized, it's hard for the listener to sympathize.

The closing track is "The Sire of Sorrow (Job's Sad Song)"; and it is deeply depressing, not so much because of its subject matter—death, suffering, more death—but because Mitchell uses global concerns to mask her own disappointments. She bleats on about a modern world of "trash," "breathtaking ignorance" and so on, but refuses to let the undercurrents of her own fear of aging and death get through and give the song some emotional honesty.

If you don't listen too hard, you might like *Turbulent Indigo*. It's simply a new Joni Mitchell record that sounds a bit like her old ones. Listen closer and what's on offer is not that comfortable. Neither, sadly, is it that pleasurable.

BY BARNEY HOSKYNS

OUR LADY OF SORROWS

From the vantage point of 1994 and the release of Turbulent
Indigo, *Joni takes a hard-headed look over the course of her career.*
Note Joni's sharp edge here, something only hinted at in interviews
past.—SFL

Mojo, December 1994

She almost bounds into the room, this dowager duchess of American rock,
fresh from whooping it up for *Mojo's* photographer on the street outside
manager Peter Asher's West Hollywood offices. Where lesser mortals
would have been wiped out by the session, she seems to have found it positively rejuvenating.

After this exuberant entrance, however, Joni Mitchell plunks herself
down at the substantial oak table and proceeds to fire up the first of the
many cigarettes she will have on the go through the course of our conversation. I'd heard whisperings that she was seriously ill, possibly even dying
of lung cancer; if there's any truth to them they've made little difference to
her prodigious intake of nicotine.

She's just released *Turbulent Indigo*, the seventeenth album in a career
that surely stands as one of the most distinguished (and diverse) in the
whole rock canon. As *Mojo* reviewer Charlotte Greig pointed out last
month, it's been a very long journey from *Blue* (1971) to *Indigo*—the
indigo of the tormented Vincent Van Gogh, a Mitchell pastiche of whose
famous self-portrait sans ear graces the album's cover. But the woman is
still making music of great authority, still writing songs full of beguiling
beauty and trenchant indignation.

If occasionally she oversteps the mark and strays into the self-righteousness that made early champion David Crosby say she was "as humble
as Mussolini," the best of the album's songs—"Sunny Sunday," "Sex
Kills," "The Magdalene Laundries," "Not to Blame," "The Sire of
Sorrow"—rank with the most compelling and compassionate musical
statements ever made about the things human beings do to themselves and
to each other.

Recorded at her Bel Air home with her husband, Larry Klein—from
whom, in rather typical Mitchell style, she separated the day before the
sessions for the album began—*Turbulent Indigo* was, for a moment at
least, conceived as a virtual swansong to her entire career. Released on

Charismatic Siren . . . Doom-Laden Seer

161

Reprise, the label to which she was first signed back in 1967, it is an even sparser affair than her last album, *Night Ride Home*. It also boasts fewer of the guests to which we became accustomed with her '80s records: only guitarist Bill Dillon, sax god Wayne Shorter and backing vocalist Seal (on a cover of James Brown's "How Do You Stop") got the call this time. . . . The album finishes with "The Sire of Sorrow (Job's Sad Song)," an astonishing distillation of the Book of Job which literally raised the hairs on the back of my neck the first time I heard it . . .

——

Barney: "Sire of Sorrow" must be one of the most harrowing things you've ever recorded.

Joni: Well, in a lifetime, I think everyone sinks to the pits, and without that you don't really have powers of empathy. You may have powers of sympathy, but if you've been to the bottom you have an opportunity to be a more compassionate person. I have had a difficult life, as most people have—no more difficult than anyone else's, but peculiarly difficult all the same. A life of very good luck and very bad luck, with a lot of health problems and therefore a lot of conduct with medical carelessness. But I don't think I've ever become faithless; I've never been an atheist, although I can't say what orthodoxy I belong to. Many of the themes and images on this album have been with me for a long time, but it wasn't until now that I was cheerful enough to tackle the Book of Job.

B: The line about spitting out bitterness made me remember things you said at the time of Blue *about perceiving that you had a lot of hate in your heart.*

J: Oh yeah, you've got to cleanse yourself. Krishnamurti said an interesting thing, which was that the man who hates his boss hates his wife, and I think that's true. If you're holding dark feelings about anyone, they carry over into your relationship; you burden them with your bitterness. The '80s were very difficult for me, physically and emotionally. A lot of financial betrayal, a lot of health problems. My housekeeper sued in a version of the new palimony; simultaneously I was butchered by a dentist. I don't want to get into the 'poor me' syndrome, but the '80s for me were like being a prisoner of war, what with the physical and mental pain and general climate of mistrust.

B: *Have the '90s been better so far?*

J: Oh yeah. Even the yuppies seem to have noticed that goodies only make you so happy! All human relationships are so malformed at this point, especially heterosexual relationships. Every other woman is raped in her lifetime, and generally if she's raped once she's raped many times because it's by a man who has repeated access to her, either a father or a brother or a priest. And if she's raped as a child she will not be a well-formed adult woman. You have to wonder why it is that men are so frustrated that they're beating on women, and feel they have the license to do so. Contemporary music is full of woman hatred. Rap grew out of the pimp tradition: "My bitch is badder than yours."

B: *There does seem to be a new note of compassion for your sex sounded on this record, particularly on "Not to Blame" and "The Magdalene Laundries."*

J: I've never been a feminist—I've always been a tomboy, a companion to men—but as I get older I have more women friends. Also, things between men and women have gotten so out of line in America. Wife-battering is now a national pastime. As regards "Not to Blame," we don't know if O.J. Simpson killed his wife, but we do know that he battered her frequently and was kind of smug about it, like he was above the law. So the precariousness of my gender at this particular time was something that was hard for me to sidestep: precariousness in the office, in the streets, even in public swimming pools, which I talk about on "Sex Kills."

B: *That song takes one back to the rage and despair of* Dog Eat Dog.

J: Yes, but no one was ready for that at the time. They were all into ra-ra-Ronnie Reagan, whereas I was one of 12 artists in the state who had 85 percent of our income taxed in a kind of experimental levy. Maybe the greed of that decade was supposed to descend on me more heavily, or more irrationally, than on other people. But I did feel like Alice with the Red Queen; I felt I was in a world where irrational law was coming at me from all directions.

B: *There's a new huskiness and vulnerability to your voice on this record.*

J: I'm finally developing enough character in my voice, I think, to play the roles I write for myself. A song like "Cold Blue Steel and Sweet Fire" [from *For the Roses*] should have been sung by a man, but I think I could probably sing it better now. That was a song about the seduction of heroin, which I never did but which I was around. There are other songs in which I think I was miscast, songs I performed as an ingenue—even "Both Sides, Now," which I wrote when I was 21 and which I think is better sung by a person in their fifties or sixties reflecting back on their life.

B: *Sinatra did it, didn't he?*

J: Poor Frank, though, they gave him this folk-pop arrangement that was all wrong for him. I would love for him to have been able to really stretch out and sing the song.

B: *You sang "Woodstock" at the Edmonton Folk Festival. What were your thoughts about Woodstock II?*

J: Oh, the whole thing was just silly.

B: *That's it?*

J: Uh huh.

B: *You said before the Edmonton festival that you didn't want people to use you as "a sentimental journey." Have you always tried to resist the nostalgia of your fans?*

J: I understand how people's memories—particularly of their youth and their best years—are wrapped up with the music they listened to then. They also tend to listen to music less and less as they get older. But I'm a maker of music, and I have a painter's spirit even more than a musician's, and I like to keep moving forward. I don't like to get stuck in regurgitative situations. I don't want to become a "duty player," as Miles Davis would have said.

B: *What did you feel about, say, the Eagles' so-called "Greed" tour?*

J: I don't know, it's hard for me to imagine a "Greed" tour. People think we make a lot of money out there, but they forget that the artist is the last to get paid. By the time you've paid all the people who have a piece of you, there isn't a lot left. Unless you get some kind of sponsorship. And who's gonna sponsor me apart from tobacco companies, right? (raucous laugh)

B: *John Martyn says the problem with folk was that it didn't "swing." When you look back on the folkie days, would you agree with that?*

J: Yes, but you have to remember that I was born in a swing era. When I got my legs back after I had polio, I rock 'n' roll-danced my way through my teens. My music was always very rhythmic, it just had no drums. But as I began to write my first songs, they were quite intricate and classical, so they went back to my first roots, which were classical. My friends who only knew me as a party doll thought, "What is this and where is it coming from?" My music started off as folk music because that was a good place to get in on the guitar, but then it got more Celtic, and even like German lieder when I added the piano. Only then did it really begin to swing. Sometimes it takes a long time for your influences to show up.

B: *Do you ever look on songs such as "The Circle Game" and think, God, how maidenly and virginal that girl sounds now?*

J: I sang "Circle Game" as an encore in Edmonton, but I usually try to avoid it. What I realize now is that songs like "Circle Game" and "Big Yellow Taxi" have almost become nursery rhymes, they've become part of the culture. I didn't write "Circle Game" as a children's song, but I'm very pleased to see it go into the culture in that way. Anyway, I'll sing those songs, but I'm more tempted to run by the songs that no one ever seemed to notice. "Moon at the Window" was one I did in Edmonton, and it was very well received, despite the fact no one noticed it on *Wild Things Run Fast*.

B: *The conflict between the temptation of fame and the fear of the crowd was a preoccupation of yours through the '70s. When did it stop troubling you?*

J: At the time of *For the Roses* I was really mad at show business. I realize now that I'd entered into show business with a bad idea of what it was about. To give you some idea of how I saw show business, I wrote a poem when I was 16 called "The Fishbowl," based on my perception of what the press were doing to Sandra Dee and James Darren at a time when they were having marital difficulties. It went like this:

The fishbowl is a world reversed
Where fishermen with hooks
That dangle from the bottom up
Reel down their catch on gilded bait
Without a fight.

Pike, pickerel, bass, the common fish
Ogle through distorting glass,
See only glitter, glamour, gaiety,
Lunge towards the bait
And miss and weep for fortune's loss.

Envy the goldfish? Why?
His bubbles breaking round the rim
While silly fishes faint for him and say,
"Oh look, I think he winked at me?"

So now, with that insight, why in blazes would you go into this business?
I've always been somewhat reluctant. I liked small clubs, I am a ham and
I am an enjoyer. But on the big stage you get sonic distortion, and my
open tunings are a pain in the butt, so it's not very enjoyable.

Yes, at a certain point I became contemptuous of my audience.
Critics seemed to praise me when I felt I was poor and slam me when I
felt I was at my peak, so that also fed my bad attitude to the business. I've
always loved making the albums and the writing, because that's more like
the painting process. The self-promotion used to be distasteful; now it's
just kind of funny to me. I guess that's one of the beauties of getting older.

—

*B: Tell me about leaving Geffen and moving back to Reprise after 23
years.*

J: I had the choice to give this record to Geffen and call it my swansong
to head up into the Canadian backbush and get on with my painting. But
because Geffen hadn't done much with me in the time I was with them—
I was just kind of hired and forgotten, on a lot of levels—the feedback
from everyone around was that that would be a shame. And Mo Ostin at
Warner's was very enthusiastic about having me back. See, in my entire
career there hasn't been a lot of excitement about my albums coming out.

There is excitement about this one, for some reason. People are ready to listen, they're more ready to take something a little more to heart and to mind than they have in the past. And unlike some of my peers I haven't hit a writer's block: when I hit a block I just paint, which is an old crop rotation trick. So since I haven't lost my voice, and since I'm over the middle-age hump and at peace with becoming an elder . . . although, of course, I did ask myself whether a woman of my age could continue in this youth-oriented genre. As a painter you're just beginning to ripen at 50, but as a musician there's a lot of scrutiny as to how you look and so forth. It's such a shallow and fickle business.

B: *Is it true that David Crosby used to show you off to his superstar cronies—bring you out to play a few songs?*

J: David was very enthusiastic about the music—he was twinkly about it! His instincts were correct: he was going to protect the music and pretend to produce me. So we just went for the performance, with a tiny bit of sweetening. I think perhaps without David's protection the record company might have set some kind of producer on me who'd have tried to turn an apple into an orange. And I don't think I would have survived that. The net result of that was that [engineer] Henry Lewy and I made 13 albums together without a producer.

B: *You were never really a hippy, were you?*

J: I was the queen of the hippies, but in a way I wasn't really a hippy at all. I was always looking at it for its upsides and its downsides, balancing it and thinking, here's the beauty of it and here's the exploitative quality of it and here's the silliness of it. I could never buy into it totally as an orthodoxy.

B: *Do you feel your earliest fans had you pegged as a paragon of purity and introspection and then found it hard to adjust to the chic, jazzy Joni of the '70s?*

J: I can't speak for how you're perceived. I can only say that you write about that which you have access to. So if you go from the hippy thing to more of a Gatsby community, so what? It's not a Zelig thing: life is short and you have an opportunity to explore as much of it as time and fortune allow. No subject matter ever seemed barred to me, and no class ever seemed barred. In a way, there is no region for me in the way there might be for someone like Tom Waits. There are some people who want to make a documentary about me, and I don't really know how they would do that. I don't want to bring them into my homes, because you don't really want the lunatic fringe to know where you live. I feel like I belong to everything and nothing, so how could you define my environment?

B: Who do you regard as your real peers as writers?

J: Dylan, Leonard Cohen . . . that's about it as far as lyricists go. I'm influenced by Shakespeare, not so much by the reading of him as by the idea that the language should be trippingly on the tongue, and also by the concept of the dark soliloquy, with a lot of human meat in it. Obviously it has to be more economical and direct, and that's Dylan's influence on me.

B: Does it ever strike you as strange that Canadians such as yourself and Cohen and Neil Young and The Band have made some of the most powerful music about America?

J: Fresh eyes. [David] Hockney made great paintings of L.A. The Swiss photographer Frank documented America in the '50s at a time when nobody noticed how culturally peculiar it was. People sometimes don't know what's happening under their noses.

B: Do you find Los Angeles inspires the kind of apocalyptic ruminations that other songwriters do?

J: Well, "Sex Kills" was written on the last night of the riots. To see a license plate with "Just Ice" on it at that time was so poignant. I mean, did you ever think of "justice" as two words? From the rappers, maybe . . .

B: There was an early gangsta rapper called Just Ice, as it happens.

J: Maybe that was his car! Anyway, it got me writing.

B: Has it been strange watching your rock contemporaries turn into virtual Hollywood deities over the course of 25 years?

J: I'll tell you a funny tale, and then we'll think about whether we should print it or not. I don't like ragging on people and making 'em look bad.

Bonnie Raitt and Joni Mitchell performing in Illinois, 1985. © Corbis/Neal Preston

This makes [Don] Henley look kinda like a jerk, but shall I tell you it any-way? OK, to me this is kind of funny.

I go to see Sting because my beloved Vinnie [Coluita] is drumming with him, but poor Vinnie's all alone up there, there's no one with him. So it put me in kind of a bad mood, this show. I kept going out and smoking in the wings. Anyway, afterwards there was a party and I was the first to get there. By now I was real cranky. I see Henley sitting by himself in a long, long, long booth. So I walk over as if to sit down with him and I say, "Hi, Henley," and he does this thing where he looks left and right, with a very worried look on his face. And I know exactly what that means, that he's saving the place for Sting. So I say something casual and go sit at another table with Vinnie and Bruce Springsteen and his wife.

Finally, Sting comes in and sits next to Henley and the room fills up with people. At that point, Henley sends an emissary, a woman, to my table who says, "You can come and sit with Sting and Henley now." So, I launch myself into the air and I yell at Henley over at the end of the room: "Never!"

I mean, the whole idea of that kind of political lamination, frankly, gags me with a spoon. It's so tragically hip, and I think it's the enemy of art. I'm not impressed by stars, you know? I never was as a kid. I'm impressed by heart, and fun, and a lot of things, but stardom in and of itself?

B: *How have your worldview and standpoint changed since* Dog Eat Dog?

J: I'm more comfortable in my own skin than I've been in my entire life: I wouldn't trade my fifties for my twenties for anything in the world. No way. In fact I probably went through most of my fear in my twenties and I'm a good deal more fearless today as a result. There are things I have to work on, like I get pugnacious and impatient. I'm impatient with human beings for being stupid assholes.

I'm an elder now! I should still be swinging at things to a certain degree, but you need to serene on down a little bit. So I would say that nothing much about the world shocks me as much as it used to. I was enraged at the time I wrote *Dog Eat Dog*, but I'm very cheerful now. I think I'm in a good place in my own spirit, even if I still get mad in traffic. But I still think you have to tackle the deeper topics.

They say that as a writer you're a lyric poet in your youth, in your thirties epic poetry appears because you're going over changes repeatedly. In your fifties, so the theory goes, you become a tragedian. Many of the themes and images on this album have been with me for a long time, but it wasn't until now that I was cheerful enough to tackle the Book of Job.

B: *Have you been disappointed by the sales of your albums since* Mingus? *You've described yourself as a "radio orphan."*

J: I was completely out of whack with public taste throughout the late '70s and the '80s. People aren't always going through changes at the same time as me, and sometimes I get so far ahead I look like I'm behind. The warp with public taste on *Wild Things*, for instance, was twofold. I loved the band on that record, we were all in love with each other, but that was the beginning of drum machines, so no one wanted to hear live playing. Now it's just the opposite. If you put on *Hissing* now, the playing is beautiful.

With *Dog Eat Dog*, the press went to sleep en masse: Ronnie Reagan could do no wrong. It took a few years for the press to wake up. This Japanese interviewer said to me, "Joni, you used to be a poet and now you're a journalist." And I said, "That's because America is a land of ostriches and somebody's gotta be Paul Revere." People didn't like the politics on that album. *Time* magazine called it an adolescent work, yet it contained two of their subsequent cover stories.

B: How did you feel when Rolling Stone *dubbed you "Old Lady of the Year" back in 1972?*

J: Oh, it was a low blow, and it was unfair. I was not abnormally promiscuous, especially within the context of the free love experiment, so to be turned on by my peer group and made an example, made me aware that the whore/Madonna thing had not been abolished by that experiment. People who were legitimately on that list, like Graham Nash, were gonna call and complain, but then they figured it would fan the flame. There were people on that list like B. Mitchell Reed, whose radio show I'd done and that was all. Assumptions were made in interpreting the lyrics, as they always were, that this was about so-and-so . . . all that nonsense that destroys the ability of the listener to identify with a song. Plus they were misinterpretations. So that was painful and unnecessary, and *Rolling Stone* had a policy for years after that to get me.

B: Still, you have to admit the irony of a song like "Man to Man" [Wild Things Run Fast], a song about serial monogamy which features not only your husband but two ex-lovers, James Taylor and drummer John Guerin.

J: Oh, I always do that, I'm terrible at that! I've got a new boyfriend now, and John played some drums on one song on the record, and [Larry] Klein was the producer! And they're all looking at me like, "You asshole," because the boyfriend and I wrote the song, and the old boyfriend who introduced me to Klein is on the drums. . . . I don't know, artists are a strange lot.

B: But you clearly stay friends with these guys.

J: Whenever possible. See, my mother says things to me like, "Ducks mate for life," but I guess I am a serial monogamist. Klein and I spent 12 years together. We were good friends in the beginning, then we were lovers, then we were husband and wife. I love Klein: there's a mutual affection there and I can't imagine what would destroy it.

B: *Is there a fundamental frustration about creating art—a restlessness, as you've described it—which makes it hard to live with people?*

J: My main criterion is: am I good for this man? If at a certain point I feel I'm causing him more problems than growth, then if he doesn't have the sense to get out I have to kick him out! The "Mr. Mitchell" thing, of course, is prevalent. I was in New Orleans one night and we were partying, and this Greek guy came up and asked me to dance. And he said to me, "In Greece they say Joni Mitchell, she doesn't need a man." I said, "Oh, is that right? All of Greece says this?"

I started in the business kind of ultra-feminine, but as I went along I had to handle so many tough situations for myself—had to be both male and female to myself.

So it takes a specific kind of man who wants a strong and independent woman. Klein did, but at the same time there were things about living with "Joni Mitchell"—not with me—that pinched on his life in a certain way that made me think he needed a break. Our separation, I think, was wholesome—painful and occasionally a little mean, but never nasty or ugly. There was a certain amount of normal separation perversity—he'd spent a third of his life with me, after all, and I'd spent a quarter of mine with him—but for the most part it was a wonderful growth experience for both of us. Klein would say the friction created a pearl.

B: *Listening to "Free Man in Paris" again made me think of Dylan saying that you weren't really a woman.*

J: Yeah, they asked him about women in the business and he said, "Oh, they all tart themselves up." And the interviewer said, "Even Joni Mitchell?" And he said, "I love Joni Mitchell, but she's" . . . how did he put it? . . . "kinda like a man," or something. It was a backhanded compliment, I think, because I'm probably one of Bobby's best pace runners . . . you know what I mean, as a poet? There aren't that many good writers. There are a lot that are touted as good, but they're not literature, they're just pretty good for a songwriter.

B: *What was it like singing with Dylan at the Great Music Experience in Japan?*

J: Oh, he's such a little brat, you know. He really is. He's never been very complimentary to my face—most of the boys haven't. But he loved "Sex Kills," and was very effusive about it. Anyway, we played three concerts, and they kept shifting my position on the [mikes] and which verses of the songs I was going to sing. On the third night they stuck Bob at the [mike] with me, and that's the one that went out on tape. And if you look closely at it, you can see the little brat, he's up in my face—and he never brushes his teeth, so his breath was like . . . right in my face—and he's mouthing the words at me like a prompter, and he's pushing me off the [mike]. It's like he's basically dipping my pigtail in ink. The press picked up on it and said, "Bobby Smiles!" Yeah sure, because he was having a go at me out there.

B: *Talking of brats, did you ever actually work with Prince?*

J: No. He sent me a song once called "You Are My Emotional Pump, You Make My Body Jump." I called him up and said, "I can't sing this." He's a strange little duck, but I like him.

B: *There are far less of the guest appearances on the last two albums than we're used to seeing. Is there any reason for that?*

J: One of the reasons for that is that I put a studio in my house. I used to drag those guys in when they were recording across the hall. Billy Idol is cast as the bully in "Dancin' Clown" because his voice was right, although it was viewed in England as a political and opportunistic move because he was big at the time and my stock was down. Which was so stupid. Even Prince called me up and said, "Who is that guy whooping and hollering all over your record?" And I said it was Billy Idol. "Oh, that's a good idea," he said.

B: *What do you consider the most neglected or underrated music of your career?*

J: I would say *Hejira. Court and Spark* was about as popular as it got, although with Asylum it got lost because Geffen had just signed Dylan for *Planet Waves.* Everything after that was compared unfavorably to it.

Hissing of Summer Lawns was felt to be too jazzy, and the drums on it were misunderstood. *Hejira* was not understood at all, but that was a really well-written album. Basically it was kinda kissed off. It's a traveling album; it was written driving from New York to Los Angeles over a period of time, and people who take it with them, especially if they're driving across America, really find it gets to them. Given the right setting, all of my albums have a certain power. I wouldn't recommend them for certain moods, I'd say, "Take this pill and stay away from that one!"

B: How do you feel about the countless female singer-songwriters you've influenced? You are sure the template for a certain kind of soprano-voiced siren, from Rickie Lee Jones to Stina Nordenstam.

J: I haven't heard them all, but the one show I heard where this DJ was likening them to me unfavorably, I couldn't see it. He'd say, "This girl has been listening to *Court and Spark*," and I could not see it. Harmonically there was no resemblance. I mean, I've had girls come up to me and say how influenced they are by me, and then they get up and play and they sound like the Indigo Girls!

B: Do you find it easier or harder writing songs these days? Do you still, as you once put it, have to be "hot on the trail"?

J: It's no easier or harder. It's still a matter of collecting the material and having the time. It will be difficult from here till next February because I'm in the harness promoting this record. Which is unfortunate because I've got ideas. Will they go up into the ether and get lost, or will they yet emerge? I don't know. That's the trouble with the process.

B: Do you ever regret not having had kids?

J: I think the children of artists are frequently malformed. You can't really do justice to both. My grandmothers both were frustrated musicians in different ways. My paternal grandmother came from Norway, and the story has it that the last time she cried in her life she was 14, and she was crying because she knew she would never have a piano. And she became a stoic. She had a miserable, nasty life. She had 11 kids and married a mean, poor drunk, but she never wept through all the hardship in all her adult life that anyone knows of.

My maternal grandmother, on the other hand, was a classical musician who came east when the Prairies opened up by train. She was Scottish-French, and they brought an organ in for her and a gramophone. She was a poet and musician, but she still kicked the kitchen door off its hinges out of her frustration at being trapped in the role of a housewife. So the creative gene then fell upon me, in a woman's form, and in a way you have to safeguard that and do it for them, because after 1965 it was really the first opportunity that women had had in history. There were the George Sands and Georgia O'Keefes who [plowed] against the grain. But even Georgia said to me, "Well, I would like to have been a painter and a musician, but you can't do both." I said, "Oh yes, you can!" In the end, I'm happier and better off with cats and godchildren. I have a lot of god-children.

B: *Twenty years after writing "People's Parties" [Court and Spark] are you still "living on nerves and feelings"?*

J: No. I still swing by them, but I don't live there.

BIRTHDAY SUITE

A tale of two impromtu performances—one by Joni, and another by two celebrities in her audience.—SFL

The New Yorker, December 11, 1995

One recent evening, Joni Mitchell, whose autobiographical lyrics and jazz-inflected acoustic guitar are largely responsible for folk music's staying power, celebrated her 52nd birthday with what she called "an informal open rehearsal" at Fez, the downtown watering hole. Mitchell's appearance was not announced in the press. Then hours before she had decided to perform, after a twelve-year absence from touring and just an hour after she informed Ellen Cavolina, who books the acts at Fez, of her decision ("I played for a group of seventy-year-old intellectuals at the Waldorf-Astoria last night; tonight I want to do something different," she said), word of Mitchell's impromptu concert spread throughout Manhattan. "When I heard she was performing, my whole *body* filled up with this. . . Joni feeling," Katerine Dieckmann, a *Village Voice* writer, said as she waited in line. "I almost passed out. Joni's been incredible for thirty years."

Of some two hundred fans who gathered in the dark, cavernous space where Mitchell was to perform, many were women, including the novelist Susan Minot; the Pretenders' lead singer, Chrissie Hynde; Carly Simon; and Natalie Merchant. Hynde, who was sitting in a banquette, raised her hands in the air as Mitchell made her way to the stage. "Let it out, Joni!" she shouted. Mitchell smiled, strapped a green guitar across her chest, and bowed.

She looked like any number of her photographs: long blond hair with bangs, long pallid face, equine mouth. On a stand to Mitchell's right, there was a vase filled with sunflowers, which evoked van Gogh, one of Mitchell's favorite painters; in fact, the cover of her latest album, *Turbulent Indigo*, executed in oil, is a self-portrait with a bandaged ear. "I have this little house in Canada," she told the audience, rubbing her right hand against her black-jeaned thigh. "And there's this man who looks after my land. He's a melody man. He hums all the time, like my grandmother did. He thinks Frank Sinatra is an amateur. He said to me, 'Joni, I know you're not sad like you are in your songs all the time. Write me something different.'" Mitchell smiled her muted Stan Laurel-like smile. "I sat on a rock and tried to tune my guitar to the sound of squawking birds near the sea. I tried to write a happy song, but it didn't turn out that way." Mitchell then began to sing "The Magdalene Laundries," which is about discrimination against single women in Ireland in the early part of this century.

During certain songs, Mitchell rocked her hips back and forth, in a modified version of the Elvis swivel. Between songs, the only sound besides Mitchell's voice and the audience's applause was Chrissie Hynde intermittently shouting, "Let it out, Joni!" When Carly Simon, who was seated in the booth beside Hynde's, asked her to stop, Hynde held Simon tightly around the neck, pointed to Mitchell, and stage-whispered, "That's a *real* singer up there."

"Why don't you have another drink, Chrissie?" a male member of the audience yelled to Hynde after Mitchell completed "Turbulent Indigo" and moments before Simon picked up her coat and left. Hynde ignored everyone except Joni Mitchell. She cheered, "Happy birthday, Joni!" Mitchell looked out into the audience and bowed again. The audience began singing "Happy Birthday." Looking pleased and embarrassed, Mitchell said, "The one good thing about this birthday thing is that I don't have to say I'm fifty-one and a half anymore." She paused and strummed a few chords on her guitar. "Maybe I've made it."

BY DANIEL LEVITIN

A CONVERSATION WITH JONI MITCHELL

Miles Davis is one of Joni Mitchell's earliest, most powerful, and most ever-present influences. This piece, an excerpt, gives surprising details found nowhere else—at least, nowhere I've seen—about the relationship between Joni Mitchell and Miles Davis.—SFL

Grammy Magazine, Spring 1996

Isles of Miles

GM: *You've recorded with some of the best jazz musicians in the world. I'll bet you would have loved to work with Miles [Davis].*

JM: Oh, yes, I would have loved to. I approached him many a time.

GM: *Was it because you are white?*

JM: I originally thought that, but that wasn't it. When Miles died we went to an art opening, his brother Eugene was there, his son and one of his wives, Shirley, a lot of people were there. And I said to his brother Eugene, "Miles would never play with me because I was white."

And Eugene said, "No, Joni, it wasn't *that*. It was because you are a singer. Miles would say (whispers, imitating Miles' voice), 'Singers! [contemptuously] They got *words* to do it with. I don't have words. I've got to do it without the words.'"

I said, oh God, if I'd known that when he was living I would have just stayed out. I would have approached him differently. I would have given him the bare track [without vocals on it] because, see, a lot of my taste in music comes from loving Miles. I tried everything. I bribed him, I was at his house one time . . .

GM: *His beachfront place in Malibu?*

JM: Yeah, he liked my painting and he'd seen this print that a mutual friend of ours had and he called me up (whispers) "Joni, I like that paint-

Singer Joni Mitchell at home in California, 1989. © Corbis/Neal Preston

ing that you did. Nice colors. I want to come over and watch you paint."
So he would talk painting but he wouldn't talk music with me. He never
would talk music.

GM: *So you knew him?*

JM: A little bit. I approached him on many occasions to play with me, see,
and he wouldn't play with me. When he died, his son inherited his record
collection, and he said to me, "Joni, did you give Dad all your records?"

I said "No, on a couple of occasions I gave him just a tape that I
wanted him to play on and an art print to bribe him, or something
(laughs) . . ."

He said, "Well, he had *all* your records. And at the end he moved
your print from the bathroom up to the side of his bed."

And I thought he must have just been getting ready to play with me
when he died.

I went to see him four days before he died, along with Wayne Shorter
and a whole group of us. He was playing at the Hollywood Bowl, and I
walked into the dressing room, and Miles had his hand on Wayne's shoul-
der and he was talking music to him.

This was unusual, because Miles never talked music; he ordinarily
didn't give a lot of instruction. After the show I asked Wayne what they
were talking about, and Wayne said that Miles was kind of passing the
baton to him. He must have known he was gonna die. . . .

GM: *A spiritual guy like that would know, I guess . . .*

JM: Yes, and he didn't even look sick that night; I didn't notice anything
about his energy that was failing or abnormal. But, anyway, he basically
told Wayne—as near as I can figure out because Wayne is a very cryptic
speaker sometimes—that he was one of the last giants left and that he was
undervalued and he shouldn't let people undervalue him. . . . He kind of
gave him a pep talk but there was more to it than that. I heard little bits
and pieces of it, but I really wanted to be a fly on the wall for that conversation (laughs).

Miles has always been one of my inspirations. My favorite band of
Miles is on the *Nefertiti* album with Ron Carter on bass, Wayne Shorter
on saxophone, Herbie Hancock on Fender Rhodes, and the 16-year-old
Tony Williams on drums. That's some of my favorite music in life! I've

played with all that band with the exception of Ron Carter. I basically got that band together for my *Mingus* album.

The song "Nefertiti" is unusual for a jazz piece; the structure of the arrangement is the simplest of folk song forms—verse, verse, verse, verse, verse—there's not really an "ABC" structure to it. Wayne and Miles are playing the melody in tight unison in the first verse. (Sings melody.) So you can hear, the melody begins with a note of inquiry and it ends with a note of inquiry, leaving it wonderfully unresolved. Then boom, it starts off again. With each module that they go through, Miles and Wayne shift slightly off sync with each other. So they're still playing the melody, but it's like a silk screen, it's like they . . .

GM: Timing-wise, rhythm-wise . . .

JM: They begin to phrase *individually*, more so with every take, while still playing the melody. It's an usual piece of music. The melody is so unusual in the first place and they begin to shadow each other—they even clash sometimes. And the bass as I recall is pretty much just anchoring, it's not doing anything too showy. Herbie is scattering colors in, little punctuations. As the song progresses, the drums become more and more and more expressive. When I hear that piece of music, it always evokes this image of late at night in New York City; some guy is coming up from Chinatown and he's pissed off and drunk and he's knocking over garbage cans and yelling, like, all the way up town (laughs). It's like that. There's an increasing kind of anger. It's a remarkable piece of drumming.

At the time that I first fell in love with Miles' music my music bore no resemblance to it. As I went along as a songwriter, it leaked more and more into the way that I would voice chords and so on, but not necessarily the way I would move them.

I don't think Miles ever became uninteresting, but I think that over time his bands became less interesting. It began to take him longer and longer on stage to find his inspiration because he was so pure . . . he'd stand there for half an hour until he heard a riff that he felt like playing.

So he'd stand there a long time waiting for something to feel, I think.

GM: With a less interesting band, it would be harder for him to pick up on something to play. . . .

JM: Mmm-hmm. Miles has been a big inspiration, but I never copied him. I picked up a lot about how to voice chords, but not necessarily how to move them. Miles' music is so full of space, but I know it's true that my stuff is choked with words. There's a favorite piece of Miles' from much earlier called "It Never Entered My Mind." At the end of the piece he draws a flat note. He goes out totally flat for I don't know how many bars. The power of that pitch for inducing melancholy is amazing.

GM: No words, just one note. Singularly among instrumentalists for me, I hear him talking to me when he's playing.

JM: Yes, that's exactly it! He is playing words with notes! We did a jam one time, Herbie and Wayne and a bunch of people. It was a medley of two of my songs, "Hejira" and "Furry Sings the Blues." And the band was so star-studded, so jam-packed and my words were taking up so much space, that I remember being disappointed when I first heard it and wishing we could have done a second take. Now we had two saxophonists, two drummers, two vocalists, me and Bobby McFerrin—it was like a Cecil B. DeMille production! And I felt there was no room for anybody to get in because my damn words were choking it. So here were two horn players and, well, with Bobby singing you have basically three horn players in this jam—where are they going to get in with all these words?

GM: Your songs do have a lot of words, but I don't see that as a negative; it's just a different style. Miles would play very spare lines most of the time, and Cannonball [Adderley] was the perfect foil for that. In vocal music, that "wordiness" is certainly a valid form: look at Lambert, Hendricks and Ross. Your lyric writing is something like Hendricks'.

JM: Oh, very much so. In high school I had *Lambert, Hendricks and Ross: The Hottest New Sound In Jazz.* I was very influenced by that; that was my Beatles. [Joni covered two of their songs, "Twisted" on *Court and Spark* and "Centerpiece" on *The Hissing of Summer Lawns.*]

Blue and Purple Rain

GM: From your first album in 1968 up through Hejira *in 1978, there's an optimism—an undercurrent of optimism in most of your songwriting—even the more serious and introspective songs. Since then, and starting with* Don Juan's Reckless Daughter, *the optimism seems to have been . . .*

JM: Eclipsed?

GM: *Yes. And around the same time the songs became less about your personal experience—there was less "I." Was this conscious?*

JM: Yes. I did make a conscious lyrical shift to "you," which is a device that [Bob] Dylan used for a lot of his autobiographical stuff, I suspect. That has a certain amount of self-protection built into it.

GM: *Were there experiences around the mid-'70s that caused you to put up a wall? To guard yourself more?*

JM: Well, I had no wall then, and I still really have no wall. But I was at my most defenseless during the making of *Blue*. Now, to be absolutely defenseless in this world is not a good thing. I guess you could say I broke down, but I continued to work. In the process of breaking down there are powers that come in, clairvoyancy and . . . everything becomes transparent. It's kind of an overwhelming situation, where more information is coming in, more truth than a person can handle.

So it was in the middle of all this that I wrote the *Blue* album. It is a very pure album; it's as pure as Charlie Parker. There aren't many things in music that pure. Charlie Parker played pure opera of his soul—especially the times that he was extremely sick. He had no defenses. And when you have no defenses the music becomes saintly and it can *communicate*. As one group of girls in a bar that accosted me put it (laughs), "Before Prozac, there was you," and especially that album. Somehow it had more power than an aspirin for the sufferer, and I think part of it is because it's extraordinarily emotionally honest; I had no defenses. But you cannot go around with no defenses, so defenses had to be built.

GM: *And one of them was this lyrical shift.*

JM: Yes. I tried with Dylan's device to switch from "I" to "you" on *Hissing of Summer Lawns*, but people didn't like it. In my case, the device failed because people said suddenly, "Why are you *pointing* at us?" In other words, with the "I" device—which wasn't a device, it was just a way I wrote—when I said "I" the listeners could see themselves in it if they wanted to, but they could always say "it's her" because of the "I."

GM: *It's safer for the listener . . .*

JM: It's safer for the listener. I have a friend who was raised on my music and I've been trying to get him into Dylan. But he doesn't like Dylan because he says Dylan is preaching at him, and that's the "you" device.

I still write a lot of personal songs. But *Blue* was, I gather, shockingly intimate for the time.

GM: *I'd say not just* Blue *but the two albums on either side of it, from* Clouds *up to* Hissing. *There was something not just in the songwriting but also in the vocal delivery that made a lot of people feel like you were singing just to them. They're sitting home in their room listening to your records and they feel a very intimate connection to you, like you're singing only to them.*

JM: Well, that's one of the tests for schizophrenia, isn't it? "Do you hear people speaking to you from the media?" (laughs)

Unfortunately, a lot of people holed up in their room, and, yes, they become obsessive because of that intimacy. Prince was one of those people (laughs), oddly enough, who holed up in his room with *Hissing of Summer Lawns* . . .

GM: *He heard you singing just to him?*

JM: Well I don't know about speaking *just* to him, but he became quite obsessive about *Hissing of Summer Lawns*.

GM: *How do you know this?*

JM: Because he told me.

GM: *How do you do that as a singer and as a writer? How do you get that sincerity?*

JM: Well, if it sounds sincere, it's because I have a really fine jive detector. I'll give you an example. Let's talk about [Charles] Mingus for a minute.

Okay, so Mingus gives me these six melodies and he flattered me by calling them Joni One, Joni Two, and so on. Of the six melodies, two stood out to me and the other ones sounded kind of idiomatic to me, and I couldn't really grab onto them. But the one that interested me the most was the first one that I wrote words to and it was called "Chair in the

Sky." I said, what do you want on this one? And he looked at me really wryly and he said (in a deep voice), "I want you to write about all the things I'm gonna miss when I'm gone."

GM: *Wow! That's a difficult assignment.*

JM: Well, I wrote it as best I could, and when I recorded it I recorded two takes. In take one, I had interpreted two notes toward the end—

GM: *Two of his notes, because he wrote the music—*

JM: Right, and I was sure he would rap my knuckles for that, so I recorded another take. Take one he loved—he wanted to send it to the moon in a capsule. The reason that take affected him in that way was because when I sang it, I sang it only to him. But when I sang take two, I was singing to a greater audience. And he could perceive the difference. I can perceive that difference.

GM: *In your own singing?*

JM: Absolutely. So in answer to your question, what I consider great singing is between the singer and God, not an audience necessarily, I mean there are exceptions, there are showy, fun songs that will accommodate a certain amount of winky-wink, nod-nod from the stage, but on these intimate things you almost have to sing with a method acting kind of way— you have to find your sincerity like an actor does. Like Meryl Streep. You have to sing from the heart.

GM: *Can you do that on stage?*

JM: I can do it. I can go into myself and find it there. I can do it anywhere unless I have a heckler; I'm real sensitive, I need a quiet house. Many a time I've had to stop and say, "Oh, come on, I can't do this if you're doing that, because it will throw me out of myself."

Poets Like Us

GM: *You said "Great singing is between the singer and God." Are you actually singing to God?*

JM: Well, it's something like that. I don't know. I don't really call in spirits or deities, or anything. I just quietly center myself; I sober myself.

I just know that this is a very mysterious place we're in, and I hardly ever use the word "God." As a matter of fact I asked Dylan one time, "What do you mean by 'God,' 'cause if you read the Bible, I can't tell God from the devil half the time! They seem to me to act very similarly."

And Dylan said, "Well, it's just a word that people use."

I said, "Yeah, but when *you* use it, what do *you* mean?"

And he never answered me.

GM: *Were you talking to Dylan during his Christian phase, his Orthodox Jewish phase, or . . .*

JM: Prior to all of it. Then, a couple of years later, when he went through his Christian period prior to his Judaic return, he came up to me and said, "Remember that time you asked me about God and the devil? Well, I'll tell you now." And he launched into this fundamentalist crap, and I said "Bobby, be careful. All of that was written by poets like *us*; but this interpretation of yours seems a little brainwashed."

"Poets like *us* . . ." he said. He kind of snickered at that.

But there certainly is a creative spark whether or not it has gender or personification. And I thought, when I write, I could go back over it and say, "Joni wrote that, Joni wrote that, ohhh, divine intervention, Joni wrote that, Joni wrote that . . ."

GM: *What's a line that was divine intervention?*

JM: Oddly enough, most of *Shadows and Light*, but I know that would seem like blasphemy to many.

GM: *It's some beautiful poetry, though.*

JM: Thank you. But philosophically it is a kind of secular humanism, if you're a fundamental Baptist or a Catholic: these are really dangerous thoughts. I am forbidden literature on a lot of church lists because I raise doubt, and because I'm opposed to blind faith.

GM: *"Blindness, blindness and sight. . . ."*

JM: I know the power of blind faith and it's a beautiful power. Don Juan in the [Carlos] Casteneda books has a beautiful, unifying line: I believe, not because I *care*, but because I *must*.

GM: *Do you have the self-awareness that you are one of the best at sincerity?*

JM: Yes, I do know that. I know because I can't hear it except in primitives, in primitive music.

GM: *You don't hear it in some other singers?*

JM: Not much pop music.

GM: *You don't hear it in Bob [Dylan]?*

JM: Well, I do hear it in Bob, absolutely. Bob can connect up to his stuff really sincerely. In that way he's a great singer. And then he puts his jive in where it belongs. Bob's a great singer.

Orchestral Maneuvers

GM: *How do you approach recording a new song? Do you make demos?*

JM: In a sense I never make demos because the demos are always incorporated into the final piece. It varies from project to project, but for many albums, I would lay down my voice and piano, or voice and guitar. That's my sketch. From that I know where the "height" has to come in, and where the "depth" has to come in. I imagine my cast of characters, my guest performers, and I add them last.

GM: *How much do you direct them?*

JM: It depends on the performer. Wayne Shorter is a great metaphorical thinker, and he composes from metaphor, as do I. So I can tell him things like "You're the bird!" He's a pictorial thinker. And he plays off lyrics well.

For the first eight albums or so I was directing bass players and annoying them to death with it. I wanted them to stop putting dark polka dots all over the bottom and instead to treat it like symphony. When you listen to a symphony, the bass is not always in, it gets light and airy for a while and then boom, it anchors again. And most bassists go plodding along there at the bottom like all pop music does. Finally, someone said "There's this bass player in Florida; he's really weird, you'd probably like him. . . ."

GM: *Jaco [Pastorius]!*

JM: Jaco. So Jaco was a natural for me; we were on the same wavelength as far as that went.

In later years, I got addicted to perfect time. I would build kind of a skeleton track of programmed drums . . . I'd set up the high hat pattern and set up the low end with Larry [Klein]'s help on the Fairlight. Then we'd play the part to a real drummer and have them play it, to loosen it up and put some grease on it. We did "Chalkmark in a Rain Storm" that way, for instance.

GM: *You talked about a recording verité. But there's a thing that I love in modern recordings, which is that you can create something that would never exist in the real world.*

JM: Yes.

GM: *You can put a pair of [mikes] on each end of a piano, and then pan them so that one [mike's] all the way to the right and the other's all the way to the left. Sitting at home in your living room with the speakers ten feet apart it sounds like the piano is ten feet wide!*

JM: I have a new guitar, and the way I have set the sounds up is the three bass strings go to the left speaker and the treble goes to the right. Now, I have always heard the treble as my "brass section," and if you listen to it closely it's just like this train . . . it's moving like a triad of muted trumpets because that's how I'm hearing it even though it's an acoustic instrument.

GM: *So suddenly the guitar sounds ten feet wide. . . .*

JM: It's an orchestra . . .

GM: *. . . And your head's in the middle of it.*

JM: Yeah—I like that. *Up on Old Beale Street.*

Joni Mitchell playing air guitar in her recording studio, 1989. © Corbis/Neal Preston

GM: *What has been your happiest moment in music?*

JM: When I wrote "Shadows and Light," which came out intact, verse by verse by verse with no rewrites; that was a thrill.

Also, when I wrote "Furry Sings the Blues." When the second verse came that was a thrill 'cause it all just poured out at once.

BY DANIEL LEVITIN

JONI MITCHELL

We think of Joni Mitchell as a singer, a songwriter, a musician, and, for those who know her better, as a painter. But she has another professional identity: producer. Joni is listed in Daniel Levitin's book, The Billboard Encyclopedia of Record Producers *(1999), as one of the top 500 record producers of the pop music era 1950–1997. Here is an excerpt from her entry in that book.—SFL*

The Billboard Encyclopedia of Record Producers (1999)

Joni Mitchell (b. Roberta Joan Anderson, 1943, Fort MacLeod, Canada).

Though known primarily as a singer and songwriter, Joni Mitchell has produced or co-produced nearly all of her recordings. The consistency of quality makes it clear that she has been far more than a nominal producer, and has been involved in shaping the overall sound, feel and presentation of her songs. *Blue* is the archetypal "confessional singer/songwriter" album, establishing a strong bond of intimacy between the performer and the listener that set the standard for dozens of artists who wanted to pour out their most private feelings to a mass audience. On a technical level, *Court and Spark* is one of the finest recordings of the last forty years, a musically and sonically ambitious opus that combines a variety of different textures on one album, and still—remarkably—expresses itself cohesively. If Mitchell's only production credit was for this album, she would be deserving of a place in the present volume. But 1975's *Hissing of Summer Lawns*, followed in 1978 by *Hejira*, her musical diary of a cross-country drive, brought a new sophistication to her work as a producer, with even more ambitious soundscapes and strongly image-filled moods.

Mitchell's early albums were inappropriately dubbed "folk" by reviewers unable to hear beyond the simple instrumentation to the more complex harmonic structure underneath. As Mitchell notes, "they just saw a girl with a guitar." For the aforementioned *Court and Spark* Mitchell brought in some of the best jazz musicians in Los Angeles, including Tom Scott and the L.A. Express, and brought lush arrangements to songs such as "Down to You" and "Car on the Hill." ("Car" featured such complex rhythms that notating its bridge has been used as a final exam question in theory classes at the Berklee College of Music.)

In the following years she worked with some of the best jazz musicians in the world, including Wayne Shorter, Herbie Hancock, Eddie Gomez, and Jaco Pastorius. Her explorations brought her into the jazz world at the cost of alienating many of her original fans. Yet the songs continued to grow musically and thematically, and the new players helped her to better fill out the harmonic complexities that were latent in the early albums, and had always been implied. Years of cigarette smoking have had a profound affect on her voice; Mitchell argues it has been for the better. *Night Ride Home* featured a darker, and at times more haunting-sounding Mitchell, far less likely to engage the pellucid and seraphic high register of her youth, preferring instead to explore the huskier timbres of her instrument. The title track featured a sequenced loop of crickets and other insect sounds that functioned as the rhythm track for the song.

BY BRIAN D. JOHNSON, WITH DANYLO HAWALESHKA AND DALE EISLER

JONI'S SECRET: MOTHER AND CHILD REUNION

The story finally became public: Joni has a daughter—and a grandson. The following article describes how Joni and Kilauren came to separate in 1965 and how they reunited in 1997.—SFL

MacLean's, April 21, 1997

It is all there, encoded in the song [Joni Mitchell's "Little Green," from her 1971 album, *Blue*]. A true story of secrets and lies. The child "born with the moon in Cancer" is the baby that Joni Mitchell gave up for adoption. She felt she had no choice. At 21, she was Joan Anderson, dirt poor and pregnant, an unknown folksinger in a Toronto rooming house. The girl was born on Feb. 19, 1965. The child's father, a Calgary artist named Brad MacMath, had, as the song says, disappeared "to California / hearing everything was warmer there." Joni balked at the prospect of being a single, destitute mother, and was not prepared to ask her parents back in Saskatchewan for help—they did not even know she was pregnant. She tried a desperate marriage of convenience, to a fellow folksinger named Chuck Mitchell, but it would soon collapse, leaving her nothing but a new surname. "Weary of lies," as Joni sings in "Little Green," she "signed all the papers in the family name," and sent her baby, Kelly Dale Anderson, into the unknown. Kelly, as in kelly green.

. . . Penned two decades before Mitchell's secret was finally exposed in a tabloid newspaper four years ago, "Little Green" was part private confession, part wishful prophecy. And the "happy ending" hoped for in the song had already begun to unfold. At the age of six months, Kelly—renamed Kilauren Gibb—found a home as the adopted daughter of two teachers, David and Ida Gibb, in the cozy Toronto suburb of Don Mills. Kilauren grew up in a world of private schools and country clubs and tropical vacations. She landed a career as a fashion model. . . .

But, as the song predicted, there was also sorrow. The mystery of Kilauren's adoption cast a lengthening shadow over her life. She says that her parents did not tell her she was adopted until she was 27 and pregnant with her own child. Kilauren then embarked on a frustrating five-year quest to track down her birth mother. Now 32, she is separated from the father of her son, Marlin, who is almost 4. And a "happy ending" quite different from the one envisioned in "Little Green" has come to pass. In the past few weeks, amid a blaze of media attention, mother and daughter have reunited, their high cheekbones, blue eyes and long blond hair framed side by side. "I've had pain and joy in my life, but nothing like this," Mitchell told a reporter in Los Angeles, where she has lived since 1968. "It's an unparalleled emotional feeling."

The story reads like a fairy tale. But the tale is beginning to show some tarnish. Mitchell, who is twice divorced, has not just gained a daughter, she has inherited an entire family, innocents who have found themselves in the spotlight at a time of tremendous emotional upheaval. Losing Kilauren to her birth mother "was our greatest fear," adoptive mother Ida Gibb told *Maclean's* last week. "It was a nightmare that this would happen to us when she was little and when she was a teenager. Now, it is easier to take. But it's still hard."

Kilauren, meanwhile, has had to cope with the excitement of finding her birth mother and becoming famous all at once. Hounded by reporters, she disconnected her phone last week and abandoned her apartment. Soon, she had handlers marketing her, selling interviews and juggling requests from the likes of Barbara Walters, Oprah Winfrey and Larry King. "You can't imagine the onslaught of press from all over the world," says Mitchell's Vancouver-based manager, Sam Feldman. "It's so bizarre. It's something out of a movie."

The Joni-Kilauren saga is a story that has become too good for its own good. Its appeal obviously goes beyond Mitchell's mellowing stardom. It is about seeing the destinies of the famous and the unknown thrown together in a lottery-like twist of fate. It is also a fable for the baby boom generation, one that suggests miracles can still be salvaged from the emotional losses of the Sixties. But above all it has played out as a very public adoption drama—and shed light on the dilemma faced by families whose adopted children seek out their biological parents.

What really complicates an already sensitive issue, however, is the fact that Kilauren Gibb's story has become a property. Swamped by interview requests, Gibb put Mitchell's manager in charge of her publicity. And she also had her boyfriend, an orthopedic parts salesman named Ted Barrington, act as a go-between. After several days of trying to set up an interview with Gibb last week, *Maclean's* finally received a call from Barrington, who said it could be arranged for $10,000. When told that *Maclean's* does not pay for interviews, he became impatient. "It's all business to me," he declared. "The money's for Kilauren. She doesn't have a pot to piss in. She's a student right now [living on student loans while studying desktop publishing at George Brown College in Toronto], and she should really be able to profit from this, at least monetarily."

But what about her newfound birth mother? "Joni's asset-rich but not cash-rich," replied Barrington. Kilauren is getting "quite anxiety-ridden. If you were in her position, and you were being hounded all day long, you'd say what the f———am I getting out of this, except a real bad headache." Then he added, before hanging up, "If you've got an offer, let us know. You have my pager number." Later, after talking to Feldman, Barrington phoned back to apologize. "I was out of line," he said, adding: "All the good stuff is at the back end with book deals and all that. I'm just worried about Kilauren being exploited. I'm just worried about my girl-friend."

Even Mitchell's octogenarian parents, Bill and Myrtle Anderson, have been swept up by the media blitz. "It's sort of a fairy-tale thing," Bill told *Maclean's* from his home in Saskatoon, "but some of the publicity isn't so entertaining as far as we're concerned. It's been hectic, especially for Myrt. The phone's been ringing off the wall." Myrtle and Bill both say they are happy to discover their granddaughter, and a great-grandson. "But I feel sorry for the adoptive parents," says Myrtle. "They do all the work and then suddenly they have a rival." Her husband concurs: "The parents who brought the child up deserve a lot of credit, and sometimes we feel they're being overlooked," he says. "I hope they don't lose her."

Kilauren's parents live on a quiet crescent in Don Mills, in the same grey-brick bungalow where they raised their children. They invite a visitor down to the basement, into a classic Fifties rec room with wood panelling and a red shag rug. Framed photographs of Kilauren and her older brother, David (now a 36-year-old Toronto advertising executive), cover the walls. Although David is not adopted, the siblings look remarkably matched, both blond and long-limbed. There are glamour shots from Kilauren's fashion portfolio. David, who dabbled in modelling himself, strikes a muscled pose in white underwear. There is also a picture of a beaming David, as captain of the football team at Upper Canada College, being introduced to Prince Philip. Kilauren was educated just down the road from U.C.C., at equally exclusive Bishop Strachan School.

More photographs, hundreds of them, in albums stacked on the rec room table, showing the children frolicking on beaches from Maine to Florida. A number of the pictures are inscribed with loving captions such as "my two chickadees," and they are all meticulously dated. "I would say we had a happier family life than average," says Ida. "We were very fortunate." Before retiring, she taught teenagers with learning disabilities and her husband taught at a teachers college and worked at the Ministry of Transportation. "When David was 3 1/2, we were doing very well, and we wanted to share it with someone," explains Ida. "Taking a child into your home seemed like a good way of doing it. We just phoned the agency, and what surprised us is how quickly it came through," recalls Ida, who had to drop out of a postgraduate course in education to take care of their new charge.

Ida seems puzzled by Kilauren's claim that she did not find out she was adopted until she was 27. "She knew when she was a teenager," she says. "Her friends told her. But maybe the full significance didn't sink in." Kilauren's father, meanwhile, says: "The mistake we made was in trying to say she's not adopted, that she's one of us and let's forget the whole thing and put it away somewhere, because we wanted her to be part of the family." Then he adds: "People are born. They are a life. They belong to nobody."

Kilauren's brother, David, expresses empathy for his parents. "There's a lot of fear there," he told *Maclean's*. "They're thinking, 'My gosh, are we going to lose her? Are we being replaced?' On top of that, you add the fame component. They're very modest, very quiet people, and all of a sudden there are people knocking on their door at seven in the morning wanting to take their picture. It's a lot to deal with. But it's all turned out better than you could have hoped for."

Ida is getting over her shock. "The thing is, Joni phoned me and we had a good chat," she says. "I found her to be quite a nice person, and that made all the difference in the world to me. She assured me that there weren't going to be any big changes, that nobody's going to lose anything."

Mitchell also put in a call to Kilauren's biological father. She had her first conversation with Brad MacMath in 32 years. "It was very weird," says MacMath, 56, who runs a Toronto photo studio with his wife. "But there was no animosity." Last week, MacMath also met his daughter for the first time. "I was elated," he says. "But it was very strange. We had fun noticing the mannerisms we have in common. We walk the same, have the same dimples, the same little knobs on our shoulders—surfer knobs."

In the excitement surrounding Kilauren's reunion with her birth mother, meeting her birth father almost seemed an afterthought. Trying to contact MacMath, Ted Barrington phoned Linda Miller, an old acquaintance from Don Mills—without realizing that she was MacMath's wife. "I'd photographed Ted's wedding five years ago," Miller laughed. "The marriage only lasted six months. So yesterday he phoned me up out of the blue, because I'm the only photographer he knew, and he said, 'Have you heard of this Brad MacMath guy?'"

That, as it turns out, is just one in a trail of bizarre coincidences linking Kilauren to her past—slim degrees of separation between Sixties abandon and the Nineties commitment.

Kilauren's biological parents were both art students in Calgary when she was conceived. They moved to Toronto during the pregnancy and discussed settling down. "Oh yeah," sighs MacMath, "we had to go through all that. But we were not communicating." He went back to Saskatchewan, then on to California. "I was trying to be an artist," he says, "and when she got married to some other guy, I just divorced myself from the whole situation. That was the last straw."

Mitchell, in a recent interview with the *Los Angeles Times*, says that her main concern at the time was to conceal her pregnancy from her parents. "The scandal was so intense," she recalls. "A daughter could do nothing more disgraceful. You have no idea what the stigma was. It was like you murdered somebody." Mitchell's mother, however, now says, "If we had known she was expecting a baby, we would have helped. I'm sure we would have encouraged her to keep the baby, but we didn't know anything about it until several years later when she and Chuck separated and she was home and told us about it."

Mitchell remembers giving birth in a Toronto hospital, where "one of the barbaric things they did was they bound the breasts of unwed mothers to keep the milk from coming," she says. Complications, she adds, kept her in the hospital for 10 days with her child. During the early years after the adoption, Mitchell told the *Times*, she "worried constantly" about the child's health because her pregnancy diet had been "atrocious." In an interview on CBC Newsworld's "Pamela Wallin Live"—broadcast, by coincidence, on Feb. 19, 1996, Kilauren's 31st birthday—the singer explained that she had no recourse but adoption. "I didn't have a penny," she said. "I had no money for diapers, or a room to take her to. There was no career on the horizon. Three years later, I had a recording contract and a house and a car, but how could I see that in the future?"

In 1968, Mitchell's career began to take off. She won a Grammy for her album *Clouds*, and singer Judy Collins turned one of its songs, "Both Sides Now," into a hit. Another cut, "Chelsea Morning," would later inspire Bill and Hillary Clinton in naming their daughter. In 1970, Mitchell released *Ladies of the Canyon*, which featured such classic songs as "Big Yellow Taxi," "Woodstock" and "The Circle Game." The same year, she recorded *Blue*, an intimate excursion into loneliness and loss, which many consider her masterpiece.

Although Mitchell kept her secret from her parents for several years, and from the media for almost three decades, those close to her knew. "It was very much part of her life," singer Murray McLaughlan told *Maclean's*. "I think she was always looking for the child." Another friend, Toronto music manager Bernie Fiedler, remembers being with her at the Mariposa Folk Festival about four years after Kilauren's birth. "There was a couple with a little girl wanting to speak to Joni. We went over and talked to the girl, who must have been 4 or 5, and afterwards Joni turned to me and said: 'That could be my daughter.' I will never forget that. She was obviously suffering tremendously."

Over the years, Mitchell made some quiet attempts to track down her daughter, without success. But while promoting her album *Turbulent Indigo* (1994), she fielded questions about a tabloid report of a "love child," and took her search public for the first time.

Kilauren, meanwhile, was already looking for her mother. She says it took nearly five years for the Children's Aid Society to produce the adoption documents that she requested. Even then, the papers offered non-identifying information, just dates and some telling biographical details. A Joni Mitchell fan could have matched the profile to the singer without much trouble. But what finally led Kilauren to identify her birth mother was a tangled thread of coincidence winding all the way back to the birth of the Sixties counterculture.

The maze of events begins with Duke Redbird. Now a Toronto CITY TV entertainment reporter, in 1964 he was writing and reading poetry at folk festivals. Redbird moved into a Victorian rooming house on Huron Street, and Mitchell, already pregnant, moved in across the hall. Most of the boarders were broke. "It was a very sad and lonely time for her," Redbird says. "I remember Joni being a very private person. I would hear her singing in that beautiful voice of hers, strumming her guitar behind the closed door of her room."

One day, Redbird's brother, John (now deceased), came by and gave Mitchell a couple of apples, a gesture that she never forgot. Years later, she met Redbird at a concert and asked him to convey her thanks to his brother.

Cut to 1988. Redbird meets Annie Mandlsohn while both are studying at York University. "Never tell this to anybody," he told her, "but I lived in the same house as Joni Mitchell; she had a baby and nobody knows." Late last year, Mandlsohn's current boyfriend, Tim Campbell, introduced her to Kilauren Gibb—Campbell, Gibb and Barrington had all grown up together in Don Mills. Gibb showed Mandlsohn the Children's Aid information describing her mother as a Saskatchewan folksinger who had moved to the United States. "That was the key," says Mandlsohn. "I said, 'Kilauren! Your mother is Joni Mitchell!'"

Gibb was stunned. Mandlsohn sent Gibb to Redbird. "I said, 'Kilauren, you've got to go down and see Duke Redbird and ask him one question: what was the season that she was pregnant?' If it was winter, it's bingo." Gibb met Redbird in early March. "When I talked to Kilauren, she was hesitant," Redbird says. "She had suspicions, but I mean it's like you and I having suspicions that Donald Trump was our father." Gibb also looked up a Joni Mitchell home page on the Internet and was struck by details matching her Children's Aid information. Finally, she phoned the singer's manager, whose office had been flooded with calls from would-be Joni offspring. She could not get through, but she sent off a package of information, including her birth date—and the fact that she had been named Kelly Dale. Before long, Gibb and her son were on a plane to Los Angeles, where they spent 19 days getting acquainted with the singer in her $9 million mansion.

In the Coloured Stone, a club that Redbird co-owns, he found a note pinned to the bulletin board. "Hi Duke, it's Kilauren," the note read. "I wanted to see you today because I'm on my way to L.A. on March 13 to visit Joni. She remembers you and your brother and your kindness during her time of need. She couldn't believe that I had met you. She is my mother and she has sent me and my son tickets to visit her. Sorry I missed you and I will try again soon. Thanks for being so kind. Love Kilauren Gibb."

Born of coffeehouse romance and California dreaming, raised in the suburban conformity of a model family, Kilauren has come full circle. Adopted by show business, she is now entering a new circle game, a world where there are few secrets and too many lies.

BY JODY DENBERG

TAMING JONI MITCHELL—
JONI'S JAZZ

Joni talks with Jody Denberg about the music biz, her daughter, her 1998 album Taming the Tiger, *and the recent honors that have been heaped upon her.—SFL*

Austin Chronicle, October 12, 1998

Joni Mitchell recently read in a book of birthdays that she was born on the day of the discoverer in the week of depth, and her more than 30 years' worth of songs and paintings certainly prove the astrologers right. During an hour-long interview conducted last month at Los Angeles' plush Bel Air Hotel for a promotional compact disc, Mitchell, who turns 55 November 7, seemed eager to not only express her triumphs and frustrations, but also to learn about herself in the process.

Though she smokes one cigarette after another and her voice maintains its native Canadian lilt, Mitchell's glowing face still appears quintessentially Californian as she recounts the endless litigation she endured during the Eighties (related to tax woes and battles with her bank and business manager). The last decade has also found the iconic singer-songwriter's albums critically and commercially underappreciated. More troubling, perhaps, is Mitchell's faltering health, due in part to five years of "dental hell" coupled with post-polio syndrome—the fallout from a childhood bout with polio that made it difficult for her to even hold a guitar.

Mercifully, Mitchell's life in the Nineties has moved her to write in a new song that "happiness is the best face lift." Having abandoned Western medicine for a "Chinese mystic acupuncturist," Mitchell now feels fine, and a wafer-thin guitar has made it easier for her to hold the instrument. A slew of accolades came in the wake of her last album of new material, 1994's *Turbulent Indigo*: induction into the Rock and Roll Hall of Fame, two Grammys, *Billboard*'s 1995 Century Award, and the National Academy of Songwriters' 1996 Lifetime Achievement Award. Two career compilations followed (*Hits* and *Misses*), and when Mitchell was finally

Joni Mitchell playing guitar in her home in Bel Air, 1989. © Corbis/Neal Preston

reunited with the daughter she gave up for adoption at birth—and found out that she was a grandmother to boot—her physical, emotional, and artistic facelift was complete.

Now comes Mitchell's new album, *Taming the Tiger*, brimming with the first-person revelations her longtime fans crave and chock-full of the melodies her critics claim are absent from much of her later work. Yet *Tiger* is not a compromised capitulation; in fact, Wayne Shorter's sax playing is in the tradition of his work with Weather Report and Miles Davis, while the disc's opening track echoes Duke Ellington and Cab Calloway. "Harlem" starts the album as if it were an invitation to a big bash, and Mitchell agrees.

"Oh, I was a dancer in my teens and kind of a party animal," she explains. "I think it was a shock to my friends when, suddenly, I bought a guitar, introverted, and began thinking somewhat deeply.

"After all," she laughs, "I was a blonde!"

The Austin Chronicle: It was four years ago that you released your last album of new studio material. It not only won a couple of Grammys, but there were honors coming at you from every direction. Did you anticipate the higher profile and recognition that followed Turbulent Indigo?

Joni Mitchell: No, no. One would never anticipate this. I was fed up and I put a black joke on the cover, a van Gogh with his ear cut off, because I was that frustrated. So I kind of cut my ear off in effigy. And I don't know whether people got it or whether it was [a] catalyst to change, but things did begin to change. I felt that I had been doing good work for 20 years and that it was not being recognized at all. Of course, it was by my fans. I have a loyal body of people that look forward to the next album in the same way, I suppose, that I look forward to [Carlos] Castaneda's next book.

AC: Did you feel vindicated by the accolades?

JM: Yes and no. I mean, the reviews of this last concert tour, for instance, were very schizophrenic. The laments for the lack of early material in this last performance were accompanied by some strange statements. For 25 years, the public voice—in particular the white press, let's say—lamented the lack of four-on-the-floor and major/minor harmony as my work got more progressive and absorbed more black culture, which is inevitable because I love black music, Duke Ellington, Miles Davis.

Not that I set out to be a jazzer or that I am a jazzer. Most of my friends are in the jazz camp. I know more people in that community, and I know the lyrics to Forties and Fifties standards, whereas I don't really know Sixties and Seventies pop music. So I'm drawing from a resource of American music that's very black-influenced with this little pocket of Irish and English ballads, which I learned as I was learning to play the guitar. Basically, it was like trainer wheels for me, that music. But people want to keep me in my trainer wheels, whereas my passion lies in Duke Ellington more so than Gershwin—with originators like Charlie Parker. I like Patsy Cline. The originals in every camp were always given a hard time.

Believe me, I get my strokes on the street, but I don't generally in the press. The press has a tendency to listen to it, not like it, and then it appears at the end of the year in their top ten list. But they kill it for sales somehow or another with their expectation for it to be something else.

AC: *What about your latest batch of songs on* Taming the Tiger? *Did these songs come from a specific period or were they written following the last album?*

JM: Well, I've been struggling to write since the last record came out. And it's four years, but I turned this in quite a while ago. And I did *Hits* and *Misses*, which took a lot of research; I had to listen to everything I ever did in the middle. There was a lot of thought that went into that, also.

And then all these honors came. Well, the honors kind of fell short. It seemed like it was kind of a copycat crime, that once one was given to me, the others felt the necessity to do it, but they didn't really know why. And once the honors had kind of passed, we went back into this thing, "Your later work isn't as good as your older work," which isn't true. There's been a tremendous amount of growth.

Besides, an actress is not expected to continue to play her ingenue roles. I've written roles for myself to grow into gracefully, but there is no growing gracefully in the pop world, unfortunately, because of the airwaves—everybody is in the same bind. You know this. We're all in this same bind. Since the record business went public and the men at the top want the graph to go up and nothing else, everybody's getting the squash, including the record company executives. From the top of the business down, we're all in the same boat, so I'm not just a whiny artist. The business is sick.

And for the genuinely gifted, such as myself, being shunned from the airwaves in favor of tits-and-ass bubble gum kind of junk food is a tragedy. And there is no other arena for me to make music in. So I feel constantly in a position of injustice. There's a civil liberties thing here. Is it my chronological age? That should never be held against an artist. We're all going to grow middle-aged. We need middle-aged songs. I'm an unusual thing. I'm a viable voice. For some reason, even though I want to quit all the time, you know, I still have a driving wheel to do this thing.

AC: Sometimes, in interviews, you seem a little put out by those female singer-songwriters who claim you as an influence. Do you feel like you compete with them in the pop arena?

JM: Well, no. I'm forced to compete by the interview system. I have no problem. I'm honored to be an influence. I think art should beget art and spark it. And I'm always looking for something to spark me. But I'm less likely to be influenced by a tributary of myself. I mean, you can learn from students from time to time, but what I resent, in a nutshell—and this has been done to me—is to be pitted against them intentionally and be told I'm not as good.

Like, there was a radio show, for instance, that was done a while ago that somebody gave me thinking I'd be honored. It was a lot of the new women coming up. And the interviewer began by saying, "There are a lot of women coming onto the scene these days, all of them claiming Joni Mitchell as an influence. You can even tell what albums they've been listening to. Take this one." And they would play it. "She's been listening to *Court and Spark*." And they'd play the record. The harmony the girl was using was very primary colors. I thought, "How can you say she's been listening to *Court and Spark*? It's an insult to *Court and Spark*, because this is so rudimentary."

One thing that I do get tired of is all the "Women of Rock" articles, you know, always lumping me in with the women, which the white press does and the black press doesn't. The black press recently, in *Vibe* magazine, had an article where they singled out Miles Davis, Santana, and myself, and said, "All you kids with your tight little abs and your two hits, take a look at these guys." I feel that that is a more accurate museum grouping for me. And genderization is a form of bigotry and (a result of journalists) not really hearing what I'm doing.

AC: There's a line in the title track from your new album wherein you describe some popular music as "genuine junk food for juveniles." Hasn't pop music like that always existed?

JM: Yeah, it has. But the difference has been radio. In Toronto—or rather, when I lived in New York—I was on the road most of the time playing little clubs. And when I had time off and came back to New York, I would run into the house and I would turn on the radio and disc jockeys back then were creative. If it was raining, and the disc jockey was an audiophile who had been hired for his talent and his scope, he could play a rain piece by Charlie Parker. If his scope embraced some bubble gum, he could follow it up with that, so that you could have an afternoon of rain montage all over the place. I just don't like the segregation that has occurred for the sake of commerce in music. I don't like being told that this album doesn't fit any format, that music of this caliber doesn't fit into a format. I will not pander to a format. Does that mean I never get on the airwaves? If music of this caliber is being made, don't you think it's kind of a crime that it has no outlet that will accept it?

AC: *You painted a beautiful self-portrait for the cover of* Taming the Tiger. *And on this new album there's a couple of songs that share qualities with your artwork: "Harlem in Havana" and "Love Puts on a New Face," in particular. Sometimes they're austere, other times they're bright and bursting with color and imagery. Does painting offer you similar rewards as making music?*

JM: Well, I'm a painter first and a musician second, as it turns out. I had impulses to create classical music when I was seven or eight, but I had my love of it taken away by raps on the knuckles from my piano teacher saying, "Why would you want to play by ear when you could have the masters under your fingertips?" So the impulse to compose in the community that I grew up in was thwarted, and it didn't come out for quite a while later. I switched to the guitar with no ambition to be in show business. As a matter of fact, as a teenager, I felt sorry for the stars for their loss of privacy, and I wrote a poem about it in high school. So I'm an odd candidate for celebrity in that I didn't practice in front of the mirror and I'm not addicted to applause. But I have a painter's ego and I get a thrill of juxtaposing one color against another. I get, like, a private rush. I'm an only child. It's a form of solitary play. If I put that color next to that color and add another color, you know, I get a buzz.

It's the same with music. I don't have any of the musician's languages. I read as a child, but I let the reading ability go. I don't use it in the recording process, because I fiddle around with the guitar so much that I'm not playing it normally anyway; the numerical language that some musicians have doesn't mean anything within my system, nor does the alphabetical system. I don't know what key I'm playing in. So I'm a sophisticated ignorant is basically what I am. But there are people who can come in, listen to what I play, write it out, and follow it. My harmony is selected by my own interest in the same way that I would select to put that color next to that color. I think of myself as a painter who writes music.

AC: *You use color in your paintings in a unique way, and you play unusual guitar tunings in your songs. How did your tunings develop? Were you just looking for different ways to do things, rather than just playing the standard major chords?*

JM: Well, I wrote my first song, "Urge for Going," in standard tuning, and I guess it's because of the stars; in the folk houses, the chords that everybody played sounded the same, while the chords that I heard in my head you couldn't get off the neck, even with tremendous facility. The chords that I play, if you don't twiddle the strings, you don't get them. I've made the guitar kind of orchestral. It's down into the territory of the bass in some cases. And the chords are very, very wide relative to what guitar chords usually are. You couldn't get that without the tunings.

And there are traditions of tunings. The Hawaiians, for instance, played in slack key and they were usually major chords. The old blues guys tuned in banjo tuning, which is open G tuning, which is what Keith Richards plays in. He doesn't even play the sixth string on the guitar. He plays the guitar like a five-string banjo. So, most of the old blues men, coming from banjo to guitar, not knowing anything about Spanish tuning, tuned the guitar into open G, D modal, which is just a dropped D. These tunings were kicking around the coffeehouses. There were about three of them. It was Eric Andersen that turned me onto them one night in Detroit. Well, soon they seemed to be explored and I didn't seem to be able to get any fresh colors out of them. So then I started tuning the guitar to chords that I heard in my head. And that's the way it went.

AC: *You've said, "My chords reflect my complex life, which is why my simple, old songs don't suit me." When you hear one of your older songs, do you ever feel like rediscovering them?*

JM: First of all, my voice has changed. Secondly, the way I played guitar back then is completely foreign to me. I have no idea how I did it. It's how

I did it then. It's like, as a painter, if you ask Picasso to go back and paint in an early period of his, I doubt that he could. You're moving forward and it's always evolving. Basically, the reason I'm so unruly in this business is because I think like a painter, not like a musician. And I never wanted to be a human jukebox. I think more like a film or a dramatic actress and a playwright. These plays are more suitable to me. I feel miscast in my early songs. They're ingenue roles.

AC: *Maybe Bob Dylan, Van Morrison, and Neil Young don't think like painters, because they seem to have no problem playing their earlier songs . . .*

JM: But their styles didn't change as radically as mine over time either. It's not that difficult for them to go back. They haven't changed as much.

AC: *You had a chance recently to reassess your work when you issued the* Hits *and* Misses *compilations. Did you feel like* Misses *was a way for folks to catch up with you if they hadn't been around for the whole ride or to expose people to your more difficult pieces.*

JM: It's hard to say what my reasoning was in the selection there, because most of my work was technically misses. I mean, the *Hits* is padded. I didn't really have enough hits to make a real "hits" album, really, by the *Hit Parade* measure. But like "Circle Game," which was never on the *Hit Parade*, was distributed through summer camps all across the North American continent and was a hit. It was like "Old MacDonald." The same with "Big Yellow Taxi."

I turned on the TV one day and I saw a woman holding an alligator. So I stopped. And there were a lot of New York inner-city kids around her. Turned out it was coming from the Bronx Zoo. And she said, "This is Harvey; do you want to pet him?" And all these little grade-three kids got up. And then she held up a skin, you know. And she said, "And this is Harvey's brother; look what they did to him." And they went, "Oh." And then she said, "Let's sing a song." She picked up a guitar and she sang "Big Yellow Taxi." And this little rainbow of kids, little yellow kids and white kids and black kids and brown kids started singing my song, in grade three. And they knew all of the words. And I wept.

AC: *On your most recent tour, you did play "Big Yellow Taxi" and "Woodstock." Did you feel that those were older songs of yours that still held something for you?*

Judy Collins and Joni Mitchell backstage at the Troubadours of Folk Festival, 1993. ©
Corbis/Henry Diltz

JM: "Woodstock," oddly enough, because it should be kind of a curio about an event, still has a life for me. And "Big Yellow Taxi" is just kind of cute. It's a ditty.

AC: *I wanted to ask you about some of the recent projects that you've been doing. The tour you did with Bob Dylan and Van Morrison, was it a good experience?*

JM: Yeah, well, I think it was a great triple bill. And I took it on that account. I hadn't performed in a long time and I thought, oh, that's a good show. But I had a little bad luck. Right out of the chute, I got a virus. Then, we bussed out of Vancouver to the Gorge, and the bus had new carpet with glue, and the glue was really stinky. We burnt patchouli like old hippies to kind of mask it. Also, I'm allergic to air conditioning. To make a long story short, by the time I got to the Gorge, I was really sick and the roof of my mouth was red and my throat was like hamburger. And they sent me a doctor who gave me really extraordinarily violent medicine. And, I played the two Gorge dates very ill, like delirious, but happy. I was enjoying it, but I was delirious, literally.

So I did the whole tour, really, from behind the wheel in terms of stamina. The San Jose show, in particular, I was afraid to hit a high note. It takes a lot more air to hit a high note. And every time I went to hit a high note, I'd go all pins and needles and start to black out. So I had to kind of jockey things around. And I apologized, I believe, although I don't even remember that show. I said something, but I don't know what it was. The press picked up on it and assumed it was that I was rusty from not having been out for a long time. But I was just really ill.

AC: *I was surprised that there was no collaboration between the three artists on the bill.*

JM: Well, Bobby keeps to himself. Van came to me at one point and said, "Have you spoken to Bobby yet?" And I said, "Yeah, I saw him after the Vancouver show." "Well, he hasn't spoken to me," he said. And I said, "Well, come on, let's crash his set." So there was a song in Japan that closed the show. Bob and I were in Tokyo, and he kind of short-sheeted me on stage. He pulled a number on me. So I said, "Well, we'll go out on this song of his and we'll get him." So we went out and kind of crashed the set the one night. And Bob got a big kick out of it. It was really rough and I blew the words on it and blew the rhyme and had to make one up.

And Bobby was looking at me grinning, "What is she going to rhyme with it," because I got the first rhyming line wrong.

AC: What song was it?

JM: "I Shall Be Released."

AC: You did the Walden Woods benefit in April. You sang "Stormy Weather" backed by an orchestra. Would you ever do an album of cover songs?

JM: That's what I want to do. Rather than tour this album, because I'm so far behind, because they're taking so long to release it, I want to go straight into the studio and record in that genre. As a singer, if you separate all these things, just forget Joni the writer, because I write these kinds of soliloquies which take more dramatic skills than vocal skills. There's no room to put a trill in. You've so many syllables to deal with. And you have to enact them, like an actress, as opposed to just singing a mood piece. So I need a break from my own music. And to disappear into standards would be a treat. I did two standards with Herbie [Hancock] and Wayne [Shorter] and Stevie Wonder on Herbie Hancock's album, which is coming out: "The Man I Love" and "Summertime." And my band and I now, since Woodstock, have an arrangement of "Summertime" that I think is really fresh. And I saw four chins quivering in the audience at Woodstock to that old chestnut. So I know it has a power.

AC: You didn't play the original festival. Was this summer's "A Day in the Garden" concert in Woodstock a good experience for you?

JM: Oh, it was beautiful. It was beautiful. It was a beautiful audience. They loved my band. After some of the prejudice against [my music for being] too jazzy—all that the West Coast press tends to levy against me—the East Coast doesn't so much. And there was a banner in the audience about eight foot long that said, "Joni's Jazz" and all these smiling heads above it. When I hit the stage, I thought, "Oh, good." And they applauded my band genuinely and enthusiastically every time a color entered and left, because, I mean, we took a big leap in growth, I think. It felt like the band was that much more solid. Well, I was well, for one thing. And we added [Mark] Isham and the addition of muted trumpet, which is a color that I love. It seemed to flesh everything out. And the audience was wonderful.

AC: *Recently you put out a beautiful book of your lyrics [Joni Mitchell—* The Complete Poems and Lyrics, *Crown Publishers, NY, 1997]. And I had read at that time that you might do a short story book or an autobiography.*

JM: I'm contracted for an autobiography. But you can't get my life into one book. So I want to start, actually, kind of in the middle—the *Don Juan's Reckless Daughter* period, which is a very mystical period of my life and colorful. If I was a novelist, I would like that to be my first novel. And it begins with the line, "I was the only black man at the party." So I've got my opening line.

AC: *Finally, Joni, there's a poignant song on your new album called "Stay in Touch." Last year you reunited with your daughter, who you gave up for adoption after she was born. Was that song written about your daughter?*

JM: When [they] came [to visit], Kilauren's boyfriend heard the song and said, "Kilauren, this is about you." And it is. It's about the beginnings of love, conducting yourself through it wisely. I don't think there's another song like it in existence. How foolish we all are when we're smitten. It applies. It wasn't the catalyst for it. Kilauren came in the middle of the project, and one of the reasons why there was a delay in finishing it, was because, well, we just had to spend a lot of time with each other. So we'd spend three weeks and then I'd go back in the studio and then I'd go up there and we'd spend some more time and then I'd go back in the studio. But it applies to any new, terrific attraction. It's basically how to steer yourself through that smitten period.

AC: *When you met your daughter after so many years, did you see any of your qualities in her?*

JM: Oh, well, when we first met, we walked into the kitchen. They arrived and I was upstairs and I was glazing the cover painting. I was varnishing it. So I walked out on the balcony of the house with brushes in my hand and I saw her kind of in the dark. And I ran downstairs. We went into the kitchen and we looked at each other and we said [giggles], "Hmm, hmm," exactly at the same time and in the same tone. And our speaking voices are almost identical. And in the first few weeks, well, even now, we say exactly the same thing with the same inflection, like at the same time, which people do sometimes when they're in the beginning of relationships—there's a lot of kind of psychic things. It's terrific. And we've had a couple of little skirmishes. And we're getting to know each other and it's just terrific [laughs]. And I love my grandson, and [she lets out the last word like a sigh] yeah. . . .

BY NEIL STRAUSS

THE HISSING OF A LIVING LEGEND

A glimpse into Joni's life, albeit from a dark perspective, in 1998. For a jolt, compare this point of view to the New York Times *portrayal of her in 1969, reprinted in Part One. —SFL*

The New York Times Magazine, October 4, 1998

At 54, Joni Mitchell has suddenly found herself in possession of a daughter, a grandson and a desire to write light songs. Yet she compares herself to Mozart, hates popular music and has nothing but contempt for the whole notion of the Lilith Fair.

Slices of afternoon sun cut through the blinds of a darkened second-floor room in the Hollywood Athletic Club as Joni Mitchell, cigarette hanging limply from her thick lips, bends over a pool table and meticulously lines up a shot to sink the solid yellow ball.

"You're stripes," one of her pool partners yells.

"Oh," she exclaims and switches angles. She is distracted. There is too much going on. Present in the room are a mixture of friends and family members. Her friends are all men, mostly younger, outdoor, athletic types. Her family members, by contrast, are more cerebral and artistic. Her daughter, Kilauren Gibb, whom she met for the first time a year and a half ago after giving her up for adoption in 1965, is a model (as her mother once was) whose real wish was always to be on the other side of the camera (like her biological father, a Toronto photographer). Now she takes pictures of her 5-year-old son, Marlon, who seems like a model and actor in the making.

"Pretend like you're excited," Paul Starr, Mitchell's close friend and makeup artist, tells the blond tyke as he widens his mouth and eyes adorably. Paul mimes snapping a photo.

"Now pretend like Joni's going away," he says. Marlon pauses for a moment, and then pulls a forlorn, drooping face. A faux photo is snapped again.

"That was hard," Marlon says. "I couldn't imagine why Joni would be going away." Suddenly, at 54, Mitchell has settled down. In the last two years, she has become a mother and grandmother simultaneously. Seeing the family together, one would never know that she, her daughter and grandson had ever been apart. Some musicians feel that they must sacrifice the joy of raising a family because of their commitment to their work. Mitchell always seemed like this type of artist, but now she seems to be relishing her new role. For someone whose art and life have always been intertwined, this development is bound to have implications for her music.

"The coming of the kids hasn't come out in my art yet," she says, referring to her latest projects —a new album, *Taming the Tiger*, a television special and a book of poetry. But she has recorded music with Herbie Hancock and Wayne Shorter and "they're convinced," she said, "they can hear my family in my tone. It has a more full-bodied femininity."

That's just the beginning of the new, complete, ever-changing Joni, one of the most influential and immodest songwriters of the last 30 years. Since inheriting her new family, Mitchell has suddenly become acquainted with pop culture. She watches "Taxi" reruns, reads kids' books to her grandson, spends more time shooting pool and hanging out with her family and has rediscovered Disney movies.

"I used to be monastic, almost," she explains with a touch of wistfulness. "Now I'm like a Tibetan that has discovered hamburgers and television. I'm catching up on Americana."

Disney, in many ways, is responsible for Mitchell's career. Watching *Bambi* as a child in Saskatchewan, she says, made an artist out of her, inspiring her to pick up crayons and draw forest fires, which led to art school, which led to an unwanted pregnancy (with Kilauren) that forced her to drop out and take up music in Canada's folk clubs.

Between pool shots, Mitchell, wearing a loose-knit sweater and jeans, speaks words that fans of more complex albums like *Hejira* and *Don Juan's Reckless Daughter* thought they'd never hear: "I don't like to make fluffy little songs, but now I want to make some light songs," she says. "I think that comes from watching a lot of comedy. People will probably not enjoy it as much as the deep suffering that I've done in the past. And I don't even know if I can do it."

When it comes to her music, Mitchell can be humorless. People describe her as "bitter" and a "loose cannon," and those are her friends. Over the course of three days of conversations, Mitchell will compare herself to Mozart, Blake and Picasso; she will say that the lyrics to one of her songs "have a lot of symbolic depth, like the Bible" and describe her music as so new it needs its own genre name. In discussing her autobiography in the works, she will explain that there is no way to fit her life into one volume. She needs to do it in four. (She already knows the first line: "I was the only black man at the party"; colleagues say she sometimes feels "like a black man in a white woman's body.")

Mitchell is not a forgetful woman. Like Santa Claus, she remembers who's been naughty and who's been nice. Speaking of a *New York Times* profile written in 1996, she recalls that there were "seven errors of observation in the piece." On the nice side, she let Janet Jackson sample her song "Big Yellow Taxi" for the hook of "Got Til It's Gone" because Jackson had once spoken favorably of Mitchell's album *Chalk Mark in a Rain Storm*. And she distinctly remembers being excited by seeing the chins of four people of different ages quiver during her performance of "Summertime" this summer on the original Woodstock site.

"You think I got a trap mind or something?" Mitchell asks when I make the Santa Claus comparison. "I guess I do."

Howie Klein, the president of Reprise, her recording label, says it can be a challenge working for Mitchell. "She distinctly feels her music belongs on black radio," he says. "Sometimes I get the feeling that she thinks I'm keeping it off black radio. We may not see eye to eye on every detail, but I have so much respect for her that I'm willing to subsume my own way of thinking to hers."

Yet even as she lives up to the stereotype of the difficult artist, Mitchell is "a good-time Charlie," as she puts it, in her private life. This is evident in her friends' comments about her as well as in the good-natured way she loses her pool games. Though Mitchell's most-loved work is her most melancholy (particularly her introspective *Blue* album), her music, and particularly her newest album, is also filled with joy. "I'm not a pitiable creature," she says. "It's just that I suffer very eloquently."

Taming the Tiger is a beautifully sung jazz, rock and classical fusion album, neatly extending Mitchell's body of work. In the tradition of *The Hissing of Summer Lawns* and *Hejira*, it is a self-produced, meticulous album that incorporates jazz musicians and harmonies, but stands on its own as a complete composition. Like her more recent *Night Ride Home*, the overall sound is sparse, reverberation-drenched, highbrow and contemporary. The album is simultaneously beautiful and frustrating, with moments of pitch-perfect poignance as well as moments of overwrought mood music that makes you wish that Mitchell would be more open to outside input while recording. When I dare make a comparison to New Age, she bristles, "It's composed music."

After 19 albums, many of which have been heavily criticized upon their release only to be hailed as classics years later, Mitchell is upset by the album's mixed reviews. She blames Charles Mingus, the seminal jazz bassist, and her 1979 collaboration with him, *Mingus*, which succeeded in confusing both her fans and his. (She has a habit of trying to perfect musical standards, whether putting words to Mingus's compositions or, more recently, tinkering with lyrics to Gershwin songs.)

"When I did the Mingus project, I was advised what it would cost me," she remembers. "I took that seriously but I couldn't believe that I would lose my airplay. It kicked me right out of the game. It was a great experience, one of my fondest. . . . I would do it today even knowing what it costs, but it certainly cost me. It took me some years to get back in it. And my work is still reviewed but radio stations don't play me. VH1 and MTV don't even touch me."

Despite her growing weakness for pop culture, *Taming the Tiger* is filled with disdain for the entertainment world. The title is an allusion to success and the music industry, and the difficulty of controlling them. To compose the title song, she forced herself to listen to pop radio for several days and then came up with lyrics like "I'm a runaway from the record biz / From the hoods in the hood / And the whiny white kids / Boring!"

Although Mitchell is credited as the godmother of current female singer-songwriters and the spiritual muse of the Lilith Fair, the successful all-female summer tour put together by Sarah McLachlan, she has always held such sisterhood, particularly with imitators, somewhat in contempt. ("Girlie guile / Genuine junk food for juveniles," she sings in *Taming the Tiger*.) All of her life she has been considered the grande dame of female singer-songwriters, and all of her life she has tried to be so much more.

"One guy came up to me and said, 'You're the best female singer-songwriter in the world,'" she remembers. "I was thinking: 'What do you mean female? That's like saying you're the best Negro.' Don't put a lid on it: it transcends boundaries."

Not only is Mitchell an influence on female songwriters from Jewel to Madonna to Chrissie Hynde of the Pretenders, she is also an influence on male songwriters from the Artist Formerly Known as Prince to Elvis Costello to Beck, who all sing her praises.

Yet, despite such recognition, Mitchell is remarkably discontent. Even the mention of a positive article merits the response, "It broke my heart to read it." Her ego is a complex thing. In her mind, she feels that she's one of the greatest artists of the 20th century. Yet in her heart, she must have doubts or she wouldn't need the affirmation. Much of it stems from a frustration that even as she has done better work, she still can't eclipse the popularity of her earliest music.

At lunch at the daily grill in Brentwood, her home away from home, we talk about the trappings of the popular-music game over smelly tuna fish sandwiches. For years, she rightly complained of a lack of recognition and appreciation compared with that of the male musicians of her era. But in the past four years, she has won a Grammy Award for Best Pop Album, been inducted into the Rock and Roll Hall of Fame and been honored with a Century Award from *Billboard* magazine. Still, she categorizes many of her awards as "dubious."

"It's like that line of Dylan's: 'You know something is happening here but you don't know what it is, do you, Mr. Jones?' That's what most of my honors felt like," she explains. "They knew they had to do it but they . . . weren't quite sure what to illuminate in the work."

It antagonizes her no end that the songs that have made her famous—most notably "Big Yellow Taxi"—are her least complex and innovative ones. After all, Paul Simon was praised for bringing together world music and pop in *Graceland*, and Sting bragged of doing the same for jazz in *The Dream of the Blue Turtles*. Mitchell beat them all to the punch with albums like *The Hissing of Summer Lawns, Hejira, Don Juan's Reckless Daughter* and the live album *Shadows and Light* by making music in whatever style and tuning best suited her songs.

"'Big Yellow Taxi' is nice," she says. "It's like Chuck Berry kind of skipping rope. It's a good little workhorse of a song and it's got some content. But it's a nursery rhyme. Of all the creations that are there, if you reduce it to this thing, it's a tragedy.

"Picasso was restless," she adds, her face half-shaded by a straw sun hat. "I mean, he just kept changing and changing and changing." She mentions Miles Davis as well. "So those are my heroes. The ones that change a lot."

Mitchell has always defined herself as being not who others have expected her to be. She came down with polio when she was 9. Five years later, having beaten the odds and recovered, she wasn't just walking, she was dancing. In her paintings, she has purposely made it part of her style to break the rules that she was taught at the Alberta College of Art (focusing on the same kind of stylistic combinations that can make her records seem difficult). When she dropped out of art school and committed to the folk circuit, where she traveled from Toronto to Detroit to New York City, she denied that she was ever a folksinger.

"I came into the game looking like a folksinger, but I was really playing classical art songs," she explained as she checked her watch to make sure she wasn't late to meet a friend. "Those weren't like the chords that folkies played. But I looked like a folksinger, like the girl with the guitar. And at that point I had already been a lover of classical music in my preteens, a rock-and-roll dancer in high school, and I had discovered jazz. So folk music was easy and I needed money for art school just because we were all on students' wages. It wasn't until I was 21 and the desire to compose and create came back . . . that I got caught between being pigeonholed by critics and laboring for the sake of commercial exploitation."

Mitchell traces her feeling of being misunderstood back to the first music she made, at age 7. "I had music killed by my piano teacher," she says. "She rapped my knuckles with a ruler, which was the way they taught everybody in that era anyway, and said, 'Why would you want to play by ear'—that's what they called composing—'when you could have the masters under your fingertips, when you could copy.' So you go to art school and innovation is everything, but in music, you're just a weird loner. So I have more of a painter's ego or approach, which is to make fresh, individuated stuff that has my blood in it and on the tracks."

Given all her anxiety about her career, it's perhaps understandable that the musician's life is not one she professes to relish. She regards touring as a violation of her muse and says record labels treat musicians like dumb prizefighters built to earn them purse money.

"I feel pregnant with creativity and all that touring represents to me is a delay until I can be creative," she explained as we wrapped up lunch. "I'm responsible to the company, and the company wants me to tour. In the meantime I'm probably going to lose 20 songs, by being cooperative to the game. To be responsible to the creativity, I should go on strike right now and get into my pajamas. Most of my career, right after I made an album I would run away; I'd go to Europe. I'm glad I did. While I was running away from the last record, I'd be writing the new one because I'd be having a life."

Speaking of her new album, she continues, "I'm already out of what this record is about." She pauses and lights her 5th or 11th cigarette and exhales. "I'm involved with family and the socializing process, which is something very exciting and very different."

———

The night after we wrap up our interviews, I run into Mitchell at Dominick's, a new Los Angeles restaurant so trendy that it fills up every night despite its awful food. Mitchell is sitting in the middle of a table surrounded by her daughter, grandson and friends, celebrating her friend Paul Starr's birthday. When I see her, she loops her arm around my elbow like an Auntie Mame and spirits me into the foyer.

As we walk, we talk about astrology. According to a book she has been reading, her daughter was born on the day of the explorer and she was born on the day of the discoverer. "She's a natural follower, I'm a natural leader," she says. "I can't help it, the stars put me there."

Mitchell says that their birth dates interact in a way best suited to siblings and that, in fact, they have a sisterly relationship. Not by design, they have the same handbags and shoes, wear similar clothes and share what she describes as a "crazy bravado that comes from the Irish blood."

Throughout her career, Mitchell dropped hints in her songs for her only child to find. Although Gibb knew the biography of her birth mother—that she was a Canadian folksinger— she never dreamed that she was Mitchell's child. Then, in 1996, the *New York Times* described Mitchell's search for her daughter. A friend of Gibb's, who saw the story, joked that Mitchell could be Gibb's birth mother. Gibb had only recently been told that she was adopted, and she already had a son. She decided to investigate. Eventually, she and Mitchell were united.

As for the adoptive parents, Mitchell says: "We worked through all of that. I'm totally grateful to them, and Kilauren hasn't forgotten about them."

At Dominick's, we sit down in two adjacent chairs, and she places her hand over mine on the armrest. She then proceeds to clarify comments she made in our previous interviews. Clearly, she has replayed the conversations and has tried to pinpoint where her natural frankness and expansiveness may have got her into trouble.

There is a lyric on her new album that complains, "I'm up to my neck in alligator jaws gnashing at me." She is trying to figure out if I am an alligator, too. Her fears, however, seem dated. The alligators are gnashing less and less, and at the dinner table around the corner, she has found something to protect her from them.

Joni Mitchell and Ramblin' Jack Elliott at UCLA, 1993. © Corbis/Henry Diltz

"I used to be too much of an illuminated scribe locked in my attic with a responsibility to my gifts," she says, laughing for once at herself. She stubs out a cigarette. Now, she says: "I long to live in a Chekhov play with relatives and aunties and the long white tables with green bottles on them, under the apple tree. That's really where I should be."

Part Six

THE MUSIC:
CRAFT, PROCESS, AND ANALYSIS

BY JEFFREY PEPPER RODGERS

MY SECRET PLACE: THE GUITAR
ODYSSEY OF JONI MITCHELL

The evolution of Joni's famously intricate guitar tunings: how she discovers them, how she remembers them, what they are, and what they evoke.—SFL

Acoustic Guitar, August 1996

At the heart of the music of Joni Mitchell is a constant sense of surprise and discovery. The melodies and harmonies rarely unfold in ways that our ears, tamed by pop-music conventions, have come to expect. Her guitar doesn't really sound like a guitar: the treble strings become a cool-jazz horn section; the bass snaps out syncopations like a snare drum; the notes ring out in clusters that simply don't come out of a normal six-string. And her voice adds another layer of invention, extending the harmonic implications of the chords and coloring the melody with plainspoken commentary as well as charged poetic imagery.

Even though all these qualities have made Mitchell one of the most revered songwriters of our time, an inspiration for several generations of musicians, the creative processes and impulses behind her music have always been clouded in mystery. A guitarist haunted by Mitchell's playing on an album like *Court and Spark* or *Hejira*, for instance, can't find much help in the music store in exploring that sound: what she plays, from the way she tunes her strings to the way she strokes them with her right hand, is utterly off the chart of how most of us approach the guitar. The only published documentation of her 30-year guitar odyssey is four single-album songbooks transcribed by Joel Bernstein, her longtime guitar tech and musical/photographic archivist, which show the real tunings and chord shapes. But that's a very small slice of a career that spans 17 albums, each one a departure—often a radical one—from what came before.

In the wake of her 1996 Grammy for Best Pop Album for *Turbulent Indigo*, which marked the stunning return of her acoustic guitar to center stage, Joni Mitchell met with me in Los Angeles to offer a rare, in-depth view into her craft as a guitarist and composer. To orient myself better in the world of Mitchell's guitar, I also spoke with Joel Bernstein, who's now based in San Francisco and helping to compile a Neil Young anthology. Remarkably, Mitchell herself relies on Bernstein's encyclopedic knowledge of her work: because she has forged ahead with new tunings throughout her career and rarely plays her past repertoire, Bernstein has at several junctures helped her relearn some of her older songs.

"There's a certain kind of restlessness that not many artists are cursed or blessed with, depending on how you look at it," Mitchell said. "Craving change, craving growth, seeing always room for improvement in your work." In that statement lies the key to her music: seeing it as an ongoing process of invention, rather than a series of discrete and final statements.

———

Joni Mitchell began playing the guitar like countless young musicians of the '60s, but she quickly turned onto a less-traveled path. "When I was learning to play guitar, I got Pete Seeger's *How to Play Folk-Style Guitar*," she recalled. "I went straight to the Cotten picking. Your thumb went from [*imitates alternating-bass sound*] the sixth string, fifth string, sixth string, fifth string . . . I couldn't do that, so I ended up playing mostly the sixth string but banging it into the fifth string. So Elizabeth Cotten definitely is an influence: it's me not being able to play like her. If I could have I would have, but good thing I couldn't, because it came out original."

At the same time that she departed from standard folk fingerpicking, Mitchell departed from standard tuning as well (only two of her songs— "Tin Angel" and "Urge for Going"—are in standard tuning). "In the beginning, I built the repertoire of the open major tunings that the old black blues guys came up with," she said. "It was only three or four. The simplest one is D modal [D A D G B D]: Neil Young uses that a lot. And then open G [D G D G B D], with the sixth string removed, which is all Keith Richards plays in. And open D [D A D F♪ A D]. Then going between them I started to get more 'modern' chords, for lack of a better word." As she began to write songs in the mid-'60s, these tunings became inextricably tied to her composing.

On Mitchell's first three albums, *Joni Mitchell* (1968), *Clouds* (1969), and *Ladies of the Canyon* (1970), conventional open tunings coexist with other tunings that stake out some new territory. "Both Sides, Now" (capo II) and "Big Yellow Taxi," for instance, are in open E (E B E G♪ B E—the same as open D but a whole step higher); and "The Circle Game" (capo IV) and "Marcie" are in open G. But it was more adventurous tunings like C G D F C E ("Sistowbell Lane"), with its complex chords created by simple fingerings, that enthralled her and became the foundation of her music from the early '70s on.

"Pure majors are like major colors: they evoke pure well-being," she said. "Anybody's life at this time has pure majors in it, given, but there's an element of tragedy. No matter what your disposition is, we are air breathers, and the rain forests coming down at the rate they are . . . there's just so much insanity afoot. We live in a dissonant world. Hawaiian [music], in the pure major—in paradise, that makes sense. But it doesn't make sense to make music in such a dissonant world that does not contain some dissonances."

The word dissonances seems to imply harsh or jarring sounds, but in fact, the "modern chords" that Mitchell found in alternate tunings have an overall softness to them, with consonances and dissonances gently playing off each other. It's difficult to put a label on these sounds, but Mitchell is emphatic about one thing: they're a long way from folk music. "It's closer to Debussy and to classical composition, and it has its own harmonic movement which doesn't belong to any camp," she said. "It's not jazz, like people like to think. It has in common with jazz that the harmony is very wide, but there are laws to jazz chordal movement, and this is outside those laws for the most part."

So how does Mitchell discover the tunings and fingerings that create these expansive harmonies? Here's how she described the process: "You're twiddling and you find the tuning. Now the left hand has to learn where the chords are, because it's a whole new ballpark, right? So you're groping around, looking for where the chords are, using very simple shapes. Put it in a tuning and you've got four chords immediately—open barre five, barre seven, and your higher octave, like half fingering on the 12th. Then you've got to find where your minors are and where the interesting colors are—that's the exciting part.

"Sometimes I'll tune to some piece of music and find [an open tuning] that way, sometimes I just find one going from one to another, and sometimes I'll tune to the environment. Like 'The Magdalene Laundries' [from *Turbulent Indigo*, the tuning is B F♪ B E A E]: I tuned to the day in a certain place, taking the pitch of birdsongs and the general frequency sitting on a rock in that landscape."

Mitchell likens her use of continually changing tunings to sitting down at a typewriter on which the letters are rearranged each day. It's inevitable that you get lost and type some gibberish, and those mistakes are actually the main reason to use this system in the first place. "If you're only working off what you know, then you can't grow," she said. "It's only through error that discovery is made, and in order to discover you have to set up some sort of situation with a random element, a strange attractor, using contemporary physics terms. The more I can surprise myself, the more I'll stay in this business, and the twiddling of the notes is one way to keep the pilgrimage going. You're constantly pulling the rug out from under yourself, so you don't get a chance to settle into any kind of formula."

To date, Mitchell said that she has used 51 tunings. This number is so extraordinarily high in part because her tunings have lowered steadily over the years, so some tunings recur at several pitches. Generally speaking, her tunings started at a base of open E and dropped to D and then to C, and these days some even plummet to B or A in the bass. This evolution reflects the steady lowering of her voice since the '60s, a likely consequence of heavy smoking.

When Mitchell performs an older song today, she typically uses a lowered version of the original tuning. "Big Yellow Taxi," originally in open E, is now played in a low version of open C (C G C E G C, which is the same as open E dropped two whole steps). She recorded "Cherokee Louise" on *Night Ride Home* with the tuning D A E F♯ A D, [but] when she performed it on the Canadian TV show "Much Music" last year, she played it in C G D E G C—a whole step lower. (This C tuning, also used for *Night Ride Home*, is her current favorite, according to Joel Bernstein.)

In some cases, the same relative tuning pops up in different registers for different songs: "Cool Water" (*Chalk Mark in a Rain Storm*) and "Slouching Toward Bethlehem" (*Night Ride Home*) are in D A E G A D, a half step down. C♯ G♯ D♯ F♯ G♯ C♯ is the tuning for "My Secret Place" (*Chalk Mark*): and a whole step below that, B F♯ C♯ E F♯ B, is the tuning for *Hejira*.

These connections allow Mitchell, in some cases, to carry fingerings from one tuning to another and find a measure of consistency, but each tuning has its own little universe of sounds and possibilities. "You never really can begin to learn the neck like a standard player, linearly and orderly," she said. "You have to think in a different way in moving blocks. Within the context of moving blocks, there are certain things that you'll try from tuning to tuning that will apply."

Mitchell has come up with a way to categorize her tunings into families based on the number of half steps between the notes of adjacent strings. "Standard tuning's numerical system is 5 5 5 4 5, with the knowledge that your bass string is E, right?" she said. "Most of my tunings at this point are 7 5 or 7 7, where the 5 5 on the bottom is. The 7 7 and the

7 5 family tunings are where I started from." Examples of 7 5 tunings are D A D G B D (used for "Free Man in Paris," *Court and Spark*) and C G C E G C ("Amelia," *Hejira*): in both cases, the fifth string is tuned to the *seventh* fret of the sixth string, and the fourth string is tuned to the *fifth* fret of the fifth string. Similarly, examples of 7 7 tunings are C G D G B D ("Cold Blue Steel and Sweet Fire." *For the Roses*) and C♩ G♩ D♩ E♩ G♩ C♩ ("Sunny Sunday," *Turbulent Indigo*): the intervals between the sixth and fifth strings, and the fifth and fourth strings, are seven frets.

Mitchell continued, "However, the dreaded 7 9 family—I have about seven songs in 7 9 tunings—are in total conflict with the 7 5 and the 7 7 families. They're just outlaws. They're guaranteed bass clams [*laughs*], 'cause the thumb gets used to going automatically into these shapes, and it has to make this slight adaptation." Mitchell's 7 9 songs include "Borderline," "Turbulent Indigo," and "How Do You Stop" (*Turbulent Indigo*), all of which are in the tuning B F♩ D♩ D♩ F♩ B.

Just to confuse the fingers further, Mitchell also has some renegade tunings in which she's written only one song. Consider the tuning for "Black Crow." from *Hejira*: B♭ B♭ D♭ F A♭ B♭, with the fifth and sixth strings an octave apart. By Mitchell's numerical system, this would be a 12 3 tuning—a very long way from 7 7 or 7 5, and a thousand miles from standard tuning.

An interesting tuning can be fertile ground for writing a song, but—as a whole pile of new-age guitar CDs amply illustrate—it's how you work the tuning with your hands and compositional sense that counts. Throughout her music, Mitchell makes the most of the freedom that open tunings allow in traveling around the neck. One of her stylistic signatures is the way she juxtaposes notes fretted high on the neck against ringing open strings. This is a great way to extend the range of the accompaniment, as you can hear on songs like "Chelsea Morning," (*Clouds*, open E), in which she plays a riff up high on the top two strings that dances over the open bass strings, followed by a fretted bass part that moves below the open treble strings.

In Mitchell's later songs, with their more radical tunings, the ringing open strings take on a different sort of drone quality—she uses them between chords as a sort of connecting thread in the harmony. "It's like a wash," she said. "In painting, if I start a canvas now, to get rid of the vertigo of the blank page, I cover the whole thing in olive green, then start working the color into it. So every color is permeated with that green. It doesn't really green the colors out, but it antiques them, burnishes them. The drones kind of burnish the chord in the same way. That color remains as a wash. These other colors then drop in, but always against that wash."

Upper melodies, moving bass line, drone strings: all these components of Mitchell's guitar style are rooted in her conception of the guitar as a multi-voiced instrument. "When I'm playing the guitar," she said, "I hear it as an orchestra: the top three strings being my horn section, the bottom three being cello, viola, and bass—the bass being indicated but not rooted." The orchestral effect is particularity vivid on "Just Like This Train," with its "muted trumpet parts" and independent lines on the top, middle, and bottom strings.

Mitchell compares the right-hand technique that maintains these separate voices to harp playing, with its fluid movement over the strings. Here's how Joel Bernstein describes the evolution of that style: "Her first album has some very fine, detailed fingerpicking—note for note, there are very specific figures. As time goes on, she gets into more of a strumming thing until it becomes more like a brush stroke—it's a real expressive rhythmic thing. Her early stuff doesn't really swing, there's not jazz stuff going on in it, and she's not implying a rhythm section as much, whereas now she obviously has a lot going on in the right hand. It's at the same time simpler and deeper."

Ever since the *Blue* album, percussive sounds have been central to Mitchell's guitar style—a clear influence on all sorts of tapping and slapping contemporary players. Mitchell's inspiration for these sounds came from a surprising place: an encounter with a dulcimer maker at the 1969 Big Sur Festival. "I had never seen one played," she said. "Traditionally it's picked with a quill, and it's a very delicate thing that sits across your knee. The only instrument I had ever had across my knee was a bongo drum, so when I started to play the dulcimer I beat it. I just slapped it with my hands. Anyway, I bought it, and I took off to Europe carrying a flute and this dulcimer because it was very light for backpacking around Europe. I wrote most of *Blue* on it."

For about a year, Mitchell played the dulcimer and didn't have a guitar on hand. "I was craving a guitar so badly in Greece," she said. "The junta had repressed the population at that time. They were not allowed public meeting: they were not allowed any kind of boisterous or colorful expression. The military was sitting on their souls, and even the poets had to move around. We found this floating poets' gathering place, and there was an apple crate of a guitar there that people played. I bought it off them for 50 bucks and sat in the Athens underground with transvestites and, you know, the underbelly running around—and it was like a romance. It was a terrible guitar, but I hadn't played one for so long, and I began slapping it because I had been slapping this dulcimer. That's when I noticed that my style had changed.

"I thought that slap came purely from the dulcimer until I saw a television show [recently] that I did the day after Woodstock, where Crosby, Nash, and Stills showed up. Stephen slapped his guitar, which is a kind of flamenco way of playing it, so I would have to cite Stephen Stills also as an influence in that department. But it was latent and not conscious. It wasn't like I studied him and tried to play like him, but I admired the way he played. That's the way I grow, by admiration and not by intellect. Anytime I admire something, something expands, and somewhere down the road that admiration works on me as an influence."

—

Joni Mitchell's first five albums are essentially solo works, driven by her guitar, dulcimer, piano, and voice. But the pared-down production wasn't a reflection of a back-to-basics philosophy, as one might have guessed. "There were no drummers or bass players that could play my music," she said. "I tried the same sections that Carole King and James Taylor were using. I couldn't get on the airwaves because there was no bass and drums on [my records], so I had incentive, but everything they added was arbitrary. They were imposing style on something without seeing what the something was that they were playing to. I thought, 'They're putting big, dark polka dots along the bottom of the music, and fence posts.' I'd end up trying to tell them how to play, and they'd say, 'Isn't it cute, she was telling me how to play my ax, and I've played with James Brown. . . .' So it was difficult as a female to guide males into playing [what I wanted], and to make observations in regard to the music that they had not made. Finally a drummer said, 'Joni, you're going to have to play with jazz musicians.' So I started scouting the clubs, and I found the L.A. Express, but that was for my sixth album [*Court and Spark*]. It took me that long.

"You have to understand, not only was it difficult to be a woman in the business at that time, but the camps of music were very isolated from one another. Jazzers and rockers and folkies did not mix, and I had moved through all of these camps. I was moving into the jazz camp. As far as the rockers were concerned, that was betrayal, and definitely to the folkies. But [jazz musicians] could write out lead sheets: they also could analyze my chords. They were kind of snobbish at first when they heard the music, but when they wrote out what the chord was, they were surprised, because it would be like A sus diminished—these were not normal chords. In standard tuning these chords are very difficult. They would come around with kind of a different respect, or a curiosity at least."

As Mitchell began to work with full-band arrangements, she still maintained strict control over the parts. For *Court and Spark*, she said, "I sang all the countermelody to a scribe, who wrote it out. So anything that's added is my composition. In a few exceptions I'll cut a player loose, but then I'll edit him, move him around, so even though he's given me free lines I'm still collaging them into place.

"I've tried to remain true to my own compositional instincts by eliminating the producer, who laminates you to the popular sounds of your time. I've been in conflict with the popular sounds of my time, for the most part. All through the '70s I never liked the sound of the bass or the drums, just on a sonic level, but I couldn't get any [drummers] to take the pillow out of their kick and I couldn't get [bassists] to put fresh strings on and give me a resonant sound, because they were scared to be unhip. Hip is a herd mentality, and it's very conservative, especially among boys."

Mitchell's dissatisfaction with the standard bass sounds of the '70s eventually led to one of the most extraordinary collaborations of her career. "Finally, someone said. 'There's this kid in Florida named Jaco Pastorius. He's really weird: you'd probably like him.' So I sent for Jaco and he had the sound I was looking for—big and fat and resonant."

The interplay of Mitchell's guitar and Pastorius' bass, first heard on *Hejira*, is a marvel. Pastorius both expands on her chords and harmonics and weaves melodies around her vocal line (including several Stravinsky quotes). His rhythmic/melodic approach, which revolutionized the world of the electric bass, was so thick and up-front that it demanded new approaches on Mitchell's side. "Although I wanted a wide bass sound, his was even wider, and he insisted that he be mixed up so that I was like his background singer," she said. "So to get enough meat to hold his sound, I doubled the guitar loosely—I just played it twice."

Years later, in the recording of *Chalk Mark in a Rain Storm* (1988), Mitchell carried this concept to its extreme, taking advantage of developments in studio technology that allowed the recording of 48 tracks—two 24-track tapes linked together. "I decided to use up one of the reels of the tape doubling the part 24 times. 'My Secret Place' is 24 guitars playing the same part," she said. Her reason for this experiment says as much about

Joni Mitchell. © Corbis/Shelley Gazin

her adventurousness as a musician as it does about her obsession with defying categorization. "On that whole album, all of the guitars are played 24 or 16 times, not in order to get a [Phil] Spector sound but to get people to hear my guitar playing. I thought, 'Well, maybe it's just too thin and silvery sounding. If I beef it up and make a whole section of the guitars, maybe they'll notice how these chords are moving and stop calling it folk music.'"

As the "My Secret Place" story suggests, Joni Mitchell delved deeply into studio craft during the 1980s, especially in the synthesizer-based *Dog Eat Dog*. On *Night Ride Home* (1991), her acoustic guitar rose again in the mix, paving the way for its full return in *Turbulent Indigo*, a masterpiece of instrumental understatement that ranks as some of the most haunting work of her career. *Turbulent Indigo* also received the warmest reviews she's gotten in many years, and her first Grammy victory since 1975.

Does that mean we should expect more of the same in her next album? Naturally not, because Mitchell is in the midst of yet another radical departure, one that she calls "probably the biggest break for me since *Court and Spark*."

The new influence at work is an electric guitar that Mitchell's old friend Fred Walecki built for her to alleviate her ongoing frustrations with using alternate tunings—one of the reasons why she stopped touring in 1983 and was on the verge of quitting the stage permanently in the spring of '95. Walecki, of Westwood Music in Los Angeles, designed the Stratocaster-style guitar to work with the Roland VG-8—the Virtual Guitar—a very sophisticated processor capable of electronically creating her tunings. While the strings physically stay in standard tuning, the VG-8 tweaks the pickup signals so that they come out of the speakers in an altered tuning. This means that Mitchell can use one guitar on stage, with an off-stage tech punching in the preprogrammed tuning for each song.

"This new guitar that I'm working with eliminated a certain amount of problems that I had with the acoustic guitar," Mitchell explained. "*Problems* isn't even the right word: *maddening frustrations* is more accurate. The guitar is intended to be played in standard tuning: the neck is calibrated and everything. Twiddling it around isn't good for the instrument, generally speaking. It's not good for the neck: it unsettles the intonation. I have very good pitch, so if I'm never quite in tune, that's frustrating." Over the years, Mitchell has learned to slightly bend the strings to compensate for the intonation error, but that effort is still often defeated by the extreme slackness of her tunings. "In some of those tunings I've got an A on the bottom or a B♭, and it's banging against the string next to it and kicking the thing out of tune as I play, no matter how carefully I tweak it." The VG-8 sidesteps all these problems: as long as the strings are accurately in standard tuning, she can play all over the neck in the virtual alternate tunings and sound in tune.

In every gig since the 1995 New Orleans Jazz Festival, Mitchell has used the VG-8, using its effects to build a guitar sound reminiscent of her

Hejira era. But the VG-8 is having a much more far-reaching impact on her music than just providing a workable stage setup. In composing and recording the songs for her next album, she's thrown herself into a heady exploration of the VG-8's sampled sounds. "Sonically, it's very new," she said of the tracks recorded so far. "I don't know what you'd call it. It's my impression, in a way, of '40s music. Because I don't like a lot of contemporary music—it's just so formulated and artificial and false—I kind of cleared my ear and didn't listen to anything for a while, and what emerged were these vague memories of '40s and early '50s sounds. Swinging brass—not Benny Goodman and not Glenn Miller but my own brand, pulled through Miles [Davis] and different harmonic stuff that I absorbed in the '50s. Because this guitar has heavy-metal sounds in it and pretty good brass sounds, I'm mixing heavy-metal sounds with a brass section, so it's a really strange hybrid kind of music. I'm a bit scared of it sometimes, you know. I don't know what it is."

The richest irony of Mitchell's VG-8 experience thus far is that this guitar rig, which was intended to make her alternate tunings more practical and usable, drove her to write her first song in 30 years in standard tuning. A technical barrier was responsible: the VG-8's synth patches were created to be used with a guitar in standard tuning, and initially they were not accessible in conjunction with her alternate tunings (Roland has since fixed this problem).

So Mitchell's first VG-8 composition, "Harlem in Havana," is in that vaguely remembered thing called standard tuning. "You'd never know it was in standard tuning because I haven't played in standard tuning for 30 years. I don't know how to play in standard tuning, so I treated standard tuning like it was a new tuning and used my repertoire of shapes.

"It's a strange piece of music. The guitar sound that I'm using is like a marimba, but it's not like any marimba part you've ever heard because it's fingerpicked. The bass string is almost atonal and sounds almost like a didgeridoo. But off of it I'm building huge horn sections, and the poem that's going to it is about two little girls in my hometown getting into this black revue called Harlem in Havana which was an Afro-Cuban burlesque kind of show that you weren't supposed to stand in front of, let alone go in."

Heavy metal mixed with brass, guitar-generated marimbas. Afro-Cuban and swing rhythms: all indications are that Mitchell's next creation, slated for an early '97 release [*Taming the Tiger*], will be a real ear-opener and a direct challenge to our settled perceptions of the music of Joni

Mitchell. In the meantime, a number of other projects are percolating. A best-of collection is in the works, and the VG-8 seems to be encouraging her tentative steps back onto the stage (in November '95, she played her first full-length gig in years, at the Fez in New York). Further into the future, we can look forward to a new CD anthology and probably—keep your fingers crossed—a complete songbook, with all the tunings and basic chord shapes. That book will be an invaluable map for retracing the steps of one of the most amazing guitar journeys of our time, while Joni Mitchell herself disappears around the next bend.

BY JEFFREY PEPPER RODGERS

JONI MITCHELL'S GUITARS

About the instruments she used to make the music. Originally written as a sidebar to the preceding article, "My Secret Place: The Guitar Odyssey of Joni Mitchell."—SFL

Acoustic Guitar, August 1996

Joni Mitchell has never quite gotten over the first guitar she loved and lost: a '56 Martin D-28 she got circa 1966 from a marine captain stationed at Fort Bragg, North Carolina. The guitar had accompanied him to Vietnam and was in his tent when it was hit with shrapnel. "There were two instruments and all this captain's stuff in there," Mitchell says. "When they cleared the wreckage, all that survived was this guitar. I don't know whether the explosion did something to the modules in the wood, but that guitar was a trooper, man." Mitchell played that D-28 on all her early albums. Before she recorded *Court and Spark*, it was damaged on an airline, and soon after it was stolen off a luggage carousel in Maui. Wistfully, she adds, "I've never found an acoustic that could compare with it."

As Mitchell explored jazzier sounds in the late '70s, she turned to electric guitars. From 1979 until the mid-'80s, she performed with five George Benson model Ibanez guitars, which were set up by Joel Bernstein and Larry Cragg with a range of string gauges to accommodate her tunings. At that time, the Roland Jazz Chorus amp—which was invented, Mitchell says, so she could replicate her *Hejira* sound in performance—was an important component of her live sound.

These days, Mitchell's main acoustics are a Martin D-45, a Martin D-28, and two Collings—a D-2H dreadnought and the 3/4-size Baby seen in the cover photo—that she calls "the best acoustic guitars I've found since I lost my dear one." She says, "I need really good intonation, and one of the signs of really good intonation is how flashy the harmonics are with a light touch. You should be able to get them to bloom like jewels. Both those guitars have that capacity. Of the two, the big one [which was the primary guitar for *Turbulent Indigo*] records better, but the little one is so sweet to cradle. It's just the right size for sitting. I write a lot on it and I travel with it, which is kind of scary. I carry it on board with me, because I won't take a chance on it. I won't let it go into the hold and get mushed like my beloved." For performance, her acoustics are equipped with Highlander pickups, which she uses in combination with an external microphone.

In the last year, Mitchell has almost exclusively played an electric guitar made by Fred Walecki of Westwood Music in Los Angeles, which she uses with the Roland VG-8 processor to electronically create her alternate tunings. The guitar is made with a very lightweight German spruce body and a neck that's somewhere between that of a Martin and a Stratocaster.

BY JENNY BOYD

MUSICIANS IN TUNE: SEVENTY-FIVE MUSICIANS DISCUSS THE CREATIVE PROCESS

For her book on the creative process, the author interviewed 75 musicians and divided the book into seven main categories: Nurturing Creativity, The Drive to Create, The Unconscious, The Collective Unconscious, The Peak Experience, Chemicals and Creativity, and The Creative Potential.

The following reflects Joni's contributions.—SFL

1992

The Drive To Create

Musical Rebels
Singer-songwriter Joni Mitchell was encouraged by her parents to be creative, until they no longer approved of her means of expression and withdrew their support. By this time Joni trusted her inner resolve enough that

she was undaunted by her family's disapproval, and she continued to follow her creative path. Ostracized by her peers since her early years, she was already accustomed to being different from what people expected and to heeding her inner voice. Joni described her youth in a small Canadian village: "In my early childhood because I was creative—I was a painter always—I had difficulty playing with the other children in the neighborhood, just because my games they couldn't get in on. The town I lived in was a small third-world town; the mail still came at Christmas on open wagons drawn by horses with sleigh runners. There were a lot of music lessons taking place in the town. Since mainly the kids were athletic, they were sticks and stone throwers; they were hardy, robust, physical, not very creative. The creative people in the town generally studied classical piano or classical voice, so I had a lot of friends who were considered the singers. I was always considered the painter, but I was in association with child musicians. I spent a little time in the church choir.

"At seven, I begged for a piano—I used to have dreams that I could play an instrument—so I was given piano lessons. The lessons used to coincide with the television broadcast of "Wild Bill Hickock," this was bad timing [since it was a favorite show], plus the piano teacher used to rap my knuckles because I could memorize and play by ear quicker than I could read. So she made the education process extremely unpleasant. So I quit, but I still used to sit down and compose my own little melodies; that's what I wanted to do, to compose. In that town, it was unheard of, considered inferior. The thing was to learn the masters and play them. I thought I was going to be a painter when I grew up, but I knew I could make up music; I heard it in my head. I always could do it, but it was discouraged. So when I quit piano lessons in my teens, my parents weren't supportive about my wanting to buy a guitar. Since they weren't really supportive, I had to buy my first instrument myself."

Joni managed to overcome the derision of her peers, her teacher, and her parents to pursue her own creative dreams. She seems the perfect example of the intrepid creative person, unafraid of what others think, as described by Maslow: "Perhaps more important, however, [is] their lack of fear of their own insides, of their own impulses, emotions, thoughts. They [are] more self-accepting than the average. This approval and acceptance of their deeper selves then [makes] it more possible to perceive bravely the real nature of the world and also [makes] their behavior more spontaneous." Maslow pointed out that these people are less afraid of their own thoughts, considered by others as "nutty or silly or crazy. They [are] less afraid of being laughed at or of being disapproved of."

The Unconscious

"YOU'VE GOT TO KEEP THE CHILD ALIVE, YOU CAN'T CREATE WITHOUT IT."

—Joni Mitchell

Reaching "No Mind"

Joni Mitchell, who has been a student of Zen, described the concept of no mind and its role in her painting as well as her songwriting: "When I paint for long hours, my mind stills. If you hooked me up to a meter, I don't know what you'd find, but maybe it's like a dream state. It goes very abstract. The dialogue is absolutely still, it's like Zen no mind. You hear electrical synapses, which could be cosmic electricity, snapping, and occasionally up into that void, in the Zen no mind, comes a command, 'Red in the upper-left-hand corner.' There's no afterthought, because ego is the afterthought; you paint red in the upper-left-hand corner, and then it all goes back into the zone again. You achieve that sometimes in music. I think I achieve it in the loneliness of the night just playing my guitar repetitiously. The mantra of it, the drone of it will get you there. In performance you're going down deep within and then you're coming back out to receive your applause. There's a more self-conscious art form in performance—people are applauding you.

"With writing, you have to plumb into the subconscious, and there's a lot of scary things down there, like a bad dream sometimes. If you can extricate yourself from it and face up to it, you come back with a lot of self-knowledge, which then gives you greater human knowledge, and that helps. To know yourself is to know the world; everything, good, bad, and indifferent, is in each one of us to varying degrees, so the more you know about that, the more you know about that which is external. So in that way, the writing process is fantastic psychotherapy—if you can survive. But it is tricky.

"With one particular song I wrote, when it came time to write about my experience, it was so dense with imagery that for me it was thrilling. It was hard for me to sift through it. There came one line, though, that was like a gift. It flowed out. I drew back and said 'thank you' to the room. It just came out and said so much, I felt, so economically. I'd been grinding the gray matter trying to get this thing to come, and maybe I then just relaxed or something. Whatever it was, when it poured out it did seem like it was a gift. There are pieces in a song that just seem to pour out in spite of you. I mean, you're the witness, but the language does seem to come from someplace else."

The Collective Unconscious

The Artist as Hero

Being courageous, as all heroes are, daring to look within regardless of what may be found, and expressing one's inner self to the outside world are all parts of the creative act. I got the feeling from Joni Mitchell, for example, that she has been on a lifelong quest for self-discovery and fulfillment. Through her music, the expression of her own exploration has enabled her to give others guidance and a chance to identify with what she has found: "On a spiritual or a human level, I have felt that it was perhaps my role on occasion to pass on anything I learned that was helpful to me on the route to fulfillment or happy life. [That includes] anything that I discovered about myself, even if I had to reveal something unattractive about myself, like I'm selfish and I'm sad, which are unpopular things to say. By giving the listener an opportunity then to either identify, in which case if he sees that in himself he'll be richer for it, or if he doesn't have the courage to do that or the ability, then he can always say, 'That's what she is.' So I feel that the best of me and the most illuminating things I discover should go into the work. I feel a social responsibility to that; I think I know my role. I'm a witness. I'm to document my experiences in one way or another."

The Peak Experience

The Spiritual Element

Joni Mitchell turned to a Jungian idea to help define the mystical nature of the peak experiences she has had while playing with other musicians, particularly in the studio: "For me, the spiritual experiences are synchronicity. You can't beat it. For instance, in live performance the synchronicity is the beauty of everybody being really Zen—everybody not only hearing themselves while they're playing but hearing everybody else and creating spontaneously. This happens more on recording dates than in live performance, because by the time you get to live performance the music is somewhat composed. When you're in the studio you're still in the searching mode, so you're dealing with the unknown. Therefore, luck has to come into it, and synchronicity is good luck."

Chemicals and Creativity

A Change in Consciousness

Joni Mitchell described the importance of "screwing on a different consciousness" while creating. Though she acknowledged that certain drugs can initially help in the process, she stressed the disastrous results of dependence: "Writing is a more neurotic, a more dangerous art form, psychologically speaking [than performing music], because there you have to make the mind crazy. It's the opposite of Zen mind. That's why a lot of the great writers used stimulants—*Alice in Wonderland* was written on opium, all the great Welsh alcoholics—because writers need to screw on a different head. Sometimes they get lost in the different head, but with writing, you need to create the chaotic mind, insanity almost, overlapping thoughts. You have to plumb down if you want any depth to your writing.

"During the introductory period to a new drug, it can screw on a different consciousness. Any change of consciousness is refreshing, so is the contrast between going straight to whatever elixir, say pot; it tends to make you tactile, sensual. It warms the heart, for about the first fifteen minutes. Then it starts to fog you over. You've got about fifteen minutes of really concentrated creative thought, and then it can flatten you. If you smoke that on a regular basis, you'd just be flattened, and it's anti-creative. But if you do it knowing, 'I'm stuck here,' take some pot and you'll swing into the opposite of where you are and ideas will open up. Cocaine can give you an intellectual, linear delusion of grandeur—makes you feel real smart. It can create great insanity very quickly. My definition of insanity is chaotic mind—too many thoughts in it, overlapping. For a writer, that's a lot of choices; epic thought can be very good, but if you do [too much], then it takes over and then it's anti-creative, almost immediately. For me, sake is a very warming elixir, but [with] all these things, you can't even do them two days in a row before they [begin to have] a deteriorating effect. I think they almost have to be done with a spiritual, ritualistic [feel], like a prayer."

The False Promise
Joni Mitchell has also experienced this trap: "Out of desperation, when you have no inspiration [you may try] to stimulate it with the addition of something artificial. But with the straight mind, the little shocks of daily existence can be enough. You go out the door of your house in one mood and you run into something that either elevates or depresses that mood; that change of mind could be the stimulation needed for the creative process. The straight mind is ultimately the best because it's the long-distance runner of them all. With the others, the road is too dangerous; it can burn you out and kill your talent."

Joni Mitchell at the New Orleans Jazz and Heritage Festival, 1995. © Gahr

The Creative Potential

Taking Chances

The qualities creative people need to cope with the feeling of being different as children can help them in later life to continually grow artistically. According to Joni Mitchell: "You have to be able to go out on a limb. What keeps a lot of people from being creative is the fear of failure. In creativity, the accidents and the mistakes and the coincidences—that's what keeps some people from being creative. They're afraid to take chances. They might even be considered creative by some people, but at best they're just copycats. They hear that, they like it, they'll make something like it, they can do that. But to innovate, you have to have a certain kind of fearlessness. I think it helps if at an early age you got used to being shunned and you survived that. If you had to fight some things in your childhood, you now can stand alone."

Conditions Conducive to Creating

Joni Mitchell detailed the differing mind-sets necessary—and detrimental —to creativity: "Creativity comes from an urgency to communicate; the gift can be developed in people. Anybody can make something; in that way I think anybody can be creative. The net with which you capture [creativity] is made up of the threads of your alertness. If you could walk through the world with the same attentiveness as you played a video game, for instance, so nothing could bomb you, that's kind of Zen mind. If you're really playing well at a video game and you say, 'Oh, I'm playing really well,' that will get you, because that's the entrance of the ego. Up until then, you haven't had an ego, you've been no mind. And in no mind time is huge; but [with] the entrance of one thought, then time is small. So making yourself attractive to creative inspiration, you have to train your ears to be as alert as possible and your eyes as alert as possible, it's a finer tuning.

"If you're too rational, you're not very well equipped [to create]. You need to be able to surrender to the mystic to be good, to be great, to have one foot in divinity, which is the only place that greatness comes from. You can be good, you can write a nice song; there's a lot of nice songs on the radio that don't have one foot in divinity. They can even be huge hits; it depends on your standards of creativity, what that means to you.

"If you're too reasonable, then creativity won't come around in you, because then you're not intuitive, and it requires a great deal of intuition. You need a bit of all of it: you need to be emotional, otherwise your work will be chilly. If you're too emotional, your work will be all over the place. You need to be rational for linear, architectural, orderly, structural work, but if you stay there too long, the stuff will be chilly. You need some clarity to make the thing pertinent. [Bob] Dylan will write a song and it will have abstract passages and then it will have a direct phrase—like bam—directly communicate, and then he'll go back into something more surrealistic."

BY LLOYD WHITESELL

A JONI MITCHELL AVIARY

A scholarly and absorbing look at a recurring theme in Joni Mitchell's lyrics: "the visionary flight to a better world."—SFL

Women and Music, Volume 1, 1997

Among Composers of Popular Music in North America, Joni Mitchell stands out for the consistent quality of her craftsmanship and the depth of her lyrical thought. The directions taken in her thirty-year career have had little to do with goals of commercial success; she has never hesitated to risk her marketability in the pursuit of high personal standards of artistry. In interviews, she frequently likens aspects of her songwriting craft to classical composition, claiming affinities with the expressive disposition of German lieder and the harmonic palette of Debussy.[1] Perhaps even more telling is an off-the-cuff remark made during a live concert in 1974 (captured on the *Miles of Aisles* album). As Joni[2] adjusts her guitar tuning between numbers, fans compete for her attention, calling out the names of a dozen different requests. This prompts the following philosophical observation:

"That's one thing that's always been a major difference between the performing arts to me and being a painter. Like, a painter does a painting and he does a painting, that's it, you know, he's had the joy of creating it, and he hangs it on some wall, somebody buys it, somebody buys it again, or maybe nobody buys it, and it sits up in a loft somewhere till he dies. But nobody ever says to him, you know, nobody ever said to van Gogh, 'Paint a *Starry Night* again, man!'"

Remarkably, in the context of live performance, Joni is aligning herself with a view of the finished work drawn from the plastic arts, while alluding to a personal creed of aesthetic value over market value.

This attitude has produced works distinguished by their highly crafted musical and poetic surface, works which reward the attention of an ardent, closely focused mode of listening. At the same time, individual songs are connected by a rich network of thematic associations which have resonated throughout her career. Joni revisits important symbolic articulations, placing them in new contexts and applying the pressure of dialectical perspectives. Her body of work can be seen as a philosophical exploration of recurring themes: the solitary pilgrimage, the contrary pulls of love and independence, the landscapes of the modern city and of a mythic America.

In order to begin tracing the outlines of Joni Mitchell's lyric stature, I would like to focus on one such theme: the visionary flight to a better world. This theme clearly relates to the heady climate of utopian idealism in the late-sixties community in which Joni's talent was first fostered. But

1. Joni Mitchell, interview by Liane Hansen, National Public Radio, 28 May 1995; Jeffrey Pepper Rodgers, "My Secret Place: The Guitar Odyssey of Joni Mitchell," *Acoustic Guitar* 7 (August 1996): 40–55.
2. My use of the first name ("Joni") throughout the article is meant to reflect the more intimate sense of stage persona in the popular music context. (The name Joni is in fact a stage name: the artist's given name is Roberta Joan.) I personally feel that references to "Mitchell" would come across as rather stuffy and needlessly separate the academic discourse from the fan discourse.

as we will see, utopian longing in her work is rarely free from ambivalence, and is usually tempered with an awareness of human frailty and imperfection. My focus is defined by the evocation of a transcendent perspective in either poetry or music; this perspective often coalesces into an airborne, avian persona.

I consider four songs, ranging from the late sixties to the late eighties. By maintaining a close analytical focus, I hope to illustrate Joni's technical polish and sophistication; by developing a specific thematic strand, I aim to give a sense of the depth and texture of her thought.

———

"Song to a Seagull" appears on Joni's eponymous debut album (1968), in the barest acoustic production of voice and guitar. The sentiments this song distills are pure and naive, one solitary soul calling to another. The singing is inward and sheltered, but rises to breathy crests, and here and there rings out in earnest. The guitar's emphasis on fourths rather than triads lends a spacious but stark atmosphere that is colored in by intervening harmonic turns. These harmonies are grounded on a low drone (bass string tuned down to a C)[3] tolling slowly, never relinquished. Around this primal frame the voice circles in a free, chanting rhythm. Meanwhile, Joni shades the guitar's recurring patterns with a vivid spectrum of different touches, from dulcet to merciless.

In the first verse, Joni hails the seagull as her surrogate, partaking of an unknowing, natural freedom. She sends her dreams out with that bird, who has no tie to the sphere of human contempt and misunderstanding. Here is our first example of a transcendent perspective. Three symbolic elements are crucial to its effect: first, the projection of the speaker's identity outward to a vicariously imagined subject; second, the defiance of gravity, with the physical exhilaration and widened spatial focus encompassed in that experience; third (from the refrain), the act of disappearing, flying out of reach of sight or sound. This last element, of course, signifies the ultimate freedom to rise above the limits of one's earthbound life, and leave it behind. But it's worth noticing the uncanny and melancholy ghost-effect it

3. All but a handful of Joni's songs use nonstandard guitar tunings. Only a few of the published scores include correct tunings; the best reference to date is the beautifully maintained "Joni Mitchell Home Page" on the World Wide Web <http://www. jonimitchell.com.> According to James Leahy, from that source, the tuning for "Song to a Seagull" is as follows: C G C C G C. A detailed discussion of Joni's guitar style can be found in Rodgers, "My Secret Place."

produces. That is, though the speaker's visionary desire is winging away out of sight, such a visual image depends on a residual awareness of her actual, gravity-bound position on shore (out of sight of whom?). Furthermore, there is almost no content or shape to her "dreams," the goal of which belongs to another realm of knowledge. This ineffability is exhilarating in its suggestion of an escape from mundane thought; at the same time, it implies a conceptual divide which may very well be unbridgeable.[4]

Joni goes on to place two other metaphorical sites in counterpoint with the visionary horizon. In the second verse, she cries out against the urban wasteland and its disfigured effigy of nature: no spiritual nurture here. In the third verse, she escapes to an earthly haven where the seagulls are in view.[5]

But even here, the sad facts of mortality soon intrude into consciousness: "But sandcastles crumble / And hunger is human." This vein continues into the last verse, where a question forms for the seagull, as if the bird could tell us of those who came before. Here the perspective widens once again, this time over a temporal horizon. Once again Joni summons images of disappearance: castles that crumble, footprints washed away, dreams that come to nothing.

Thus the powerful visionary urge, which always returns with the refrain, is held in tension with the knowledge of frailty and transience. The rising wing is countered by the sinking stone. At the climactic point in each verse just before the refrain, the melody rises repeatedly to the seventh degree of the scale (B-flat). In the modal language of the song this builds a questioning as well a directional force. The verse articulations are thus poised on an updraft which is carried through only in the guitar. During the aspirations of the refrain, the vocal melody is in fact sinking on its way back to the tonic.

---

4.   There are plenty of songs in which Joni spells out specific social or philosophical ideals; but these often don't coincide with a use of visionary rhetoric. For example, in "Sisotowbell Lane," also from her first album, the utopian geniality of the earthy-crunchy community she portrays consists precisely in its being realizable at this moment in the world.

5.   Joni uses these two sites to structure the entire album, prefacing its two parts with lines from this song. Part 1 ("I came to the city") has an urban setting, part 2 ("Out of the city and down to the seaside") various pastoral settings. The urban, the pastoral, and the visionary horizon are all captured in Joni's elaborate cover art for the album; the visionary portion of the cover is set off by its widened focus, its lack of color, its infinite fan of sunrays, and its flight of gulls.

Joni's persona in this song may be filled with idealistic longing, but she is well aware of how little effect such longing might have. The longed-for world is incommensurable, a world we can't share. Where are the signs of the other dreamers that have been here? Her final call to the gull goes unanswered; it seems that her wishes must also fall back to earth, leaving no sign. The final phrase "out of cry" takes on an extra resonance. Not only does it suggest the crying bird moving out of our range of hearing, but it suggests the imperviousness of the gull to the human cry. Joni portrays her visionary flight with an image that evokes both exhilaration and melancholy, transcendence and separation.

—

"Sweet Bird" appears on the 1975 album *The Hissing of Summer Lawns*. The tone of the entire album is slick and sophisticated, miles from her earnest, rough-edged debut. The lyrics in general are more difficult, allusive, and densely scaped. The title and central image of this song refer glancingly to the Tennessee Williams play *Sweet Bird of Youth*; in fact, the song spins out a meditation on the transience of youth without ever once speaking the word. Where "Song to a Seagull" moved among three symbolic poles, "Sweet Bird" is absorbed in a single dense image, suspended in time and space.

The high-flown language of the first four lines works on two levels: its most concrete subject is the passing from one's prime into middle age. Somewhere out there, it says, was a line I crossed, a moment that marked, however subtly, the onset of decline.[6] This concrete meaning is continued with the reference to age-defying makeup in the seventh line. Surrounded as it is by highly abstract utterances, the latter image ("beauty jars") is itself rather jarring, with its assumption that an ideal can be packaged or even contained. The image of facial care also has an odd retrospective on line 4, evoking oblique echoes of "vanishing" cream—one vain remedy against the effects of time.

But the concrete level of meaning is initially quite difficult to pick out, being ironically embedded within a transcendent level. The opening poetic figures are powerfully vague and abstract, placing us on some unspecified horizon, which could be in space or time. If space, it's an airless sort of limbo; if time, it's a gyroscopic balance-point. The speaker is projected or

6. The age contrast expressed here by "golden" "vanishing" was introduced in the first song of this album ("In France They Kiss on Main Street"): "Under neon signs / A girl was in bloom / And a woman was fading / In a suburban room."

abstracted "out," away from any worldly anchor; her states of sleeping and waking assume a metaphysical connotation. Metaphysical as well, it would seem, is her turn from "golden" fullness to a state of vanishing, as if her identity, with its inevitable limitations, has just dissolved in the rarefied air. With the invocation of the strange bird in line 5, we have all the signs of transcendence familiar to us from the previous song: outward projection, flight, and disappearance. One further element contributing to the transcendent perspective in this case is the poetic discourse itself. The abstractions and suggestive imprecisions—"out," "up," "somewhere," "horizon," "time and change"—continue throughout. Keeping the language consistently at such a distance from a mundane setting reinforces the effect of elevation and widened focus.

That is why the mundane "beauty jars" are so intrusive, and why the whole topic of aging stands in an ironic relation to the transcendent. The figurative language (and the music, as we shall see) gives us a taste of an expanded perspective, from which human concerns seem a small matter. This state of privileged vision is embodied in the uncanny bird, who can only be laughing at our vain anxieties. The message of the song will turn out to be our inability to grasp firmly the ideals of youth and beauty; but the musical experience extends the seductive illusion that we can inhabit a world of ideals.

The song begins with a very gradual fade-in, as if we are approaching or tuning in to something that's already there. The alternation between two chords (Bm^7 and Em^7) creates a circular rather than forward motion. Acoustic guitars lay down a mellow strumming figure, punctuated by gentle slaps on the strings. The guitar is doubled, lending it a special fullness; this is set off against a warm glow of background vocals and wailing electric guitars. The voices cluster and shift like a spatial mass; the electric guitars unfurl in a high, haunting stratum; an intermittent, rocking piano is also added to the texture. Each instrument group occupies a distinct registral layer, the rhythmic activity of which is independent of the others; the voices and high guitars are especially free floating. The entire texture creates a very special sound-world: rather static in time, with no beginning; spatially layered, with strata that hover and float; tone colors that combine a "golden" glow with eerily distant reverberations. Spacy, ungrounded, a world untarnishable, apart.

The voice enters on a melody that maintains a low range and a low expressive profile. In fact, the second section of each verse (lines 5–15, 20 to the end) hovers closely around the single note D. The relative stasis of the melody is offset by the complex harmonic progression. When the melody enters, the harmony breaks out of its alternation between minor

Introduction:

$$\text{‖: Bm}^7 \mid \text{Em}^7 \text{ :‖ Bm}^7 \mid \text{Em}^7 \text{ G} \mid$$

Line   1   2   3   4

$$\mid \text{C}^9 \mid \text{Em}^9 \mid \text{F/G} \mid \text{C}^9 \mid \text{C}^9 \mid \text{Em}^9 \mid \text{B}\flat\text{/E}\flat \mid \text{B}\flat\text{/E}\flat \mid \text{C}^9 \mid \text{G} \mid$$

Line   5   6   7   8   9

$$\text{‖: A/D} \mid \text{C/F G} \mid \text{C}^9 \mid \text{G} \mid \text{C}^9 \mid \text{G} \mid \text{F/G} \mid \text{C}^9\text{/G} \mid \text{C}^9\text{/G :‖}$$

Second time: 10   11   12   13   14

Line   15

$$\mid \text{F/G} \mid \text{C}^9\text{/G} \mid \text{C}^9\text{/G} \mid$$

FIG. 1. "Sweet Bird," chord changes, verse I. For the compound chords, indicated with slashes, the first letter is a triad, the second letter a bass note; e.g., "F/G" equals an F triad over a G bass. This is my own transcription. Guitar tuning: C G D G B D.

chords into a G-major area. The G center is held largely in suspension, however, only rarely touching down as a stable tonic (see fig. 1). At certain points in the harmonic circuit, the chords break out dramatically from the G center. The first point occurs at line 3. After "I lay down golden," the chord changes from E minor to a type of E-flat ninth chord (B-flat with an E-flat bass). The underlying voice-leading here is chromatic, but the arrival on E-flat is far down the flat side of G—the result is something like the bottom dropping out of the key. This effect is heightened by the pungent but open stacked-fifth spacing of the E-flat chord. The tonal rupture occurs at the turning moment in the opening poetic gambit—the balance-point between fullness and decline; Joni extends the duration of this line of text to linger over the effect.

At "Sweet bird" (line 5) there is another rupture, this time on the sharp side of G. This chord, on D, has the same structure as the E-flat chord.[7] Both ruptures are momentary and quickly fold back into G. They complicate the tonal space of the song in uncanny ways; at the same time, their arrangement on either side of G in the circle of fifths reflects the thematic

7.   This structure is built into the guitar tuning: C G D G B D. Laying a finger across the third fret, for instance, produces the E-flat chord of line 3; across the second fret, the D chord of line 5.

idea of balance. Balance is evident as well between the introductory material (also used as interlude and postlude) on the dominant, or sharp side, and the verse, which largely tends to the subdominant, or flat side, of G.

The flavor of sharp and flat combines with that of minor and major to further distinguish the verses from the interludes. The circling minor harmonies of the interludes imbue those sections with melancholy; in contrast, the mostly major subdominant shading in the verses gives them a certain serenity. This polarizes the tension maintained in the lyrics between an imagined sphere of Platonic perfection ("golden in time") and our real exclusion from such a sphere ("cities under the sand"). The instrumental introduction thus concentrates in itself the ache of longing, or perhaps a mourning over our shortcomings. This symbolic connotation intensifies in the central interlude, in which the regular meter is truncated, confused by cross-rhythms, and arrested by awkward accents in the guitar figuration. After the contrast of this limping, imperfect world, the second verse truly soars. At the end of the second verse, the song falls into a loop ("guesses based on . . .") of alternating subdominant chords (as in fig. 1, line 15). It repeats so many times that it seems the song will end on this serene plateau. But at the final vocal phrase the balance tips, and we return to the melancholy instrumental loop for the fade-out.

"Sweet Bird" begins from an awareness of lost youth, but this awareness is only evoked through allusion and circuitous expression. Joni exploits the indirect language in favor of an obscure meaning, one cloaked in indeterminacy. When the bird first appears it is "briefer than a falling star": it must represent youth itself. At the next invocation, it is "sweet bird of time and change"; apparently its meaning has shifted to encompass the process of loss and transience. And youth is not all that is lost; we see "power, ideals, and beauty fading." When we come to the song's final moral, it has drifted further away from the initial concern. No one can ever get that close—close to what? Once again the song has moved powerfully toward the abstract, pushing concrete circumstances to the point of disappearance. We are left with guesses, a rushing sky, shifting patterns of time and change.

"Amelia" is from *Hejira* (1976), just one year later.[8] The musical palette is similar in many ways to that of "Sweet Bird." The vocal melody is in

8.   The published score offers this translation of *hejira*: "A journey especially when undertaken to seek refuge away from a dangerous or undesirable environment."

rather low relief—restrained sighs and eddies rather than dramatic arches. Joni uses guitar to lay down a subtly looping harmonic circuit (to which I will return in a moment). The guitar is doubled in a way that sets up a live, pulsing halo of reverberation.[9] Joni uses this tone color for the whole album as a sonic evocation of the open country so important to her over-arching themes of travel, quest, and escape. Over and around the guitar background the vibraphone and lead guitar are applied like daubs of paint, creating bell-tone highlights and a swarm of subliminal "voices" that bend, croon, and soar. The sound world, as in "Sweet Bird," is both densely textured and spacy. Due to the phlegmatic rhythm, however, the emotional tone is oddly muffled and passionless.

In contrast to the other songs we've discussed, this song rambles through a string of episodes. The speaker is a woman on the road; each verse teases out a different view of travel as a metaphor for life or love. The ethereal bird character has been translated into an airplane, and by extension into the romantic figure of Amelia Earhart. A world-weary apostrophe to Amelia rounds off each verse. The visionary aspect of this poem is not as pervasive; from the mundane realm we receive intermittent glimpses of another, "higher" perspective. For this effect, it's significant that the poet is behind the wheel of a car, while her meditations are all about air travel. The poet's skyward yearnings never quite coalesce into a sustained stratum of privileged vision.

In the opening scenario, the sight of jet planes provides the occasion for Joni to project her identity outward. The image of her guitar strings (i.e., her creative/expressive persona) spreads to fill the heavens in the wake of the planes and their seductive engine drone. The effect of this

9. This effect is now commonly supplied by the chorus pedal. "In my own peculiar way, I invented the chorus. . . . On *Hejira* I doubled the guitar . . . in a way that Wayne Shorter and Miles [Davis] double up on *Nefertiti*. It's like silkscreening— it's not tight doubling. I'm playing the part twice, but there's some variations on it so they're not perfectly tight—they're shadowing each other in some places. That sound was satisfactory for me for that project, so when it came time I asked Fred [Walecki of Westwood Music], 'Do you have anything that will break the sig-nal on a guitar and double it? I need to somehow or other duplicate this sound in performance.' He said, 'Gee, I don't—there's nothing like that.' So . . . some sales-man from Roland came to see me, and I asked them. . . . They went away and in a very short space of time they came back to Fred with the original Roland Jazz Chorus amp." Joni Mitchell, interview by Chip Stern, *Musician* 195 (January/February 1995): 24.

Interlude circles around an F chord, 6 measures:

Line   1   2   3
                   | G | G | B♭ | B♭ | Am⁹ | Bm | G C⁹/G | C⁹/G |

Line   4   5
                   | C⁹ | Em⁷ | Bm⁷ | Am⁹ | Am⁹/G |

Line   6
Refrain: | F | B♭⁹/F | F | F | (back to interlude)

FIG. 2. "Amelia," chord changes. For clarity, this transcription leaves out some ornamental and passing chords. Guitar tuning: C G C E G C.

metaphoric substitution is one of brief release from a physical setting ("the bleak terrain") into a cosmic state. But the original image which triggered the vision—the "vapor trails"—is insubstantial, and already disappearing. The refrain brings this point home: "It was just a false alarm." These words signal a deflation of the transcendent perspective and an inability to sustain it for long. More devastatingly, they reflect upon Joni's artistic confidence, which has been implicated in the vision's insubstantiality. (The point is underlined by the rhyming of "guitar" and "false alarm"—and through an imperfect, failed rhyme, at that.) What if her musical achievement itself is nothing more than a vapor trail? The refrain is indeterminate enough to serve for every verse, but at each occurrence the message is one of disappointment at the deceptiveness of appearances, or the failure of hopes and dreams.

A gestural rhythm of elation and deflation is also conveyed in the song's harmonic progression. The beginning of each verse is marked by a series of harmonic upturns (see fig. 2). After the interlude in F, line 1 is introduced by an unprepared shift to a G tonic. Line 2 consists of similar material, now shifted up in a momentary tonicization of B-flat. Both shifts are accomplished by the left hand sliding on the strings. This upward voice-leading strand reaches its high point at the C chord at the beginning of line 4, after which the bass line turns back down through B, A, and G. The entire verse (the B-flat chords excepted) sits within G major; but at the end of line 5 the descending bass overshoots and falls down into F for the refrain and interlude. Verse and refrain thus exist in a false tonal relation with each other, and the slump into F corresponds to the disappointment embodied in the refrain.

The climactic emergence of the visionary occurs in the fifth verse, where Joni portrays Earhart's historical fate in mythical terms. The pilot disappears over the horizon, following her dream; Joni identifies her own sense of vision with that of the pilot. But Amelia is an Icarus figure, reckless and flawed. Joni is admitting to ambivalence about her own "beautiful foolish" aspirations. Those aspirations center on her relationships and artistic goals, and the precarious balance between the two.[10] As the following verse bears out, the special vision integral to her artistic personality entails a risk of losing perspective, of being swallowed by the dream. The harmonic overshooting at the refrain has a pointed metaphoric correspondence here to the superimposed threefold crash of Icarus, Amelia, and Joni.

Though all three of the songs we've discussed are marked by ambivalence, the signs of inner division are strongest in "Amelia." Take, for instance, the idea of disappearance. In "Song to a Seagull" and "Sweet Bird," this idea was used complexly to convey the knowledge of mortality ("where are the footprints?"; "vanishing"), and the dream of escape from mortality ("out of reach"; "vanishing"). In "Amelia," two things vanish: the vapor trails and Amelia herself. Both are instances of the failure of the visionary, and Amelia's fate offers no escape from mortality. Likewise, in verse 6, being airborne is presented in quite a negative light ("in clouds at icy altitudes"), as a hindrance to living fully on earth. The song doesn't go so far as to repudiate the visionary impulse, but it does seek to redirect it in search of a healthier, more sustainable relation between the transcendent and the mundane.

"The Beat of Black Wings" appears on the 1988 album *Chalk Mark in a Rain Storm*, an album steeped in moral indignation. The song is a third-person portrait, a common genre for Joni; but she gives it a twist by casting the bulk of the poem as a quotation, in the subject's own words.[11] The speaker is a young Vietnam veteran whose experience in the maw of the war machine has left him morally and psychologically damaged. The insidiousness of the damage is captured succinctly in the story of his girlfriend's

10. The destabilizing effect of Joni's musical career is a pervasive theme in *Hejira*. Compare the following excerpt from the song "Black Crow": "In search of love and music / My whole life has been / Illumination / Corruption . . . / Diving down to pick up on every shiny thing / Just like that black crow flying / In a blue sky."
11. Two other songs framed in this way are "Free Man in Paris" and "Raised on Robbery," both from *Court and Spark*.

abortion (in the third verse), which ruthlessly recapitulates and external-izes elements of the original trauma: death meted out in a moral void, the obviation of grief, a preemption of his powers of decision, a future scraped hollow. The soldier's words are left offensively raw, in harsh contrast with the highly crafted music. Meanwhile, Joni delivers one of the most man-nered vocal performances of her career, changing expression with every line and veering from one timbral extreme to another as if barely in con-trol of her characterization.

At this point, one might be wondering how the visionary enters into this song. True, the refrain does invoke bird imagery, but the black wings which squawk, flap, and beat belong to bats or carrion birds. Superimposed on this, of course, is the image of a helicopter; the sound of whirring rotors provides the fundamental rhythmic track for the song. None of these winged things is associated with soaring flight. Instead, they suggest a predatory hovering—a mockery of any wish for transcendence.

The surprise lies in the music, for this is where the vision is to be found. There is still an awareness of pain and outrage in the stumbling piano figures, the jabbing percussive highlights, the plosive keyboard bursts with their reedy edge, and the indecipherable background vocal mumbles. But all these elements are extremely stylized and fused into a tone of chilly ecstasy. The basic chord progression is an elated affirma-tion of D major, while the harmonic surface is iridescent and tinted with extended sonorities and oblique shiftings. There are also several metaphorical techniques of suspension at work. In the instrumental interludes, for instance, the surface harmonic phenomena change every measure, while at a deeper structural level a much slower rate of har-monic change is projected (a new chord every four measures, as follows: I V I vi). Surface motion is thus suspended over a slowly turning back-ground. In addition, the electric bass during these same passages heavily emphasizes the dominant; even during the tonic harmonies, the bass gives the strongest metric position to the dominant, thus suspending the tonal ground. Furthermore, the first and third phrases of every verse extend the regular four-bar scansion by inserting a two-bar half-caden-tial figure. The suspense just before these cadences is heightened by the sudden emptiness of texture and the momentary disappearance of the harmony (e.g., in the first verse at "name was Killer Kyle" and "tough one for me to sing"). The prolongation of such up-in-the-air qualities gives a joyous inevitability to the full cadence at each refrain. Joni caps this cadence with a high, poignant keyboard descant whose prominent, shimmering overtones resemble an unearthly organum.

One can think of the music as achieving outward projection in an emotional sense. The soldier's vortex of rage and despair hardly affects the musical environment—so polished, so transfixed. Joni's setting places a breathtaking emotional distance between her raw subject and her expressive artifice. There is also a defiance of gravity in the multiple musical suspensions, which are not hard to hear as gestures of buoyancy and release. The third element of transcendence—the horizon or vanishing point—is more difficult to conceive in musical terms, but one can interpret the moments of textural dissipation along such lines. At these moments, it seems as if the orchestral body fades to transparency. Through the aperture, we briefly hear the most basic stratum of sound—the rotor wings—unaccompanied before the orchestral substance rushes back in. This basic stratum is ongoing throughout the song but usually not directly perceptible. The aperture effect approaches a privileged perspective through points of musical vanishing.

How do the two visions square? I have just interpreted the rotor oscillation almost in spiritual terms, as an intimation of reality. Yet to the poor soldier, the wing-beats that won't go away represent the ongoing nightmare which finally subsumes his identity. The musical figure of disappearance offers an exhilarating sense of weightlessness; but the soldier's experience of disappearance (in the last verse) means the appalling loss of personal solidity. The centrifugal forces threatening to rip the young man apart (the internal "war zone") are countered by the music's sublime self-possession: even the (sinister?) helicopter track sounds like an image of perfect balance and control. What is the point of this ironic contradiction? In my view, the affective dissociation between words and music carries no cynical, neutralizing force; it doesn't deaden the pain. By surrounding the young man's harsh outpouring with a visionary joy, Joni reminds us of what he has lost. Her indictment of social ill is made all the more piercing by the distance between corrupt reality and the possibility of grace trembling in the music.[12]

One final touch remains to be mentioned. During the instrumental

12. Similar couplings of joyous music and painful words can be found in Joni's "Cherokee Louise," from *Night Ride Home*; Suzanne Vega's "Luka," from *Solitude Standing*; and (in a muted way) the title song from *The Angel in the House*, by Jonathan Brooke (of the group The Story).

interludes, Joni adds a vocal tag—"Johnny Angel"—from the 1960 hit sung by Shelly Fabares. The dissonance of the importation strikes multiple sparks. The quoted song invokes the (now-distant) time of its release, probably the young man's teen years, before going off to war. Moreover, it's a song about innocence, a simple expression of unrequited love. And it refers in its naive way to flights of celestial happiness, in stark counterpoint to the infernal apparitions tormenting the soldier.[13] Once again, music (here, a musical recollection) is the bearer of a whole pattern of lost possibility. By now we should realize the pathos behind the soldier's complaint that he "'can't hear the fuckin' music playin'.'" He has suffered a spiritual impairment, cutting him off from the innocence, hope, and wholeness which, from our favored perspective, we can hear shimmering all around him.

—

Fade-out

My survey does not exhaust the appearance of the visionary strain in Joni's work—a strain that exerts a rich fascination in many other songs. Right from the beginning, however, in the earliest example, we feel the tug of a counterweight. Following a dialectical turn of mind which remains characteristic throughout Joni's career, the visionary urge is expressed as a tension between idealism and worldliness, between abstract yearnings and concrete realities. It is this attraction to polarity which enables Joni to discover such rich sources of significance in her chosen thematic domains. She finds continued resonance in the cross-purpose, the inconsistency, the ill fit between our lofty lines of vision and the world lying within our reach.

13. Lines from the quoted song include "Every time he says hello my heart begins to fly" and "Together we will see how lovely heaven can be."

BY ROBERT HILBURN

JONI MITCHELL: BOTH SIDES, LATER

What was her inspiration when she wrote the songs? In talking about her 1996 compilations, Hits *and* Misses, *Joni recalls the stories behind some of her best-loved songs written from the late 1960s through the early 1990s. —SFL*

Los Angeles Times, December 8, 1996

You can tell a lot about Joni Mitchell's humor and spunk from just the titles of her two recent "best of" albums on Reprise Records. One is *Hits*. It contains 15 of her best-known songs—from the wistful "Both Sides, Now," which she wrote in 1967 when she was just 23, to the declarative "Help Me," a cornerstone of 1974's *Court and Spark*, the album that cemented Mitchell's reputation as one of the most influential and acclaimed writers of the modern pop era.

The other collection is *Misses*. It's a 14-song package that focuses chiefly on the post-*Court* material—from the social commentary of *Dog Eat Dog* to the ambitious narrative sweep of *Hejira*—that moved away from the accessible, folk-accented textures of the singer's earlier work.

"I tend to be dismissive of my early songs in favor of championing my underdog children," Mitchell says, explaining why she insisted that Reprise release *Misses* along with the *Hits* package. "I think the songs after *Court and Spark* show a lot of growth and I worry that much of it is destined for obscurity."

Mitchell, 53, hopes the *Misses* album and the attention she is receiving in what she calls her "season of honors" help rescue the post–*Court and Spark* material. In September, she was presented with the Governor General's Performing Arts Award in Canada, and she'll be honored Wednesday at the Regent Beverly Wilshire Hotel with a lifetime achievement award by the National Academy of Songwriters. She'll also be inducted into the Rock and Roll Hall of Fame on May 15 in Cleveland.

Despite the awards, Mitchell—rivaled perhaps only by Bob Dylan during the rock era in combining strong literary sensibilities with an uncompromising eye for life's rituals and rites—wonders whether people understand her real musical vision, which has moved freely over the years to incorporate world music, jazz and classical textures. She's well aware, for instance, that she made the Rock and Roll Hall of Fame in her fourth year of eligibility.

"Well, it's a boys' club, isn't it?" she says of the Hall of Fame. "And it's kind of a joke . . . . There are so many people in it. It's like a hockey hall of fame where they let in anyone who has ever scored a goal. But then, I never considered myself a rock artist or a folk artist. People just saw a girl with an acoustic guitar and said, 'Folksinger.' But to me, my roots were in classical music."

The Canadian-born Mitchell, a Los Angeles resident for years, declines an invitation to pick out 10 favorites from her body of work, but she agreed to react to a list of 10 of my favorite Mitchell songs. On the eve of this week's dinner, she also expressed some of her views about song-writing and tried to clear up what she feels are some misconceptions about her work. The songs are in chronological order.

CHELSEA MORNING (1967)

I wrote that in Philadelphia after some girls who worked in this club where I was playing . . . found all this colored slag glass in an alley. We collected a lot of it and built these glass mobiles with copper wire and coat hangers. I took mine back to New York and put them in my window on West 16th Street in the Chelsea district. The sun would hit the mobile and send these moving colors all around the room. As a young girl, I found that to be a thing of beauty. There's even a reference to the mobile in the song. It was a very young and lovely time . . . before I had a record deal. I think it's a very sweet song, but I don't think of it as part of my best work. To me, most of those early songs seem like the work of an ingenue.

BOTH SIDES, NOW (1967)

I was reading Saul Bellow's *Henderson the Rain King* on a plane and early in the book Henderson the Rain King is also up in a plane. He's on his way to Africa, and he looks down and sees these clouds. I put down the book, looked out the window and saw clouds too, and I immediately started writing the song. I had no idea that the song would become as popular as it did.

BIG YELLOW TAXI (1970)

I wrote "Big Yellow Taxi" on my first trip to Hawaii. I took a taxi to the hotel and when I woke up the next morning, I threw back the curtains and saw these beautiful green mountains in the distance. Then, I looked down and there was a parking lot as far as the eye could see, and it broke my heart . . . this blight on paradise. That's when I sat down and wrote the song. When it first came out, it was a regional hit in Hawaii because people there realized their paradise was being chewed up. It took 20 years for that song to sink in to people most other places in the country. That is a powerful little song because there have been cases in a couple of cities of parking lots being torn up and turned into parks because of it.

ALL I WANT (1971)

I like that song. It's got more tooth than most of the other [early] songs. But I don't know what to say about it. It's funny how people keep looking between the lines of songs to see what is hidden there. Well, I'm not an evasive writer. You don't have to dig under the words for the meaning. The meaning is all there. It's very plain-speak. When someone asks what a song like "Sex Kills" is about, I want to say, "Well, did you listen to the words?"

FOR THE ROSES (1972)

That was my first farewell to show business. I was in Canada, where I have a sanctuary where I still go sometimes, and I had decided to quit show business and get away from all the pressures I felt. I put my thoughts into that song . . . "Remember the days when you used to sit / And make up your tunes for love . . . / And now you're seen / On giant screens / And at parties for the press / And for people who have slices of you / From the company." To me, this was an unfair, crooked business and it has nothing to do with real talent . . . . I was up in Canada about a year and I guess it strengthened my nervous system a little, so I finally came back.

FREE MAN IN PARIS (1973)

I wrote that in Paris for David Geffen [the entertainment mogul and then-president of her record label], taking a lot of it from the things he said . . . . Another song about show business and the pressures. He didn't like it at the time. He begged me to take it off the record. I think he felt uncomfortable being shown in that light.

THE SAME SITUATION (1973)

I don't want to name names or kiss and tell, but basically it is a portrait of a Hollywood bachelor and the parade of women through his life . . .

how he toys with yet another one. So many women have been in this position . . . being vulnerable at a time when you need affection or are searching for love, and you fall into the company of a Don Juan.

AMELIA (1976)

That's a good choice. To me, the whole *Hejira* album was really inspired. I feel a lot of people could have written "Chelsea Morning," but I don't think anyone else could have written the songs on *Hejira*. I wrote the album while traveling cross-country by myself, and there is this restless feeling throughout it. . . . The sweet loneliness of solitary travel. What happened was I had driven across the country with a couple of friends, starting in California when they showed up at my door. One was an old boyfriend from Australia who had a 20-day visa and wanted to go to Maine to kidnap his daughter from this grandmother. You could have made a whole movie about that trip. "Refuge of the Roads" grew out of that experience. On the way back, I went down the coast to Florida and then followed the Gulf of Mexico across the country, staying in old '50s motels and eating at health food stores. In this song, I was thinking of Amelia Earhart and addressing it from one solo pilot to another . . . sort of reflecting on the cost of being a woman and having something you must do.

TWO GREY ROOMS (1991)

I had that music back around the time of [1982's] *Wild Things Run Fast*, but it took seven years to find the story to fit the music. It's a story of obsession . . . about this German aristocrat who had a lover in his youth that he never got over. He later finds this man working on a dock and notices the path that the man takes every day to and from work. So the aristocrat gives up his fancy digs and moves to these two shabby grey rooms overlooking this street, just to watch this man walk to and from work. That's a song that shows my songs aren't all self-portraits.

NIGHT RIDE HOME (1991)

That's a sweet song that was written in Hawaii when [record producer-musician Larry Klein] and I were driving along on the Fourth of July to this house we had rented. There was this big moon and the clouds moving across the island so quickly. Everything looked so magical . . . even the white line on the highway. It was as if someone had sprinkled fairy dust all around. . . .

It's interesting how people hear your sad songs and think you must be miserable or whatever. They don't think William Shakespeare was miserable just because he wrote about tragedy. I see myself as a singing playwright and an actress and I try to make plays that are pertinent to our times . . . I fully experience my anxiety and my grief, but that doesn't mean I don't also have a lot of fun . . . . I like to think of myself, in fact, as a fun-loving person.

BY JEFFREY PEPPER RODGERS

SETTING THE STAGE: THE VOCAL AND LYRICAL CRAFT OF JONI MITCHELL

Joni discusses lyric structure, melody choices, and attitude. A highlight: how she came to love those early, high-swooping melodies. This final piece is a companion to the first in this section, about Joni's guitar tunings, also written by Jeffrey Pepper Rodgers.—SFL

Acoustic Guitar, February 1997

Joni Mitchell is one of those rare songwriters whose music is created from the ground up. Her signature as a composer can be found not only in the melody and lyric, but in the idiosyncratic chord movement, the expansive guitar and piano voicings, and the chorus of supporting voices and instruments. In describing her music, Mitchell often uses the language of painting, and, indeed, all of these elements of her songs blend together very much like brush strokes on a canvas.

In *Acoustic Guitar*'s August 1996 cover story, "My Secret Place," I profiled Mitchell's radical guitar style, drawing on an interview conducted early last year. But in truth, the guitar was only one touch point of our three-hour-long conversation, and Mitchell's comments on alternate tunings sailed right into thoughts on poetry and painting and the music business and then back to the guitar again, without a pause or a break in the logic. This article will take a second look inside Mitchell's music, through the lens of the voice and lyrics.

In discussing her slant on the lyric craft, Mitchell recalled her days as an art student in Toronto, when she was performing music on the side—mainly the English folk repertoire—but had not yet started writing songs.

"I didn't really begin to write songs until I crossed the border into the States in 1965," she said. "I had always written poetry, mostly because I had to on assignment. But I hated poetry in school; it always seemed shallow and contrived and insincere to me. All of the great poets seemed to be playing around with sonics and linguistics, but they were so afraid to express themselves without surrounding it in poetic legalese. Whenever they got sensitive, I don't know, I just didn't buy it."

Outside of school, Mitchell still found herself writing poems when a strong emotion hit her, such as when a friend committed suicide. But it wasn't until she heard Bob Dylan's "Positively Fourth Street" that she finally began to understand how to tap the power of this private poetry in a song. She recalled, "When I heard that—'You've got a lot of nerve to say you are my friend'—I thought, now that's poetry; now we're talking. That direct, confronting speech, commingled with imagery, was what was lacking for me." Later, in the '70s, Mitchell found her ideal of poetry reflected in the words of Friedrich Nietzsche's character Zarathustra, who envisions "a new breed of poet, a penitent of spirit; they write in their own blood." She added, "I believe to this day that if you are writing that which you know firsthand, it'll have greater vitality than if you're writing from other people's writings or secondhand information."

Thanks in large part to Mitchell's influence, personally based writing became one of the emblems of the singer-songwriter movement that flowered in the '70s and is going strong again in the '90s. Even today, her 1970 album *Blue* (Reprise)—written and recorded, she said, in a fragile state somewhere between nervous breakdown and breakthrough—stands as one of the most emotionally naked performances ever captured on tape. The songs are unquestionably written in her own blood, and even though she has progressed through many modes of writing since then—some more obviously autobiographical than others—her personal commitment to the words always shines through.

The mixture of direct speech and more abstract imagery that Mitchell admired in "Positively Fourth Street" remains a hallmark of her writing. Matching these different lyrical styles with the right sections of the melody, she explained, is a matter of listening closely to the song as it unfolds. "Sometimes the words come first, and then it's easier, because you know exactly what melodic inflection is needed. Given the melody first, you can say, for instance, 'OK, in the A section, I can get away with narrative, descriptive. In the B, I can only speak directly, because of the way the chords are moving. I have to make a direct statement. And in the C section, the chords are so sincere and heartrending that what I say has to be kind of profound, even to myself.' Theatrically speaking, the scene is scored—now you have to put in the dialogue.

"Also, it has to be married to the inflection of English speech," Mitchell said. "Pop music doesn't carry this fine point very far, although a lot of great simple songs do. You know, [*sings*] 'Yesterday.' That's a good melody; that's a good marriage of words and melody, just that simple little piece." To underscore the point, Mitchell sang another example. ". . . So a lot of times, even though I may have written the text symmetrically verse to verse to verse, in terms of syncopation I'll sing a slightly different melody to make the emphasis fall on the correct word in the sentence, as you would in spoken English."

Throughout the interview, Mitchell described her vocal craft by using the language of theater, just as she explained her sense of harmony in terms of painting. Metaphorically, these two art forms make a lot of sense together: the chord movement is the painting of the stage scenery—the context and structure of the music—and in the vocal parts, she steps onto the stage to act out the part she has scripted for herself. Mitchell's goal as a singer, like that of a good actor, is to embody the words and rise above what she called the "emotional fakery" of pop music.

"Pop music in particular, but music in general, is full of falseness, just loaded with it," Mitchell said. "Blessedly, most people don't hear it, otherwise none of the stuff would be popular. It's contrived, false sexualness in the voice, false sorrow in the voice." This quality is as true of instrumental music as vocal music, Mitchell said, and she recalled a conversation with Charles Mingus shortly before his death in 1979, when they were collaborating on what became her *Mingus* album (Asylum). "Mingus at the end, when I went to work with him, couldn't listen to anything except a couple of Charlie Parker records. He kept saying [imitates deep, raspy voice], 'That ain't shit. He's falsifying his emotions. Pretentious motherfucker.' Charlie could hear it; I could hear it. He couldn't stand to listen to most of his records because he could perceive in the note the egocenteredness of a player. It's not pleasant to have that perception."

Mitchell cited another example of the importance of the singer's attitude and sincerity, from the sessions for her forthcoming album, the follow-up to *Turbulent Indigo* (Reprise). "I'm doing these vocals," she said, "for this song called 'No Apologies.' It's a heavy song. I've had to take four passes at it because it's so heavy that if I color it with any attitude it makes me want to get up and shut it off. I [have to] sing it absolutely deadpan, because it's got such strong language in it."

Beyond the lead vocal, Mitchell often builds elaborate backup vocal parts—usually her own voice multitracked many times over—that amplify or comment on the lyrics in highly unusual ways. She traces this idea to her childhood, when she sang in a church choir after recovering from polio. "I took on the descant part, which I called 'the pretty melody,'" she said. "Most people couldn't sing it because it jumped around too much. Most people—kids, anyway, in a children's choir—couldn't hold onto a note much beyond a third spread; these had five- and seven- and eight-note spreads [*sings*]. [The descant parts] wove all the tighter harmonies of the choral piece together. So from there I got a very unusual melodic sense."

Mitchell considers some of her songs with complex vocal arrangements to be, first and foremost, choral pieces. One example is "The Reoccurring Dream" (from *Chalk Mark in a Rain Storm*, Geffen; also included on Reprise's new *Misses* collection), in which background voices chant the seductive messages of advertising: "Latest styles and colors!" "I want a new truck—more power!" "More fulfilling—and less frustrating!" In "The Sire of Sorrow (Job's Sad Song)," the masterful closing work of *Turbulent Indigo*, the background voices are, according to Mitchell, "actually characters—they're the antagonists. They have the insulting lines that these so-called friends of Job's say to him. They augment the drama."

Another example of Mitchell's elaborate dramatic conceptions of her vocal parts is "Slouching towards Bethlehem" (*Night Ride Home*, Geffen), in which she adapted William Butler Yeats' famous poem "The Second Coming" and added some new words of her own. In the background vocals, she said, "Conceptually speaking, I wanted it to sound like a global women's lament, so I sang some of the backgrounds with the flatted African palate and some of them with an Arabic kind of [*sings warbling sound*]. I set myself up theatrical assignments like that. Whether or not I achieved that is debatable. To me I did, but then I know what the concept was and what the goal was; other people listening to it maybe think [the voices] are just not very attractive."

Mitchell took a similar type of risk in the dissonant vocal harmonies in "Ethiopia" (*Dog Eat Dog*, Geffen), a searing portrait of environmental devastation. "I had a girlfriend say, 'I just hate those harmonies,' and she squeezed her face all up," Mitchell recalled. "I said, 'Why?' and she said,

'You can't use parallel seconds.' I said, 'Well, they said, "You can't use parallel fifths" to Beethoven. You've got these women with dried-up milk glands and cadaverous babies with flies all over them, migrating to God knows what end across a burning desert. You think they're going to sing in a nice major triad?"'

On occasion, Mitchell extends the dramatic scope of a song by using guest singers. She said, "I'll need another voice to deliver a line, because [the songs] are like little plays. Like in 'Dancin' Clown' [*Chalk Mark*], Billy Idol plays the bully. He's got the perfect bully's voice. He's threatening this guy named Jesse [*imitates his voice*]: 'You're a push-button window! I can run you up and down. Anytime I want I can make you my dancing clown!' So you need an aggressive, bullyish voice to deliver that line." On that same album, Willie Nelson makes a much more low-key sort of cameo on "Cool Water," the classic song by the Sons of the Pioneers' Bob Nolan. Nelson's voice, Mitchell said, is "perfect for that song. That was a swing country era. Willie is of that era, and he's got that same kind of beautiful voice. He also sounds like an old desert rat, which is theatrically appropriate for that song."

When you take all of these sophisticated ideas related to the vocal and lyrical aspects of a song, and lay them on top of harmonies based on ever-changing guitar tunings that continually pull the rug out from under what you know and expect to hear, the possibilities of songwriting widen to a spectacularly broad horizon. Where most songwriters aim to graft distinctive words or a unique twist of melody onto a tried-and-true song structure or arrangement, Mitchell takes far more risks and far more responsibility. To extend her theatrical metaphor, she is set designer, stage manager, star actor, and supporting cast all in one. Every part of the production is open for reinterpretation and reinvention as Mitchell follows her restless muse.

Chronology

1943　On November 7, born Roberta Joan Anderson to William and Myrtle Anderson in Fort MacLeod, Alberta, Canada.

1952　Contracts polio.

1963　Buys a ukelele. Starts performing at Saskatoon coffeehouse, the Louis Riel, and with the proceeds, buys a guitar. Attends Alberta College of Art in Calgary.

1964　Leaves art school. Writes her first song, "Day After Day." Gives birth to baby girl, Kelly, and places her in a foster home.

1965　Meets and marries folk/cabaret singer Chuck Mitchell. Moves with Chuck to Detroit, Michigan. Starts experimenting with open tunings. Sings in duo with Chuck on the Toronto-Philadelphia-Detroit circuit. Puts Kelly up for adoption.

1966　Her song, "Urge for Going," recorded by George Hamilton IV, is the first commercial release of a Joni Michell song. Tom Rush and Dave Von Ronk actively promote Joni's song on their tours and in their shows.

1967　Ends marriage with Chuck Mitchell. Meets David Crosby. Moves to the Chelsea area of New York City. Performs at Cafe Au Go Go in Greenwich Village, where she is an opening act for an opening act, where she meets Elliot Roberts, who later becomes her manager.

1968　With help of Crosby, produces her first album, *Song to a Seagull* (Also known as *Joni Mitchell*). Moves to Laurel Canyon, California, with Graham Nash.

1969　Debuts at Carnegie Hall. Writes "Woodstock." Meets Bob Dylan. Sells 100,000 copies of *Clouds* in advance of its release. According to *Rolling Stone*, announces her retirement from the music business.

1970　Has first gold record with *Ladies of the Canyon*. *Melody Maker*, a British rock magazine, votes her world's top female singer, followed by Grace Slick, Janis Joplin, and Aretha Franklin.

1971   Moves to British Columbia. Leaves Warner Brothers Records and signs on with the new Asylum label, managed by David Geffen. *Blue*, her most soulful and "penitent of spirit" album yet, features James Taylor and Stephen Stills and reaches #15.

1972   Ends two-year retreat from live performances to embark on European tour. *For the Roses*, the first of her records to feature a full rhythm section, includes Steven Stills, Graham Nash, Russ Kunkel, Wilton Felder, James Burton and Tommy Scott. Writes hit single "You Turn Me On (I'm A Radio)."

1974   Reaches commercial highpoint with *Court and Spark*, a synthesis of rock, pop, and jazz and her first album to go all-electric. Musicians include John Guerin, Robbie Robertson, Jose Feliciano, and Wayne Perkins. Also produces *Miles of Aisles*, her first live album. Moves to Bel Air, California, with John Guerin.

1975   With *The Hissing of Summer Lawns*, continues jazz-pop fusion style; becomes a North American pop pioneer in the use of South African drumming as well as sampling technique; turns to narrative-style lyrics. Goes on tour with Bob Dylan's Rolling Thunder Revue.

1976   *Hejira*, written mostly on a cross-country car trip, utilizes flickering drum patterns of John Guerin and liquid fingerflow of bassist Jaco Pastorius. Album reaches #13. *The Hissing of Summer Lawns* named "Worst Album Title of the Year" by *Rolling Stone* (and not "Worst Album of the Year," as often cited).

1977   Continuing her experimentation, develops *Don Juan's Reckless Daughter* with Afro-Latin rhythms, featuring jazz heavyweight Wayne Shorter.

1978   Collaborates with legendary bassist/composer Charles Mingus, at his request.

1979   *Mingus*, a jazz album honoring Mingus and featuring Don Alias, Wayne Shorter, Jaco Pastorius, and Herbie Hancock, leads to her exile from popular radio.

1980   *Shadows and Light*, her second live album, reaches #38.

1982   Creates joyous, jazz-inflected rock with *Wild Things Run Fast*. Marries bassist Larry Klein. Leaves Asylum Records for Geffen.

1984   Breaks off with manager Elliot Roberts and signs on with Peter Asher.

1985   Makes strong political statements with *Dog Eat Dog*. Produced with Larry Klein, Mike Shipley, and techno-wizard Thomas Dolby.

1988   Continues political themes with *Chalk Mark in a Rain Storm*. Featured vocalists include Billy Idol, Peter Gabriel, Willie Nelson, and Tom Petty.

1991   Returns to love songs on acoustic guitar and piano with *Night Ride Home*.

1994   Returns to Reprise Records. The night before recording *Turbulent Indigo*, separates from Larry Klein.

1995   Wins *Billboard*'s Century Award. At New Orleans Jazz & Heritage Festival, first uses a Roland VG-8 interface with her guitar; this allows her to program and store multiple tunings and simplifies her touring.

1996   Produces *Hits* CD—along with a most-underappreciated *Misses* CD. Wins two Grammys, including Album of the Year, for *Turbulent Indigo*. Honored by the National Academy of Songwriters with a Lifetime Achievement Award; by her native Canada with the Governor General's Award and by Canadian Television with the Gemini Award; in Sweden with the Polar Music Award; by Gibson Guitar with the Best Acoustic Guitar Award.

1997   Inducted into the Rock and Roll Hall of Fame and the Songwriters' Hall of Fame. Reunites with daughter, Kilauren Gibb.

1998   Promotes new album, *Taming the Tiger*, on tour with Bob Dylan and Van Morrison.

1999   Recognized with the ASCAP Founders Award. At work recording a collection of jazz standards.

Discography

SONG TO A SEAGULL

Side One: *I Came To The City*:

I Had a King, Michael from Mountains, Night in the City, Marcie, Nathan La Franeer

Side Two: *Out of the City and Down to the Seaside*:

Sistowbell Lane, The Dawntreader, The Pirate of Penance, Song to a Seagull, Cactus Tree

Reprise 6293   1968

CLOUDS

Side One: Tin Angel, Chelsea Morning, I Don't Know Where I Stand, That Song About the Midway, Roses Blue

Side Two: The Gallery, I Think I Understand, Songs to Aging Children Come, The Fiddle and the Drum, Both Sides, Now

Reprise 6341   1969

LADIES OF THE CANYON

Side One: Morning Morgantown, For Free, Conversation, Ladies of the Canyon, Willy, The Arrangement

Side Two: Rainy Night House, The Priest, Blue Boy, Big Yellow Taxi, Woodstock, The Circle Game

Reprise 6376   1970

BLUE

Side One: All I Want, My Old Man, Little Green, Carey, Blue

Side Two: California, This Flight Tonight, River, A Case of You, The
          Last Time I Saw Richard

Reprise 2038   1971

FOR THE ROSES

Side One: Banquet, Cold Blue Steel and Sweet Fire, Barangrill, Lesson in
          Survival, Let the Wind Carry Me, For the Roses

Side Two: See You Sometime, Electricity, You Turn Me On (I'm a
          Radio), Blonde in the Bleachers, Woman of Heart and Mind,
          Judgement of the Moon and Stars (Ludwig's Tune)

Asylum 5057   1972

COURT AND SPARK

Side One: Court and Spark, Help Me, Free Man in Paris, People's
          Parties, The Same Situation

Side Two: Car on a Hill, Down to You, Just Like This Train, Raised on
          Robbery, Trouble Child, Twisted

Elektra 1001

Asylum 1001   1974

MILES OF AISLES

Side One: You Turn Me On (I'm a Radio), Big Yellow Taxi, Rainy Night
          House, Woodstock

Side Two: Cactus Tree, Cold Blue Steel and Sweet Fire, A Case of You, Blue

Side Three: The Circle Game, Peoples' Parties, All I Want, Real Good for
          Free, Both Sides, Now

Side Four: Carey, The Last Time I Saw Richard, Jericho, Love or Money

Asylum (2) 202   1974

THE HISSING OF SUMMER LAWNS

Side One: In France They Kiss on Main Street, The Jungle Line, Edith
          and the Kingpin, Don't Interrupt the Sorrow, Shades of Scarlet
          Conquering

Side Two: The Hissing of Summer Lawns, The Boho Dance, Harry's
House/Centerpiece, Sweet Bird, Shadows and Light

Asylum 1051   1975

HEJIRA

Side One: Coyote, Amelia, Furry Sings the Blues, A Strange Boy, Hejira

Side Two: Song for Sharon, Black Crow, Blue Motel Room, Refuge of
the Roads

Asylum 1087   1976

DON JUAN'S RECKLESS DAUGHTER

Side One: Overture / Cotton Avenue, Talk to Me, Jericho

Side Two: Paprika Plains

Side Three: Otis and Marlena, The Tenth World, Dreamland

Side Four: Don Juan's Reckless Daughter, Off Night Backstreet, The
Silky Veils of Ardor

Asylum (2) 701   1977

MINGUS

Side One: Happy Birthday 1975 (Rap), God Must Be a Boogie Man,
Funeral (Rap), A Chair in the Sky, The Wolf That Lives in
Lindsey

Side Two: It's a Muggin' (Rap), Sweet Sucker Dance, Coin in the Pocket
(Rap), The Dry Cleaner from Des Moines, Lucky (Rap),
Goodbye Pork Pie Hat

Asylum 505   1979

SHADOWS AND LIGHT

Side One: Introduction, In France They Kiss on Main Street, Edith and
the Kingpin, Coyote, Goodbye Pork Pie Hat

Side Two: The Dry Cleaner from Des Moines, Amelia, Pat's Solo (Pat
Metheny), Hejira

Side Three: Black Crow, Don's Solo (Don Alias), Dreamland, Free Man
in Paris, Band Introduction, Furry Sings the Blues

Side Four: Why Do Fools Fall in Love, Shadows and Light, God Must
    Be a Boogie Man, Woodstock

Asylum (2) 704   1980

WILD THINGS RUN FAST

Side One: Chinese Café, Unchained Melody, Wild Things Run Fast,
    Ladies' Man, Moon at the Window, Solid Love

Side Two: Be Cool, (You're So Square) Baby I Don't Care, You Dream
    Flat Tires, Man to Man, Underneath the Streetlight, Love

Geffen 2019   1982

DOG EAT DOG

Side One: Good Friends, Fiction, The Three Great Stimulants, Tax Free,
    Smokin' (*Empty, Try Another*)

Side Two: Dog Eat Dog, Shiny Toys, Ethiopia, Impossible Dreamer,
    Lucky Girl

Geffen 24074   1985

CHALK MARK IN A RAIN STORM

Side One: My Secret Place, Number One, Lakota, The Tea Leaf
    Prophecy (Lay Down Your Arms), Dancin' Clown

Side Two: Cool Water, The Beat of Black Wings, Snakes and Ladders,
    The Reoccurring Dream, A Bird That Whistles

Geffen 24172   1988

NIGHT RIDE HOME

Side One: Night Ride Home, Passion Play (When All the Slaves Are
    Free), Cherokee Louise, The Windfall (Everything for
    Nothing), Slouching Toward Bethlehem

Side Two: Come in From the Cold, Nothing Can Be Done, The Only Joy
    in Town, Ray's Dad's Cadillac, Two Grey Rooms

Geffen 24302   1991

TURBULENT INDIGO

Sunny Sunday, Sex Kills, How Do You Stop, Turbulent Indigo, Last Chance Lost, The Magdalene Laundries, Not to Blame, Borderline, Yvette in English, The Sire of Sorrow (Job's Sad Song)

Reprise 45786   1994

HITS

Urge for Going, Chelsea Morning, Big Yellow Taxi, Woodstock, The Circle Game, Carey, California, You Turn Me On (I'm a Radio), Raised on Robbery, Help Me, Free Man in Paris, River, Chinese Café/Unchained Melody, Come in From the Cold, Both Sides, Now

Reprise 46326   1996

MISSES

Passion Play (When All the Slaves Are Free), Nothing Can Be Done, A Case of You, The Beat of Black Wings, Dog Eat Dog, The Wolf That Lives in Lindsey, The Magdalene Laundries, Impossible Dreamer, Sex Kills, The Reoccurring Dream, Harry's House/Centerpiece, The Arrangement, For the Roses, Hejira

Reprise 46358   1996

TAMING THE TIGER

Harlem in Havana, Man from Mars, Love Puts on a New Face, Lead Balloon, No Apologies, Taming the Tiger, The Crazy Cries of Love, Stay in Touch, Face Lift, My Best to You, Tiger Bones

Reprise 46451-2   1998

Permissions

McDonald, Marci, "Joni Mitchell Emerges from Her Retreat," Entertainment Section, *The Toronto Star*, February 9, 1974. Reprinted with permission The Toronto Star Syndicate.

Mackie, Rob, "From Folk Waif to Rock & Roll Lady," *Sounds*, April 27, 1974. Copyright © 1974.

Malka, "Joni Mitchell: Self-portrait of a Superstar," *Maclean's*, June 1974. Copyright © Maclean's Magazine, June 1974.

Coppage, Noel, "More Than a Sprinkling of Symbolism in Joni Mitchell's "The Hissing of Summer Lawns," *Stereo Review*. Copyright © 1976 by Hachette Filipacchi Magazines, Inc. All rights reserved. Reprinted from *Stereo Review*, February 1976. Reprinted by permission

Meisel, Perry, "An End to Innocence: How Joni Mitchell Fails." This article originally appeared in *The Village Voice* on January 24, 1977. Reprinted by permission.

Jackson, Blair, "Don Juan's Reckless Daughter," *BAM Magazine*, January 1978. Copyright BAM Magazine. Reprinted by permission.

Feather, Leonard, "Joni Mitchell Makes Mingus Sing," *Downbeat*, September 6, 1979. Used with the permission of the Leonard Feather Estate.

Ward, Ed, "Charles, Joni, and the Circle Game," *The Village Voice*, July 30, 1979. Reprinted by permission.

Hall, Carla, "The New Joni Mitchell: The Songbird of Woodstock Soars into Jazz," *The Washington Post*, August 25, 1979. © 1979, The Washington Post. Reprinted with permission.

Garbarini, Victor R., "Joni Mitchell Is a Nervy Broad," *Musician*, January, 1983. Copyright Victor R. Garbarini, 1983. Reprinted by permission.

Passantino, Rosemary, "Joni Mitchell: 'Dog Eat Dog,' *High Fidelity*. Copyright © 1986 by Hachette Filipacchi Magazines, Inc. All rights reserved. Reprinted from *High Fidelity*, January 1986. Reprinted by permission.

Blair, Iain, "Joni Mitchell—Lucky Girl," *Los Angeles Herald*, March 9, 1986. © 1986 Iain Blair. Reprinted with permission.

Sutcliffe, Phil, "Joni Mitchell," *Q*, May 1988. Reprinted by permission.

Holden, Stephen, "Joni Mitchell Finds the Peace of Middle Age," *The New York Times*, March 17, 1991. Copyright © 1991 by The New York Times. Reprinted by permission.

Greig, Charlotte, "The Charismatic Siren Gives Way to the Doom-Laden Seer," *Mojo*, November 1994. Text by Charlotte Greig, copyright 1994, Planet Syndication, all rights reserved. Reprinted by permission.

Hoskyns, Barney, "Our Lady of Sorrows," *Mojo*, December 1994. Text by Barney

Bibliography

Atlas, Jacoba. "Joni Mitchell." *Circus* (July 1969). 4, no. 9.

Bardin, Brantley. "Interview." *Details* (July, 1996).

Bayles, Martha. "It's Not Sexist. It's Only Rock and Roll . . . " *New York Times*, September 28, 1996.

Berlin, Joey. "Another Hyphen for Joni Mitchell." *Los Angeles Times*, January 13, 1980.

Blair, Iain. "Joni Mitchell—Lucky Girl." Los Angeles Herald, March 9, 1986.

"Birthday Suite." *The New Yorker*, December 11, 1995.

Boyd, Jenny. "Musicians in Tune." *Musicians in Tune*, 1992.

Brand, Stewart. "The Education of Joni Mitchell." *CoEvolution Quarterly*, (Summer 1976).

Brown, Les. "Joni Mitchell." *Rolling Stone*, July 6, 1968.

Charone, Barbara. "Lost Innocence with a Rock and Roll Band." *The New Musical Express*, February 9, 1974.

Cochran, Connor Freff. "Joni Mitchell: Out of the Quicksand." *Roland Users Group Magazine* 14, no. 2. (1996)

Coppage, Noel. "Joni Mitchell: Innocence on a Spree." *Stereo Review* (April 1976).

Crouse, Timothy. "Joni Mitchell Blue." *Rolling Stone*, August 5, 1971.

Crowe, Cameron. "Joni Mitchell—The *Rolling Stone* Interview." *Rolling Stone*, July 26, 1979.

Dagmar. "Joni Mitchell—Soft Shades of Green and Delicate Layers." *The Music Gig* (March 1976).

Dallas, Karl. "Joni, the Seagull From Saskatoon." *Melody Maker*, September 28, 1968.

Davis, Stephen. "Joni Mitchell's 'For the Roses': It's Good for a Hole in the Heart." *Rolling Stone*, January 4, 1973.

———. "Miles of Aisles." *Rolling Stone*, February 13, 1975.

Denberg, Jody. "Taming Joni Mitchell—Joni's Jazz." *Austin Chronicle*, October 12, 1998.

DeVoss, David. "Rock 'n' Roll's Leading Lady." *Time*, December 16, 1974.

DiMartino, Dave. "The Unfiltered Joni Mitchell." *Mojo* (August 1998).

Echols, Alice. "Thirty Years With a Portable Lover." *LA Weekly*, November 25, 1994.

Ehrlich, Dimitri. "Joni Mitchell." *Interview* (April 1991).

Feather, Leonard. "Joni Mitchell Makes Mingus Sing." *Downbeat*, September 6, 1979.

Flanagan, Bill. "Lady of the Canyon." *Vanity Fair* (June 1977).

———. "Joni Mitchell: Secret Places." *Musician* (May 1988).

———. "Joni Mitchell's Home Studio." *Musician* (July 1995).

Fong-Torres, Ben. "Joni Rocks Again." *Chatelaine* (June 1988).

Gandee, Charles. "Triumph of the Will." *Vogue* (April 1995).

Garbarini, Vic. "Joni Mitchell Is a Nervy Broad." *Musician* (January, 1983).

Gordon Lydon, Susan. "Joni Mitchell: In Her House, Love." *New York Times*, April 20, 1969.

Graham, Sam. "Shadows and Light." *Musical America Back Beat* (December 1980).

Greig, Charlotte. "The Charismatic Siren Gives Way to the Doom-Laden Seer." *Mojo* (November, 1994).

Gundersen, Edna. "Joni Mitchell Still Untamed." *USA Today*, September 29, 1998.

Hall, Carla. "The New Joni Mitchell: The Songbird of Woodstock Soars into Jazz." *Washington Post*, August 25, 1979.

Hall, John T. "Joni Mitchell's Albums Trace a Coming of Age," *Ithaca New Times*, February 10, 1974.

Hilburn, Robert. "Joni Mitchell's New 'For the Roses.'" *Los Angeles Times*, November 21, 1972.

———. "Joni Mitchell: Both Sides, Later." *Los Angeles Times*, December 8, 1998.

Hinton, Brian. *Both Sides Now.* London: Sanctuary Publishing Ltd., 1986.

Holden, Stephen. "Joni Mitchell: A Summer Garden of Verses." *Rolling Stone*, January 15, 1976.

———. "Joni Mitchell—Shadows and Light." *Rolling Stone*, November 13, 1980.

———. "High Spirits Buoy a Joni Mitchell Album." *New York Times*, November 7, 1982.

———. "Joni Mitchell Takes Up Topicality." *New York Times*, October 16, 1985.

———. "Joni Mitchell Finds the Peace of Middle Age." *New York Times*, March 17, 1991.

———. "The Ambivalent Hall of Famer." *New York Times*, December 1, 1996.

Hoskyns, Barney. "Our Lady of Sorrows." *Mojo* (December 1994).

Irvin, Les. "Pass the Salt, Please." August 1997. Internet site: http://www.jmdl.com.

Jackson, Blair. "Don Juan's Reckless Daughter." *BAM Magazine* (January 1978).

Jackson, Joe. "If You See Her, Say Hello." *Hotpress*, January 23, 1999.

Johnson, Brian D. "Joni's Secret: Mother and Child Reunion." *Maclean's*, April 21, 1997.

"*Joni Mitchell.*" Rolling Stone, May 17, 1969.

"*Joni Mitchell, Folksongs, 47 Minutes, 7 of Clubs, Toronto.*" Variety, September, 21, 1966.

"Joni Mitchell Hangs It Up." *Rolling Stone*, December 13, 1969

Landau, Jon. "Joni Mitchell: A Delicate Balance." *Rolling Stone*, February 28, 1974.

———. "Top 20: The Times, They Are A-Middlin.'" *Rolling Stone*, June 6, 1974.

LeBlanc, Larry. "Joni Takes a Break." *Rolling Stone*, March 4, 1971.

Levitin, Daniel. "A Conversation with Joni Mitchell." *Grammy* (Spring 1996).

Mackie, Rob. "From Folk Waif to Rock & Roll Lady." *Mojo*, April 27, 1974.

Malka. "Joni Mitchell: Self-portrait of a Superstar." *Maclean's* (June, 1974).

Maslin, Janet. "Joni Mitchell's Reckless and Shapeless 'Daughter.'" *Rolling Stone*, March 9, 1978.

McClain, A.L. "Two Single Acts Survive a Marriage." *Detroit News*, February 6, 1966.

McDonald, Marci. "Joni Mitchell Emerges from Her Retreat." *Toronto Star*, February 9, 1974.

McGarity, Neal. "Taming the Tiger—Joni Mitchell." *Hartford Courant*, October 8, 1998.

McKenna, Kristine. "Chalking it Up to Experience." *Los Angeles Times*, March 27, 1988.

Meisel, Perry. "An End to Innocence: How Joni Mitchell Fails." *The Village Voice*, January 24, 1977.

Morrissey. "Melancholy Meets the Infinite Sadness." *Rolling Stone*, March 6, 1997.

Naedele, Walter F. "Joni Mitchell Breaks Up Opening of Folk Festival." [Philadelphia] *Evening Bulletin,* August 24, 1968.

Passantino, Rosemary. "Joni Mitchell: 'Dog Eat Dog.'" *High Fidelity* (January 1986).

Pepper Rodgers, Jeffrey. "Joni Mitchell: My Secret Place." *Acoustic Guitar* (August, 1996).

———. "Joni Mitchell." *Acoustic Guitar* (August, 1996).

———. "Setting the Stage: The Vocal and Lyrical Craft of Joni Mitchell." *Acoustic Guitar* (February, 1997).

Perry, Claudia. "Rocking Gracefully into the Golden Years." Newhouse News Service, October 15, 1997.

Ratliff, Ben. "It's All Joni Mitchell Onstage, But She's in the Audience." *New York Times,* July 3, 1999.

Reilly, Peter. "Joni Mitchell Sings Her Blues." *Stereo Review* (October 1971).

"Riverboat, Toronto, Feb. 14, Joni Mitchell: $1.50, $2.50 cover." *Variety,* February 22, 1967.

Rockwell, John. "Joni Mitchell—Recaptures Her Gift." *New York Times,* December 1976.

———. "The New Artistry of Joni Mitchell." *New York Times,* August 19, 1979.

———. "Joni Mitchell in Forest Hills Show." *New York Times,* August 27, 1979.

Ruhlmann, Bill. "Joni Mitchell: From Blue to Indigo." *Goldmine,* February 17, 1995.

Saal, Hubert. "The Girls—Letting Go." *Newsweek,* July 14, 1969.

Sandall, Robert. "Joni Mitchell." *London Sunday Times,* September 9, 1990.

Silver, Conrad. "Triumphant Return for Singer Joni Mitchell." *San Francisco Examiner and Chronicle,* September 16, 1979.

Smith, Bruce. "Joni's Present-Tense Jazz." *New York Daily News,* August 24, 1979.

"Sony/Atv Music Publishing and Joni Mitchell Enter Into Into Worldwide Agreement." *Business Wire,* August 26, 1997

Strauss, Neil. "The Hissing of a Living Legend." *New York Times,* October 4, 1998.

Sutcliffe, Phil. "Joni Mitchell." *Q* (May 1988).

Sutherland, Sam. "Joni Mitchell's Wild Things Run Fast." *High Fidelity* (January 1983).

Swartley, Ariel. "Joni Mitchell—The Siren and the Symbolist." *Rolling Stone,* February 10, 1977.

———. "Joni Mitchell's Adolescence Reenacted." *The Village Voice,* November 30, 1982.

Tipmore, David. "Joni Mitchell's New Chataqua." *The Village Voice,* November 5, 1974.

Tucker, Ken. "Joni Mitchell: The Importance of Being Joni." *Mirabella* (April 1975).

———. "Joni Mitchell: Public Invited." *The Village Voice,* March 3, 1988.

Turner, Rick. "Joni Mitchell's Custom Klein." *Acoustic Guitar* (January 1994).

Valentine, Penny. "Exclusive Joni Mitchell Interview." *Mojo,* Part 1 from the June 3, 1972 issue; Part 2 from the June 10, 1972 issue.

Ward, Ed. "Charles, Joni, and the Circle Game." *The Village Voice,* July 30, 1979.

Watts, Michael. "Joni: A Bigger Splash." *Melody Maker,* November 29, 1975, p. 50.

Whitall, Susan. "Joni Mitchell—Still Blue." The Houston Press, December 26, 1996.

White, Timothy. "A Portrait of the Artist." *Billboard,* December 9, 1995.

———. "Joni Mitchell: Billboard Honors Joni Mitchell With Its Highest Accolade, the Century Award for Distinguished Creative Achievement," *Billboard,* December 9, 1995.

———. "Joni Mitchell." *Rock Lives.*

Whitesell, Lloyd. "A Joni Mitchell Aviary." *Women and Music: A Journal of Gender and Culture* 1, 1997.

Wild, David. "A Conversation With Joni Mitchell." *Rolling Stone,* May 30, 1991.

"Woke Up—It Was a Hall of Fame Morning." Associated Press, January 16, 1997.

Wolf, Ellen. "Joni Circulates Her Soul Around." *Crawdaddy* (March 1973).

Index